The Ten PLEASURES Of MARRIAGE.

The Nuptial estate trailing along with it so many cares, troubles & calamities, it is one of the greatest admirations, that people should be so earnest and desirous to enter themselves into it. In the younger sort who by their sulphurous instinct, are subject to the tickling desires of nature, and look upon that thing called Love through a multiplying glass, it is somewhat pardonable: But that those who are once come to the years of knowledge and true understanding should be drawn into it, methinks is most vilely foolish, and morrice fooles caps were much fitter for them, then wreaths of Lawrel. Yet stranger it is, that those who have been for the first time in that horrible estate, do, by a decease, cast themselves in again to a second and third time. Truly, if for once any one be through contrary imaginations misled, he may expect some hopes of compassion, and alledge some reasons to excuse himself: but what comfort, or compassion can they look for, that have thrown themselves in a second and third time? they were happy, if they could keep their lips from speaking, and ty their tongues from complaining, that their miseries might not be more and more burdened with scoffings which they truly merit.

And tho not only the real truth of this, but ten times more, is as well known to every one, as the Sun shine at noon day; nevertheless we see them run into it with such an earnestness, that they are not to be counselled, or kept back from it, with the strength of *Hercules*; despising their golden liberty, for chains of horrid slavery.

But we see the bravest sparks, in the very blossoming of their youth, how they decay? First, Gentleman-like, they take pleasure in all manner of noble exercises, as in keeping time all dancing, singing of musick, playing upon instruments, speaking of several languages, studying at the best Universities, and conversing with the learnedst Doctors, &c. or else we see them, before they are half perfect in any exercise, like carl-cats in March run mewing and yawling at the doors of young Gentlewomen; and if any of those have but a small matter of more then ordinary beauty, (which perhaps is gotten by the help of a damn'd bewitched pot of paint) she is immediately ador'd like a Saint upon an Altar: And in an instant there is as much beauty and perfection to be seen in her, as ever Juno, Venus and Pallas possessed all together.

And herewith those Gentile Pleasures, that have cost their Parents so much money, and them so much labour and time are kickt away, and totally abandoned that they may keep company with a painted Jezebel. They are then hardly arrived at this intitled happiness, but they must begin to chaw upon the bitter shell of that nut, the kernel whereof, without sighing, they cannot tast; having no sooner obtained access to the Lady, but are as suddenly possest with thousands of thoughts what they shall do to please the Sweet object. Being therewith so tosticated, that all their other business is dispersed, and totally laid aside. This is observable not only in youth of the first degree, but also in persons that have received promotion.

For if he be a Theologue, his books drop out of his hands, and ly stragling about his study, even as his sences do, one among another. And if you hear him preach, his whole Sermon is nothing but of Love, which he then turns & winds to Divinity as far as possible it can be fitted.

If it be a Doctor of Physick, oh! he has so much work with his own sicknes, that he absolutely forgets all his Patients, though some of them were lying at deaths dore; and lets the Chyrurgian, whom he had appointed certainly to meet there, tarry to no purpose, taking no more notice of his Patients misery, and the peril of his wounds, then if it did not concern him. But if at last he doth come, it is when the wound's festered, the Ague in the blood, or that the body is incurable. So far was he concern'd in looking after that Love-apple, or Night-shadow, for the cure of his own burning distemper.

If he be a Counsellor, his whole brain is so much puzzel'd how to begin and pursue the Process for the obtaining his Mistress in Marriage; that all other suits tho they be to the great detriment of poor Widows and Orphans are laid aside, and wholly rejected. Then being desired by his Clients to meet them at anyplace, and to give his advice concerning the cause, he hath had such earnest business with his Mistress, that he comes an hour or two later then was appointed. But coming at last, one half of the time that can be spent, is little enough to make Mr. Counsellor understand in what state the cause stood at the last meeting. And then having heard what the Plaintif and Defendant do say, he only tells them, I must have clearer evidences, the accounts better adjusted, and your demand in writing, before I can make any decision of this cause to both your satisfactions.

There they stand then, and look one upon another, not daring to say otherwise, but *'tis very well Sir, we will make them all ready against the next meeting*; and are, with grief at heart, forced to see as much and sometimes more expences made at the meeting, as the whole concern of their debate amounted to. Then it is, come let's now discourse of matters of state, and drink a glass about to the health of the King & the prosperity of our Country and all the inhabitants; which is done only to the purpose, that coming to his Mistress, he may boastingly say, my dear, just now at a meeting we remembered you in a glass, & I'l swear the least drop of it was so delicious to me, as ever *Nectar* and *Ambrose* could be, that the Poets so highly commend.

If Counsellors, and other learned men, that are in love, do thus; what can the unlearned Notary's do less? Even nothing else, but when they are writing, scribble up a multiplicity of several words, unnecessary clauses, and make long periods; not so much as touching or mentioning the principal business; and if he does, writes it clear contrary to the intent of the party concern'd: By that means making both Wills and other Deeds in such a manner, that the end agrees not with the beginning, nor the middle with either. Which occasions between friends, near relations, and neighbors, great differences, and an implacable hatred; forcing thereby the monies of innocent and self-necessitated people, into the Pockets of Counsellors and Attorneys.

And alas the diligent Merchant, when he has gotten the least smatch of this frensie, his head runs so much upon wheels, that he daily neglects his Change-time; forgets his Bils of exchange; and is alwaies a Post or two behind hand with his Letters: So that he knows not what Merchandises rise or fall, or what commodities are arrived or expected. And by this means buies in Wares, at such rates, that in few daies he loses 20, yea sometimes 30 per cent. by them. Nay, this distemper is so hot in his head, that thereby he Ships his goods in a Vessel, where the Master and his Mate are for the most part drunk, and who hardly thrice in ten times make a good voyage.

And who knows not how miserable that City and Country is, when a military person happens to ly sick in this Hospital. If he be in Garison, he doth nothing but trick up himself, walk along the streets, flatter his Mistress, and vaunt of his knowledge and Warlike deeds; though he scarce understands the exercising of his Arms, I will not mention encamping in a Field, Fortification, the forming of Batalions, and a great deal more that belongs to him.

And coming into Campagne; alas this wicked Love-ague continues with him; and runs so through his blood, that both the open air, and wide fields are too narrow for him. Yea and tho he formerly had (especially by his Mistris) the name of behaving himself like a second Mars; yet now he'l play the sick-hearted, (I dare not say the faint-hearted) to the end he may, having put on his fine knotted Scarf, and powdered Periwig, only go to shew himself to that adorable Babe, his Lady Venus, Leaving oftentimes a desperate siege, and important State affairs, to accompany a lame, squint-ey'd, and crook-back'd *Jeronimo*.

And if, by favour or recommandation, he happen to be intrusted with any strong City or Fort that is besieged, he's presently in fear of his own Bom, and practises all sorts of waies and means how he shall best make a capitulation, that so leaving the place, he may go again to his fair one.

And alas, what doth not the Master of a Ship, and his Mate hazard, when they are sick of this malady? What terrible colds, and roaring seas doth he not undergo, through an intemperate desire that he hath to be with his nittebritch'd Peggy? How often doth he hazard his Owners Ship, the Merchants Goods, and his own life, for an inconstant draggle-tail; that perhaps before he has been three daies at Sea, hath drawn her affection from him, and given promise to another? Yet nevertheless, tho the raging Waves run upon the Ship, and fly over his head, he withstands it all. Nor is the main Ocean, or blustering *Boreas*, powerfull enough, to cool his raging fire, and drive those damps out of his brain. The tempestuousness of the weather, having driven him far out of his course; his only wishes and prayer is, oh, that he might be so happy, but for a moment to see his Beacon, those twinkling eys of his dearly beloved Margery Mussel! Then all things would be well enough! Tho he and all that are with him, were immediately Shipwrackt, and made a prey for the Fishes. And if, unexpectedly, fortune so favour him, that he happens to see the Coast, oh, he cannot tarry for the Pilot! but tho it be misty weather, and he hoodwink'd by Venus, still he sails forward, running all in danger, that before was so far preserved.

And if the Shop-keeper once sets foot into this destructive Wilderness, he doth nothing less then look to his shop, and wait upon his Customers. Spending most part of his time in finical dressing himself, to accompany his Mistriss, and with a Coach or Pair of Oars to do her all manner of caresses. Then his whole discourse is, with what good custom he is blest above others; but seldom saies, that with waiting upon his Lady, and by indeavouring to please her above all things, how miserably he neglects it, by which means, shop's not only found without a Master, but the servants without government. And at New-year, the day-book is not written fair over; and if any body desires their reckoning, the squire is so full of business, that he can't spare half an hour to write it out: For where he goes, where he stands, what he thinks, what he does, all his cogitations are imploi'd to think how delicious it is to press those soft lips of his beloved, and then out of an unfeigned heart to be lov'd again, sometimes receiving a kiss. Thus he idles away all his time, and all his business with his sences runs a wool-gathering.

To be short, let it be what sort of person it will, they no sooner touch the shell of this Marriage-nut, but before they can come to tast the kernel they look for; they feel nothing else then thorns and briars of sorrow and misery. If there be any one that thinks he is gotten a footstep further then another, in the favour of his Mistriss, and that in time he questions not th' obtaining his desired happiness; immediately, that imagined joy, is crush'd with an insuing despair; being presently molested with a fear, that Father, Mother, Uncle, or Tutor will not like his person, or that he has not means enough; or else either they, or the Gentlewoman, will make choice of another in his place. Or, if he sees another have access to the Lady as well as himself, at the same moment he's possessed with jealousie, and falls a pondering how he shall make this Rival odious in the eys of her. And if the other get any advantage of him; then he challenges him to fight; hazarding in that manner his precious life, for the getting of her, who when he had her, would perhaps, occasion him a thousand torments of death and misery. Pray observe what pleasures this introduction imparts unto us; alas, what may we then expect from the marriage it self?

Really, those that will take this into due consideration, who would not but curse the Gentlewoman that draws him into such a raging madness? yet Lovers go forward, and please your selves with this imagined happiness; but know, that if according to your hope, you obtain her for a Bride, that at the least you must expect a sence and feeling of the Ten insuing Pleasures.

Folio 10.
Published by the Navarre Society, London.

THE FIRST PLEASURE.

The Consent is given, the Match concluded, and the Wedding kept.

Now, O Lover, till this time you have been indeavouring, slaving, turmoiling, sighing, groaning, hoping and begging to get from those slow and tardy lips, that long-wish'd for word of Consent; you have also sent many messengers to your Mistriss, to her Parents and Tutors, who were as able to express themselves as the best Orators, but could obtain nothing; yet at last that long desired Word, is once descended by the Draw-bridge of her lips, like a rich cordial upon your languishing heart. You have vanquish'd all your Rivals. Oh who can imagine your joy! What you think, or what you do, still your thoughts glance upon your happiness! your Mistriss now will be willing; denials are laid aside: only ther's a little shame and fear, which canot of a sudden be so totally forgotten, because the marriage is not yet concluded. Well, O Lover, who could desire a greater happiness then you now possess! For what you will, she will also: and what she desires, is all your pleasure. You may now tumble in a bed of Lillies and Roses; for all sour looks, are turn'd to sweet smiles, and she that used to thrust you from her, pulls you now every foot to her. Yea, those snow-white breasts, which before you durst scarce touch with your little finger; you may now, without asking leave, grasp by whole handfuls. Certainly, they that at full view, consider all this rightly; who can doubt but that you are the happiest man in the World? O unspeakable pleasure!

But, O triumphant Lover, let not however your joyfull mind run too much upon these glistering things: be a little moderate in your desired pleasures, if it might happen that there come some cross-grain'd obstructions; for I have oftentimes seen, that all those suspected roses, come forth with many pricking thorns; insomuch that the mouth which at first was saluted with so many thousand kisses, and appear'd as if it had been cover'd with the dew of heaven; was compared to be the jaws of *Cerberus*. And those breasts, which before were the curded *Nacter*-hills, and called the Banket of the Gods, I have seen despised to be like stinking Cows-Udders, I, and call'd worse names to boot. Be therefore, (I say) somewhat moderate and prudent, for fear it might happen that the prices of this market might fall very suddenly, though perhaps not so horribly.

Nevertheless you have great reason to be merry, for this week, 'tis hop'd there'l be a meeting to close up the match; and it is requisite, that you should go unto all the friends, that must be present at the meeting, to hear when their occasions will permit them, and what day and hour they will appoint to set upon the business, herewith you have work to traverse the City, and who knows whether you'l find half of them at home. And then those that you do find, one is ready to day, another to morrow, a third next day, or in the next week. So that by this first Pleasure, you have also a little feeling of the first trouble. Which, if you rightly consider, is to your advantage, because you may the better use your self to the following. And of how greater State and Quality the person is whom you have chosen, so accordingly this trouble generally happens to be more.

But the mirth increases abundantly; when, after your indeavours, troubles and turmoils, you finally see all the friends met together, and you doubt not but the match will be closed and agreed upon. But be here also a little moderate in your mirth, because oftentimes the friends handle this matter like a bargaining; and will lay the mony bags of each side in a balance, as you may see by the Plate.

In the mean while you may be kissing and slabbering of your Mistris in the next room; or contriving what's to be done about the marriage, and keeping of the Wedding; but perhaps, through the discord of the friends, it will not be long before you are disturb'd; the differences oft rising so high, that the sound thereof, clatters through the Walls, into the ears of the Lovers. For many times the Portion of one is too great, and what's given with the other is too little; or that the Parents of the Bridegroom, promise too little with their Son; and the Brides Parents will give too little with their Daughter. Or else that by some subtle Contract of Matrimony, they indeavour to make the goods of each side disinheritable, &c. So that it appears among the friends, as if there could be nothing don in the matter.

And in plain truth, the Parents and friends, who know very well that it is not all hony in the married estate; see oftentimes that it were better for these two to remain unmarried, then to bring each other into misery; and can find no grounds or reasons, but rather to disswade then perswade the young folks to a marriage.

But tho, on each side, they use never such powerfull arguments, to the young people, 'tis to no purpose; for there's fire in the flax, and go how it will, it must be quencht. For the maid thinks, if this match should be broke, who knows but that all the freedom that we have had with one another, might come to be spread abroad, and then I am ruined for ever. And the young man, seeing that his Mistris is so constant to him, not hearkning to the advice of her friends, is so struck to the heart with such fiery flames of love, that he's resolved never to leave her, tho he might feed upon bread and water, or go a begging with her: So, that he saies, Bargain by the Contract of Matrimony for what you will, nay tho you would write Hell and Damnation, I am contented, and resolve to sign it: but thinking by himself, with a Will all this may be broken, and new made again: hardly beleeving, that this fair weather, should be darkned with black clouds; or that this splendent Serenissimo, would be obstructed by Eclipses.

But finally, there comes an appearance of the desired pleasure; for the knot is tied, and the Publick Notary doth at large and very circumstantially write the Contract of Matrimony, which is signed by both parties. Oh Heavens! this is a burthen from my heart, and a Milstone removed out of the way. Here's now right matter for more then ordinary mirth; all the friends wish the young couple much joy; about goes a health, the good success of the marriage, and every one wishing them tubs full of blessings, and houses full of prosperity,

> *If ev'ry one that wish, did half but give,*
> *How richly this young couple, then might live.*

Yet it e'en helps as much as it will; if they get nothing, they lose nothing by it. And thinking by themselves, you'l in time see what it produces. Then if there be but one among them who is talkative, and that by drinking merrily the good success of the approaching marriage, his tongue begins to run; he relates what hapned to him at the closing of his marriage, keeping of his wedding, and in his married estate; and commonly the conclusion of his discourse is, that he thought at first he had the World at will; but then there came this, and then that, and a thousand other vexatious things, which continually, or for the most part of the time with great grief and trouble had kept him so much backward, that it was long before he could get forward in the World.

Well, M^r. Bridegroom, you may freely tickle your fancy to the top, and rejoice superabundantly, that the Match is concluded; & you have now gotten your legs into the stocks, and your arms into such desired for Fetters, that nothing but death it self can unloosen them.

And you, M^{rs}. Bride, who look so prettily, with such a smirking countenance; be you merry, you are the Bride; yea the Bride that occasions all this tripping and dansing; now you shall have a husband too, a Protector, who will hug and imbrace you, and somtimes tumble and rumble you, and oftimes approach to you with a morning salutation, that will comfort the very cockles of your heart. He will (if all falls out well) be your comforter, your company-keeper, your care-taker, your Gentleman-Usher; nay all what your heart wish for, or the Heavens grant unto you. He'l be your Doctor to cure your palefac'dness, your pains in the reins of your back, and at your heart, and all other distempers whatsoever. He will also wipe of all your tears with kisses; and you shall not dream of that thing in the night, but he'l let it be made for you by day. And may not then your Bride-maids ask, why should not you be merry?

But alas you harmless Dove, that think you are going into Paradice; pray tell me, when you were going to sign the Contract of marriage, what was the reason that you alter'd so mightily, & that your hand shook so? Verily, though I am no Astronomer, or caster of Figures; yet nevertheless me-thought it was none of the best signs; and that one might already begin to make a strange Prognostication from it; the events whereof would be more certain then any thing that *Lilly* or any other Almanack maker ever writ. But we'l let that alone, for in a short time it will discover it self.

Therefore, Mistress Bride, make you merry, and since you have gotten your desire to be the Bride before any of your Bridemaids; it would be unreasonable that you should be troubled now with any other business. And indeed here's work enough for the ordering of things that you must trouble your head with; for the Brides Apparel must be made, and the Stufs, laces, lining, cuffs, and many other things are yet to be bought. Well, who can see an end of all your business! There's one piece of stuf is too light, and another too dark; the third looks dull and hath no gloss. And see here's three or four daies gon, and little or nothing bought yet.

And the worst of all is, that whil'st you are thus busie in contriving, ordering and looking upon things, you are every moment hindered, & taken off from it, with a continual knocking at the dore to sollicite one to deliver all sorts of Comfits, another to deliver the ornaments for the Brides Garland, Flowers, &c, a third to be Cook, & Pastryman, & so many more, which come one after another thundering so at the door, that it is one bodies work to let them in, and carry their message to the Bride.

Oh, call the Bride, time will deceive us! The Semstress, Gorget-maker, and Starcher, must be sent for, and the linnen must be bought & ordered for the Bridegrooms shirts, the Brides smocks, Cuffs, Bands; and handkerchifs; & do but see, the day is at an end again: my brains are almost addle, and nothing goes forward: For M^{rs}. Smug said she would bring linnen, and M^{rs}. Smooth laces, but neither of them both are yet come. Run now men and maids as if the Devil were in you; and comfort your selves, that the Bride will reward you liberally for your pains.

Well, M^{rs}. Bride, how's your head so out of order! might not you now do (as once a Schoolmaster did) hang out the sign of a troubled pate with a Crown upon it? How glad you'l be when this confusion is once over? could you ever have thought that there was so much work to be found in it? But comfort your self therewith, that for these few troublesom daies, you'l have many pleasant nights. And it is not your case alone, to be in all this trouble, for the Bridegroom is running up and down like a dog, in taking care that the Banns of Matrimony may be proclaim'd. And now he's a running to and again through the City, to see if he can get Bridemen to his mind, that are capacitated to entertain the Bridemaids and Gentlewomen with pretty discourses, waiting upon them, & to make mirth & pleasure for them and the rest of the Company. Besides that he's taking care for the getting of some good *Canary, Rhenish* & *French* Wines, that those friends which come to wish the Bride and Bridegroom much joy, may be presented with a delicate glass of Wine. And principally, that those who are busie about the Brides adornments, may tast the Brides tears.

But really friends, if you come to tast the Brides tears now, 'tis a great while too soon: But if you'l have of the right and unfeigned ones, you must come some months hence.

O Bridegroom, who can but pitty you, that you must thus toil, moil, and run up and down, and the Jeweller and you have just now mist one another; he is doubtless chatting with the Bride, and shewing of her some costly Jewels, which perhaps dislike her ne'r a whit the worse; and what she has then a mind to, you'l find work enough to disswade her from, let them cost what they will; for she'l let you take care for that. And it is time enough to be considered on, when the weddings over. For now you have as much work as you can turn your self to, in getting all your things in a readiness from the Tailor, Semstress, and Haberdasher. And herewith, alas, you'l find that oftentimes two or three weeks are consumed in this sort of business, with the greatest slavery imaginable.

Yet, M^r. Bridegroom, for all these troubles, you may expect this reward, to have the pleasure of the best place in the Chancel, with a golden Tapistry laid before you, and for your honour the Organs playing. The going with a Coach to marry at a Country Town, has not half so much grace, and will not at all please the Bride: it is therefore requisite to consult with the friends on both sides, who shall be invited to the wedding, and who not. For it seldom happens, but there is one broil or another about it; and that's no sooner don, but there arises a new quarrel, to consider, how richly or frugally the Guests shall be treated; for they would come off with credit and little charge. To this is required the advice of a steward, because it is their daily work. And he for favour of the Cook, Pasterer, and Poulterer (reaping oftentimes his own benefit by it) orders all things so liberally as he can make the people beleeve that is requisite. And the Bride thinks, the nobler it is, the better I like it, for I am but once the Bride. But this matter being dispatcht, there's another consideration to be taken in hand, to know how the Bride & Bridegrooms friends shall be plac'd at the Table, the ordering whereof, many times causes such great disputes, that if they had known it before, they would rather have kept no Wedding. In somuch that the Bridegroom and the Bride, with sighing, say to one another, alas, what a thick shell this marriage nut hath, before one can come to the kernel of it. But Bridegroom to drive these damps out of your brain, there's no better remedy then to go along with your Bridemen to tast the Wedding wine; for there must be sure care taken that it may be of a delicate tast and relish; Because that which was laid in before, was not so delicious as is required for such a noble Wedding, where there will be so many curious tasters. Ha! riva! Look to't Bride and Bridemaids, you may now expect a jolly Bridegroom and Bridemen, for the Wine-Merchant is such a noble blade, that none of them all shall escape him, before they have drunk as many Glasses, as there are hoops upon the Wine-cask that they tasted of.

Adieu all care! the Wedding is at hand, who thinks now of any thing but superfluity of mirth? Away with all these whining, pining Carpers, who are constantly talking & prating that the married estate brings nothing but care and sorrow with it; here, to the contrary, they may see how all minds & intentions are knit together, to consume and pass away these daies with the most superabounding pleasures. Away with sorrow. 'Tis not invited to be among the Wedding guests. Noct there is nothing else to be thought on, but to help these Lovers that they may enjoy the kernel of the first pleasure of their marriage.

But really, there's poor Mally the maid, is almost dead with longing, and thinks her very heart in pieces, scarcely knowing when the first Wedding-night will be ended, that she might carry up some water to the young couple, and have a feeling of those liberal gifts that she shall receive from the Bridegroom and the Bride, for all her attendance, running and turmoiling. And her thoughts are, that no body has deserved it better, for by night and by day she waited upon them, and was very diligent and faithfull in conveyance of their Love-Letters; but all upon fair promises, having carried her self in the time of their wooing almost like a Bawd to the Bride; for which she never had in all the time but three gratuities from the Bridegroom,

> *And now the Bride is in the bed,*
> *The former promises are dead.*

Make your self merry amongst the rest of the Wedding guests, so far as is becoming you: who knows, but that some brave Gentlemans man,

Coachman, or neighbors servant, may fall in love with you; for many times out of one Wedding comes another, and then you might come to be a woman of good fashion. Udsbud Mally! then you would know, as well as your Mistress, what delights are to be had in the first Wedding night. Then you would also know how to discourse of the first Pleasure of marriage, and with the Bride expect the second.

THE SECOND PLEASURE.

The Woman goes to buy houshold-stuf. The unthankfulness of some of the Wedding-guests, and thankfulness of others.

Well, young married people, how glad you must needs be, now the Wedding's over, and all that noise is at an end? You may now ly and sleep till the day be far spent! And not only rest your selves quietly; but, to your desires, in the Art of Love, shew one another the exercise and handling of Venus Weapons.

Now you may practise an hundred delicious things to please your appetites, & do as many Hocus Pocus tricks more. Now you may outdo *Aretin*, and all her light Companions, in all their several postures. Now you may rejoice in the sweet remembrance, how sumptuous that you were, in Apparel, meat and drink, and all other ornaments that my Lady *Bride*, and Madam *Spend-all*, first invented and brought in practice. Now you may tickle your fancies with the pleasures that were used there, by dansing, maskerading, Fire-works, playing upon Instruments, singing, leaping, and all other sort of gambals, that youth being back'd with Bacchus strength uses either for mirth or wantonness.

Folio 30.
Published by The Navarre Society, London.

O how merry they were all of 'em! And how deliciously were all the dishes dress'd and garnisht! What a credit this will be for the Cook and Steward! Indeed there was nothing upon the Table but it was Noble, and the Wine was commended by every one. They have all eaten gallantly, & drunk deliciously. Well, this is now a pleasant remembrance.

And you, O young Woman, you are now both Wife and Mistris your self; you are now wrested out of the command of your grinning and snarling narrow-soul'd Tutors (those hellish Curmugions) now you may freely, without controul, do all what you have a mind to; and receive therewith the friendly imbracings, and kind salutes of your best beloved. Verily this must needs be a surpassing mirth.

And you, O new made husband, how tumble you now in wantonness! how willingly doth liberal Venus her self, open her fairest Orchard for you! Oh you have a pleasure, that those which never tried, can in the least comprehend.

Well, make good use of your time, and take the full scope of your desires, in the pleasant clasping and caressing of those tender limbs; for after some few daies, it may be hungry care will come and open the Curtains of your bed; and at a distance shew you what reckonings you are to expect from the Jeweller, Gold-smith, Silk-man, Linnen-Draper, Vinter, Cook and others.

But on the t'other side again, you shall have the pleasure to hear your young Wife every moment sweetly discoursing that she must go with her Sister and her Aunt to buy houshold-stuf, Down-beds, dainty Plush and quilted Coverlets, with costly Hangings must be bought: And then she will read to you, her new made Husband, such a stately Register, that both your joy of heart, and jingling purse shall have a fellouw-feeling of it.

For your Sweetest speaks of large Venetian Looking-glasses, Chiny-ware, Plush Chairs, Turkish Tapistry, Golden Leather, rich Pictures, a Service of Plate, a Sakerdan Press, an Ebbony Tabel, a curious Cabinet and child-bed Linnen cupboard, several Webs for Napkins and Tabel-cloaths, fine and course linnen, Flanders laces, and a thousand other things must be bought, too long to be here related: For other things also that concern the furnishing of the house, they increase every day fresh in the brains of these loving and prudent Wives.

And when the Wife walks out, she must either have the Maid, or at least the Semstress, along with her; then neighbour John, that good carefull labourer, must follow them softly with his wheel-barrow, that the things, which are bought, may be carefully and immediately brought home.

And at all this, good Man, you must make no wry faces, but be pleasant and merry; for they are needfull in house-keeping, you cannot be without them;

and that mony must alwaies be certainly ready, get it where you will. Then, saies the Wife, all this, at least, there must needs be, if we will have any people of fashion come into our house.

You know your Beloved hath also some Egs to fry, and did bring you a good Portion, though it consist in immovable Goods, as in Houses, Orchards, and Lands that be oftentimes in another Shire. Thither you may go then, with your Hony, twice a year, for the refreshing of your spirits, and taking your pleasure to receive the House-rents, fruits of the Orchards, and revenues of the Lands. Here every one salutes you with the name of Landlord; and, according to their Country fashion, indeavour to receive you with all civilities and kind entertainment. If, with their Hay-cart, you have a mind to go and look upon the Land, and to be a participator of those sort of pleasures; or to eat some new Curds, Cream, Gammon of Bacon, and ripe Fruits, all these things; in place of mony, shall be willingly and neatly disht up to you.

For here you'l meet with complaints, that by the War the Houses are burnt, the Orchards destroied, and the growth of the Fields spoiled! therefore it is not fit that you should trouble the poor people, but think, this is the use, custom, and fruits of War. If the Impositions and Taxes run high, the Country Farmer can't help that; you know that the War costs mony, and it must be given, or else we should lose all.

At such a time as this, your only mirth must be; that, through this gallant marriage, you are now Lord of so many acres of Land, so many Orchards, and of so many dainty Houses and Land. If your mony bags don't much increase by it at present, but rather lessen, that most no waies cloud your mirth. Would you trouble your self at such trivial things, you'd have work enough daily. We cannot have all things so to our minds in this World. For if you had your Wives Portion down in ready mony, you'd have been at a stand again, where, without danger, you should have put it out at interest; fearing that they might play Bankrupt with it. Houses and Lands are alwaies fast, and they will pay well, when the War is done.

Therefore you must drive these vapors out of your head, and make your self merry, with the hearing that your friends commend the entertainment they have had to the highest; and that two or three daies hence; the merry

Bridemen and Bridemaids, with some of the nearest acquaintance, will come *a la grandissimo* to give you thanks for all the respect & civilities that you have so liberally bestowed upon them; which will be done then with such a friendly and affectionate heart, that it will be impossible for you, but you must invite them again to come and sup with you in the evening, and so make an addition to the former Pleasure; by which means pleasantness, mirth, and friendship, is planted and advanced among all the friends and acquaintance.

'Tis true, you'l be sure to hear that there were some at the Wedding who were displeased, for not being entertained according to their expectations; and because their Uncle, a new married Niece, and some other friends were not seated in their right places; that M^{rs}. *Leonora* had a jole-pate to wait upon her; and M^{r}. *Philip* an old *Beldam*; M^{r}. *Timothy* was forced to wait upon a young snotty-nose; and that Squire *Neefer* could not sit easily, and M^{rs}. *Betty's* Gorget was rumbled; and that *Mal*, and *Peg Stones*, and *Dol Dirty-buttocks*, were almost throng'd in pieces; and could hardly get any of the Sweetmeats; but you must not at all be troubled with this, for 'tis a hard matter to please every body. 'Tis enough that you have been at such a vast charge, and presented them with your Feast.

Truly, they ought to have been contented & thankfull to the highest degree; and what they are unsatisfied with needed not to have cost you so much mony; for if you had left them all at home, you could have had no worse reward, but a great deal less charge. Comfort your self with this, that when it happens again, you will not buy ingratitude at so high a rate. 'Tis much better to invite them at two or three several times before hand, and entertain them with a merry glass of Wine, up and away; and then invite a small company which are better to govern and satisfied.

'Tis a great deal more pleasure for you, to see your Wives friends animate one another, to come, a fortnight after the Wedding, and surprize you; with shewing their thankfulness and satisfaction for the respect they have received from you; and that they are alwaies desirous to cultivate the friendship, by now and then coming to give you a visit.

This is here again a new joy! and as long as you keep open Table and Cellar for them, that reception will keep all discontent from growing among them.

Yes, and it will please your Wife too, extraordinary well.

And by thus doing, you will not be subject to (as many other men are) your Wives maundring that you entertained her friends so hungrily and unhandsomly; but, for this, you shall be both by her, and her friends, beloved and commended in the highest degree: Yea it will be an incouragement that they in the same manner, will entertain your friends like an Angel, and be alwaies seeking to keep a fair correspondence among them. So that in the Summer time, for an afternoons collation you'l see a Fruit-dish of Grapes, Nuts, and Peaches prepared for you; which cold Fruits must then be warm'd with a good glass of Wine. And in the Winter, to please your appetite, a dish of Pancakes, Fritters, or a barrel of Oisters; but none of these neither will be agreeable without a delicate glass of Wine. Oh quintessence of all mirth! Who could not but wish to get such Aunts, such Cousins, & such Bridemen and Bridemaids in their marriage?

Therefore, if you meet with one or t'other of your Cousins, press him to go home with you, to refresh himself with a glass of Wine; O it will be extreamly pleasing to your Wife, and a double respect paid to him; because you bring him to a collation among other Cousins, and pretty Gentlewomen, where the knot of friendship and familiarity is renewed and faster twisted. And who knows, if you bring in a Batchelor, but there may perhaps arise a new marriage, which would be extraordinarily pleasing to your Wife; for there is nothing more agreeable to the female sex, then that they may be instrumental in helping their Bridemaids to husbands. And thus you will see a double increase of your Minions, and your Wife get more friends to accompany her, and drive fancies out of her head.

If your Wife should fail in her choice of houshold-stuff, and other sort of those appurtenances; doubt not but these will be prudent School-Mistresses for her, if she be unexperienc'd, to counsel and advise her to buy of the richest and newest mode, and what will be neatest, and where to be bought. Oh these are so skilfull in the art of ordring things, that you need not dispute with your Wife about the hanging of a Picture above the Chimney-mantel! for they'l presently say, there's nothing better in that place then large China dishes; and that Bed-stead must be taken down, and another set up in the place with curious Curtains and Vallians, and Daslles: And thus, they will deliver themselves, like a Court full of wise Counsellors, for the pleasure and instruction of your Beloved. Well, what could you wish for more? D'ye talk of mony? Pish, that's stamp'd with hammers: give it liberally; the good Woman knows how and where to lay it out. If there be but little mony by the hand; be silent of that, it might happen to disturb your Dear, and who knows wherein it may do her harm. It is not the fashion that Women, especially young married ones, should take care for that. 'Tis care enough for her, if she contrive and consider what must be bought, and what things will be most suitable together. For this care is so great, that she never wakens in the night, but she thinks on't; yea it costs her many an hours rest; therefore ought not to be so lightly esteemed.

And now, O young husband, since you are come to the first step of the School to exercise your patience; it is not fit that you should already begin to grumble and talk how needfull it is to be sparing and thrifty; that Merchandising and trading is mighty dead; that monies is not to be got in; and that here and there reckonings and bills must be paid: O no! you must be silent, tho you should burst with discontent. For herewith, perhaps, the whole house would be out of order; and you might get for an answer, How! have I married then a pittifull poor Bridegroom? This would be sad to hear.

Go therefore to School by *Pythagoras* to learn silence; and to look upon all things in the beginning with patience; to let your Wife do her own pleasure; and to mix hony with your words. Then you shall possess the quintessence of this Pleasure fully, and with joyfull steps enter upon the folowing.

THE THIRD PLEASURE.

The young couple walk daily abroad, being entertained and treated by all their friends and acquaintance; and then travell into the Country for their pleasure.

If it be true that there is a Mountain of Mirth and pleasure for young married people to ascend unto, these are certainly the finest and smoothest conductors to it; that, because it was impossible to invite every one to the Wedding, this sweet *Venus* must be led abroad, and shewed to all her husbands friends & acquaintance: yea, all the World must see what a pretty couple they are, and how handsomly they agree together. To which end they trick and prick themselves daily up in their best apparel; garnishing both the whole city and streets with tatling and pratling; & staring into the houses of all their acquaintance to see whether they are looked at.

Folio 52.
Published by The Navarre Society, London.

Do but see what a mighty and surpassing mirth! for they hardly can go ten or twelve furlongs but they constantly meet and are saluted by some of their acquaintance, wishing them all health, happiness and prosperity; or by others invited to come in, and are treated according as occasion presents, wishing them also much joy in their married estate; Yea the great Bowl is rins'd, and about goes a brimmer to the good prosperity of the young couple. Well, thinks the young woman, what a vast difference there is between being a married woman & a maid! How every one receives &

treats you! What respect and honour every one shews you! How you go daily in all your gallantry taking pleasure! And how every where you are fawn'd upon, imbrac'd and kist, receiving all manner of friendship! It is no wonder that all womankind are so desirous of marriage, and no sooner lose their first husbands, but they think immediately how to get a second? Oh, saith she, what a fulness of joy there is in the married estate, by Virginity! I resolve therefore to think also upon my Bridemaids, and to recommend them where ever there is occasion.

And this is the least yet, do but see! what for greater pleasure! for every foot you are invited out here & there to a new treat, that is oft-times as noble and as gallant as the Wedding was, and are plac'd alwaies at the upper end of the Table. If next day you be but a little drousie, or that the head akes; the husband knows a present remedy to settle the brain; and the first thing he saith, is, Come lets go to see Master or Mistriss such a one, and walk out of Town to refresh our selves, or else go and take the air upon the *Thames* with a Pair of Oars. Here is such a fresh mirth again that all *Lambeth*, the *Bankside*, and *Southwark* shakes with it. Oh that *Apollo* would but drive his horses slowly, that the day might be three hours longer; for it is too soon to depart, and that for fear of a pocky setting of the Watch. So that its every day Fair-time. Well, who is so blind that he cannot see the abundant pleasures of marriage?

To this again, no sooner has the young couple been some few daies at rest, and begin to see that the invitements decline; but the young woman talks of going out of Town together, and to take their pleasures in other Towns and Cities, first in the next adjacent places, and then to others that ly remoter; for, because she never was there, and having heard them commended to be such curious and neat places, she hath a great mind to see *Oxford* and *Cambridge*.

Yea, and then she saith, my dear, we must go also to see *York*, *Glocester* and *Bristol*, and take our pleasures those waies; for I have heard my Fathers Book keeper often say, that it is very pleasant travelling thither, and all things very cheap. And when he began to relate any thing of Kent, and its multiplicity of fruit, my very heart leapt up for joy; thinking to my self, as soon as I am married, I will immediately be pressing my husband that we may go thither; because it seem'd to me almost incredible. And then again he would sometimes relate of *Herefordshire* what delicious Syder and Perry is made there, which I am a great lover of; truly Hony, we must needs go that way once, that I may say I have satiated my self with it, at the Fountain-head. Ah, my dearest, let us go thither next week.

It is most certain that the Good-man hath no mind at all to be thus much longer out of his house, & from his vocation; by reason he is already so much behind hand with his loss of time in Wooing, Wedding, Feasting and taking pleasure; but alas, let him say what he will, he cannot disswade her from it.

> *You may as soon retort the wind,*
> *As make a woman change her mind.*

In the night she dreams on't, and by day she talks on't, and alwaies concludes this to be her certain rule. "The first year won't come again. If we don't take some pleasure now, when shall we do it! Oh, my Dear, a year hence we may have a child, then its impossible for me to go any where, but I shall be tied like a Dog to a chain: And truly, why should not we do it as well as they & they did; for they were out a month or two, and took their pleasures to the purpose? my Mother, or my Cousin will look to our house; come let us go also out of Town! For the first year will not come again."

Well, what shall the good man do? if he will have quietness with his wife, he must let her have her will, or else she will be daily tormenting of him. And to give her harsh language, he can't do that, for he loves her too well. His father also taught him this saying, for a marriage lesson, *Have a care of making the first difference.* If he speak unkindly to her, his Love might be angry, and then that would occasion the first difference, which he by no means willingly would be guilty of; for then these Pleasures would not have their full swing.

Well, away they go now out of Town: But, uds lid, what a weighty trunk they send the Porter with to the Carriers! For they take all their best apparel with them, that their friends in the Country, may see all their bravery. And besides all this, there must be a riding Gown, and some other new accoutrements made for the journy, or else it would have no grace.

Now then, away they go, every one wishing them all health and prosperity upon their journy, & so do I.

But see! they are hardly ridden ten mile out of Town, before the young woman begins to be so ill with the horses jolting, that she thinks the World turns topsie-turvy with her. Oh she's so ill, that she fears she shall vomit her very heart up. Then down lights her husband, to take her off, and hold her head, and is in such a peck of troubles, that he knows not which way to turn or wind himself. Wishing that he might give all that he's worth in the World to be at a good Inn. And she poor creature falling into a swoon, makes him look as if he had bepist himself, & though he sighs and laments excessively she hears him not; which occasions him such an extremity of grief that he's ready to tear the hair off of his head. But the quamishness of her stomack beginning to decline, she recovers; and rising, they walk for a little space softly forwards; the good man thinking with himself how he shall do to get his dearly beloved to an Inn, that she may there rest her distempered body. And then getting her up again, they ride very softly forwards, to get to the end of their journey.

Truly, I must confess, that amongst the rest of the Pleasures of marriage, this is but a very sorry one. But stay a little, yonder me thinks I see the Steeple, we shall be there presently; the little trouble and grief you have had, will make the salutations you receive, and the scituation of the place seem so much the pleasanter. And these dainty green Meadows will be a delicate refreshment. You'l find your stomack not only sharpned, but also curiously cleansed of all sorts of filthy and slimy humours. And you light not sooner from your horse then your appetite is ready to entertain what ever comes before you: The good Man in the mean while is contriving at whose house he shall first whet his knife, and where he thinks his poor wearied wife will receive the best entertainment and caresses, to drive out of her imaginations the troubles and wearisomness of her journy; which will the easier be dispensed with, when she walks out to see the rarities of the place, and to visit your Cousins and relations. And so much the more, because every one will be wishing the new married couple much joy, receiving them kindly, and doing them all manner of pleasures and civilities: which I assure you is no small matter of mirth.

But every thing must have an end. It is therefore now very meet to speak of removing to some other City. But let the husband say what he will of travelling by horseback, she is struck on that ear with an incurable deafness.

They must have a Coach to themselves, and the great Trunk must go along with them, or else the whole journy would have no grace. Neither would it be respect enough for them in the presence of so many good friends and acquaintance, unless the Coach come to take them up at the dore. And it must be done to. Here now one is returning thanks for th'entertainment, and the other for their kind visit, and withall wish the young couple that all content, pleasure, and delight may further attend them upon their journy, &c. Then it is Drive on Coachman, and away fly the poor jades through the streets, striking fire out of the liveless stones, as if Pluto just at the same time were upon the flight with his Proserpina through the City.

But, O new married couple, what price do you little think this mirth will stand you at? What man is there in the World, that hath ever an eye in his head, but must needs see, that if he tarry out long, this must be the ready way to Brokers-Hall. Yet nevertheless I confess you must do it, if you intend to have any peace or quietness with your new wife.

These are the first fruits and pleasures of marriage, therefore you must not so much as consider, nay hardly think, of being so long from home, though in the mean while all things there is going also the ready way to destruction; for it is the fashion, at such times, that maid, man, and all that are in your service, to act their own parts; and so merry they are that they possess their own freedom, and keep open Table, that the whole neighbourhood hears their laughter. Ask the neighbours when you come home, and you will quickly hear, that by them was no thought of care or sorrow; but that they have plaied, ranted and domineer'd so that the whole neighbourhood rung with it; and how they have played their parts either with some dried Baker, pricklouse Tailor, or smoaky Smith, they themselves know best.

Down goes the spit to the fire; the pudding pan prepared; and if there be either Wine, Beer or any thing else wanting; though the Cellar be lockt; yet, by one means or another, they find out such pretty devices to juggle the Wine out of the Cask, nay and Sugar to boot too; that their inventions surpass all the stratagems that are quoted by the Author of the English

Rogue; of which I could insert a vast number, but fear that it would occasion an ill example to the unlearned in that study. Howsoever they that have kept house long, and had both men & maid-servants, have undoubtedly found both the truth and experience hereof sufficiently. And how many maids, in this manner, have been eased of that heavy burthen of their maidenheads, is well known to the whole World.

These are also some of the first fruits and delights of marriage; but if they were of the greatest sort, they might be esteemed and approved of to be curable, or a remedy found for prevention. Yet let them be of what state and condition they will, every one feels the damage and inconvenience thereof, ten times more then it is outwardly visible unto him, or can comprehend. For if you saw it you would by one or other means shun or prevent it. But now, let it be who it will, whether Counsellor, Doctor, Merchant, or Shopkeeper; the one neglects his Clients Suit, the other his Patients, the third his Negotiation & Trade, and the fourth his Customers; none of them all oft-times knowing from whence it arises that their first years gain is so inconsiderable. For above the continual running on of house-rent, the neglect and unnecessary expensive charge of servants; you consume your self also much mony in travelling and pleasure; besides the peril and uneasiness that you suffer to please and complaite your new married Mistris. O miserable pleasure!

But you will be sure to find the greatest calamity of this delight, as soon as you return home again; if you only observe the motions of your wife, for whose pleasure and felicity you have been so long from home. Alas she is so wearied and tired with tumbling and travelling up & down, that she complains as if her back were broke, and it is impossible for her to rise before it is about dinner time; nay and then neither hardly unless she hear that there is something prepared suitable to her appetite. If any thing either at noon or night is to be prepared and made ready, the husband must take care and give order for the doing of it; the good woman being yet so weary, that she cannot settle her self to it; yea it is too much for her to walk about her chamber, her very joints being as it were dislocated with the troublesomness of the journy.

In the mean while the servants they ly simpring, giggling, and laughing at one another, doing just what they list, and wishing that their Mistris might be alwaies in that temper, then they were sure to have the more freedom to themselves: the which, though done by stealth, they make as bad as may be: and yet hardly any man, tho he had the eyes of *Argolus* can attrap them; for if by chance you should perceive any thing, they will find one excuse or another to delude you, and look as demure as a dog in a halter, whereby the good man is easily pacified and satisfied for that time.

And these things are more predominant, when there is a cunning slut of a Maid, that knows but how to serve and flatter her Mistris well, getting her by that means upon her side: in such cases you'l generally see two maids where one might serve, or else a Chair-woman; the one to do all the course work, the other to run of errands and lend a helping hand (if she hath a mind to it) that all things may the sooner be set in order; & she then with her Mistris may go a gadding.

And because Peggy & her Mistris, do in this manner, as it were, like a Jack in a box, jump into each others humour, the good woman may take her rest the better; for she hath caretakers enough about the house. And if the husband, coming from the Change or other important affair, seems to be any waies discontented, that all things lies stragling about the house, & are not set in order, presently crafty Peggy finds a fit expedient for it with complaining that her Mistris hath had such an insufferable pain in her head and in her belly, that it was beyond imagination; & also she could get no ease for her, unless she had prepared her some butter'd Ale, and a little mul'd Sack; and this is the reason why all things were not so ready as they ought to have been.

Herewith the good mans mouth is stopt. If he begins afterwards to speak with his wife concerning th'unnecessary Chair-women; his answer is, prithee Sweetheart, don't you trouble your self with those things, leave that to me, I'l manage that to the best advantage; men have no understanding about house-keeping; & it is most proper for a woman to have the governance of her Maids. And also Sweetheart, if there be now and then occasion for a semstress or a Chair-woman, they are things of so small importance, that they are not worth the speaking of.

Now, if he will have peace and quietness at home, this reply must give him full satisfaction; and tho he be never so patient, viewing all things at a distance; yet the maids behind his back, that their Mistris may more then overhear it, dare call him, a Tom *Peep in the pot,* or *Goodman busiebody.* And before dinner is fully done, he must hear *Peg* asking her Mistris; Mistris, wont you please forsooth, to go by and by and give Mistris *Moody* a visit, or discourse a little with Madam Elenor? As long as you have nothing to do, what need you ty your self to any thing? Pray tell her that story that the North Country Gentleman related, which you laught at yesterday so heartily. Madam *Elenor* will admire at it. And I'm sure she hath something that she will relate unto you. Herewith the good Mistris begins to get a drift, and away she goes with *Peg* out of dores. Let it go then as it will with the house keeping.

This is also no small pleasure, when the Mistris and the Maid alwaies agree so lovingly together! then the husband need not go any more out of Town to please his wives fancy; for she can now find pleasure enough by her old acquaintance sweet Mistris *Moody,* and courteous Madam *Elenor.*

Do but see now, O Lovers, what multiplicity of roses, and thistles there are in the very Porch of the Wilderness of Marriage; you may think then what the middle and end must be.

Folio 52.
Published by the Navarre Society, London.

THE FOURTH PLEASURE.

The Wife goes a pratling by her Neighbours; complaining of her barrenness, and takes Physick for it.

Verily it is a great pleasure for the new married couple, that they have been up and down taking their pleasure, and have been feasted by all their acquaintance.

Now they have travelled from place to place, and taken a full view of what friends and relations each other hath; and seen also the great difference there is in the ornaments, neatness, manners and deportments of each place, and also how pleasant the *Hills*, *Dales* and *Meadows* lie, with their silver streaming Brooks; but most particularly, how neatly and compleatly one may, for their money, be treated. Yet come finally to a consideration within themselves of the weakness and vanity of this pleasure; perceiving that all those who possess it, at last conclude it burthensom, and have a longing desire to be at home again in a frugal management of house-keeping at their own Tables.

Verily, this is that happy hour of pleasure that the new married man hath been long seeking for; to the end he might once be freed from all such idle expences, and be again carefully looking after his affairs and vocation. Now he begins to hope that all things will come into a handsom posture; also not doubting, but that his wife will, having had her full swing and hearts content of treats and all other sorts of pleasures, begin like a House-Wife, to order her self to take some care for the concerns of the Family, which indeed oft-times falls out so, to the great joy, profit, and tranquility of the good man.

But can it be possible that this sweet pleasure should be so disht up, without some bitter sauce of discontent? O kind Husband, if you will beleeve that, then you may well think the whole state and term of your marriage to be a Paradice upon earth; and that you have already got footing in the high-way to all fullness of pleasures and contentments: Yet tarry a few daies, and then experience will give you a better understanding of further pleasures.

For the new Wife is no sooner come to be at quiet; but she begins to complain, that she can hardly addict her self to this new way of life; that it appears very strange and odly to her to converse with a new Maid, by reason she must be telling her this thing, and commanding her the t'other; and have a regard of all what she does, which are things that she before never used to trouble her self with; and that it is such a trouble to her to be out of her Parents house, in a strange dwelling place: Nay, this oft-times surges so high, that the good man hath his hands full of work to comfort her, and to talk these foolish fancies out of her noddle; and verily, unless he can bridle her frivolous humour with some pleasant discourses, and dry up her tears with no small number of kisses; oh then he'l be sadly put to't. And if this all falls out well, before six weeks are at an end, there'l appear another dark cloud again, to eclipse this splendant Sunshine.

For behold, within a very small time the good woman begins to scrape acquaintance, and get some familiarity with her neighbours, which increaseth from day to day more and more; nay oftentimes it comes to that height, she's better to be found among her neighbours, then at home in her own family. Here she sees Mistris Wanton playing with her child that is a very pretty Babe. There she sees Mistres *Breedwell* making ready her Child-bed linnens and getting of her Clouts together. Yonder Mistris *Maudlen* complains that she doth not prove with child; & then Mistres *Young-at-it* brags how nearly she could reckon from the very bed-side. Oh then she thinks I have been married this three months, and know nothing at all of these things; it is with me still as if I were yet a maid: What certainly should be the reason thereof?

This is the first occasion that begets a great disturbance in the brain-pan and imagination; and wo be to the good man, if he doth not understand his Py-work well! Then to the end she may hear the better how things goes; she inquires very earnestly amongst her acquaintance what caresses they receive from their husbands; and most shamlesly relates what hath passed between her and her husband, twixt the curtains, or under the Rose; which she doth to that purpose, that she may hear whether her husband understands his work well, and whether he doth it well, and oft enough; and also whether he be fully fit for the employ, &c. for the verification whereof the Councel of women bring so many compleat relations, that it is a shame to think, much more to speak of them.

Whosoever she speaks with every one pities her, and gives her their advice: And the best sort will at the least say to her, I would oftentimes treat my husband with such sort of spices as were good for my self, *viz.* Oisters, Egs, Cox-combs, sweet breads, Lam-stones, Caveer, &c. and counsell him every morning to go to the Coffe-house and drink some Chocolate; & above all things advise him to desist from Tabacco and drying things, or any other things that are too cooling for the kidneys. And then I would many times my self by dallying with him, and some other pretty Wanton postures, try to provoke him to it; whereby he should surely know that it was neither your coolness, nor want of desire that might be blamed in it; but rather alwaies confess, that you had sufficiently done your indeavour.

Who will doubt but that she puts this advice, in operation? O happy man, who art now every foot treated with some new sorts of kickshaws at your Table; and have free leave to frequent the Coffy-house, which other women grumble and mumble at. And besides all this, you find that your dearest embraceth you as if you were an Angel, and shews you a thousand other friendly entertainments that are beyond imagination to express: it is alwaies in the evening, my Dear come to bed: and in the morning, pray Love ly a little longer. These are most certainly very great pleasures.

But if the Woman marks that this helps not, and that all things remain in the old posture, then she begins to mump and maunder at her husband; vaunting much of her own fitness, and not a little suspecting her husbands; oftentimes calling him a Fumbler, a dry-boots, and a good man Do-little, &c.

This makes him look as if he had beshit him self. And though he never so much indeavours to vindicate himself; and also to perswade her from the reasons and examples given by several learned Doctors; Culpepper; the Queens Midwife; and some others of his friends and acquaintance that he demonstrates unto her; it is all but wind. She still complains, I must have a Child, or else I shall run distracted.

And this manner of frantickness hath so vehemently struck into her brains, that the very house seems to burn over her head: Insomuch that she's no sooner risen from her bed or from the Table, but immediately she goeth a gadding amongst the neighbours; and takes other peoples children in her arms, kissing and slabbring of them so unmeasurably, as if she would almost devour them with love; nay she useth more simple and childish actions with them, then ever own mothers have done. By which means the children have many times as great an affection for their neighbour, as they have for their own Father and Mother.

This gadding out of dores doth undoubtedly a little trouble her husband: But when he begins to consider, that his wife by this means knows how to handle, and make much of children; and then again, that she thus beforehand learns it for nothing; it must of necessity be no less then a great pleasure for him. And so much the more, whilest she is pratling with her neighbour, and playing with her child; he is freed from the curse of hearing her sighs and complaints to have a child. For she's no sooner within the dores, but she talks of her neighbours child, and wishes with the loss of all that shes worth in the World that she had such a one too; which continues alwaies so long, that finally she bursts out into the like former frenzy against her husband: see there I must have a child also, or else I shall run distracted.

But what remedy? which way he turns or winds himself, he finds no means or way how to pacifie his wife. And therefore thinks it best himself to take th'advice of Doctor, and most especially with that French Doctor, who is so renowned for his skill of making many men and women that before were barren and unfruitfull to conceive children: Insomuch that they do now every year precisely bear a young son, or a daughter, yea somtimes two at a time. It is thereby also very necessary that the good woman her self consult with some experienced Midwives, and old Doctresses; to the end, that those distempers which are the occasion of barrenness, might be the better removed and taken away.

To this end there are almost as many Boxes and Gally-pots brought together, as would near upon furnish an Apothecaries shop: Then to work they go with smearing, anointing, chafing, infusing, wherewith (as they term it) the good woman is to be made fresh and fit; but they make the bed and whole house so full of stink and vapours, that it may be said they rather stop the good and wholesom pores and other parts of the body; then to open those that were stopt and caused Distempers.

But in the conclusion we find it to be both fruitless and miserable, where the good woman goes to seek it by th'Apothecary; even as her husband doth out of the Oister and Eg-shels.

And if this will not do now; where shall the poor man hide his head next? What shall he do more to please and pacifie her? He thinks upon all the ways and means possible to entertain her to content. If she will have costly things, he will buy them for her; and dissimulately saith that all what she practiseth for her content, is his only pleasure and delight: yea, although her pride and ambition many times in several things flies too high, and ofttimes also doth not happen to be very suitable with the constitution of the cash; he dares in no wise contradict her, for he fears that she will presently be at variance with him again: And thinks in the interim, whilest her mind hangs upon these things, she forgets her maunding and mumbling for a child. Still hoping that there will come one happy night, that may crown his earnest desires with fructivity; this it is that makes him that he dares not anger her or give her a sour countenance; fearing that if she might have conceived, that would be the means of turning the tide.

To be short, it is his only and greatest delight to see that his wife is well satisfied and receiveth her content and pleasure; which is very hard to be practised, so long as she is not with child.

But O what a joy there will be if he may be but once so happy as to hit that mark! How will the first day of her reckoning to ly in stand in his Almanack, as if it were printed with a red Letter! Well young people, be contented; Long look'd for comes at last to the satisfaction of the Master.

THE FIFTH PLEASURE.

The young Woman proves with Child, and longs.

The old Proverb tels us, that after the sour comes the sweet; and I find, jolly couple, that it is so with you also; for I hear finally that your wife is big with child: Well what a Pleasure is that! Certainly, now you see that all your Doctoring and medicining hath been to some purpose, and now you feel also that all herbs were made for some good effects.

How happy a thing it is that you have made use of a learned Doctor, and an experienced Midwife. Now is the only time to be very carefull, for fear the least accident might turn the tide with the young woman, and so she get a mischance, or some other sad mishap; and a mischance is worse for her than a true Child-bearing; for that weakens nature abundantly, and oftentimes brings with it several sad consequences, & Thus the women talk.

Folio 85.
Published by The Navarre Society, London.

But you, O noble Champion, who have behaved your self so gallantly; continue now to reap the further conquests of your honour. Look not at any small matters; and most especially if you hope or desire to gain the principal prize of your pleasure. For be assured, that you must suffer much, and see through a perspective glass all things at a distance; because you never before saw your wife in so gallant a state and condition as she now is in; and therefore you must cherish and preserve her much more then formerly you have done. If you hear her often grunt and groan, mumble and chide, either with the men or maid-servants; nay, though it were with your own self, you must pass it by, not concerning your self at it; and imagine that you do it for the respect you bear your wife, but not by constraint; for it is common with big-bellied women to do so.

But most especially rejoice in your self, if this grunting and groaning happen only by day time; because then you may somtimes avoid it, or divertise your self with other company. Yet by night generally shall the good woman be worst of all? therefore be sure to provide your self well with pure Aniseed, Clove, Cinamon-waters, and good sack, that you may therewith be ready to strengthen and assist her. For it will often happen that when you are in your best and first Sleep, that your dearest wil waken you and complain of pain at her heart, of dizziness and great faintness; then all what is in the house must be stirring, and you your self also, though it be never so cold, out of the bed you must with all the speed possible. Comfort your self herewith, that this was one of the pleasures which you got with your wife, though it was not set down in the Contract of marriage.

Now for this again you alwaies receive the honour, that when you are invited with her to any place at a treat, the best that is upon the Table shall be presented to the big-bellied woman: Yea if she long or have a desire to any thing; immediately every one that observes it, are ready to serve her with it; nay, though there were never so little in the Dish, her longing must be fully satisfied, if no body else should so much as tast of it. And by this means oftentimes the good woman is so ill and disturbed, that she is forced to rise from the Table, and falls from one faintness into another; which for civilities sake, is then baptized, that she hath sat too high or been throng'd, or that the room being so full, the breath of the people offended her.

And though she perceives that this very food makes her so ill; yet for the most part she will be so choice and so dainty, that she seldom knows her self what she will eat or hath a mind to; but generally it tends to some thing or other that is delicate: Upon this manner again, according to the former custom, she tumbles it in till she is sick with it; and if any one looks but very wishly at her; immediately another saies to them; she must eat for two, nay perhaps for three.

And not only that in this manner she grows so delicate and gluttonous; but is thereby so easie and lazy, that she can hardly longer indure her sowing cushion upon her lap. Also sitting is not good for her, for fear the child thereby might receive some hindrance and an heartfullness. Therefore she must often walk abroad; and to that end an occasion is found to go every day a pratling and gossiping to this and then to another place; in the mean while leaving her husband without a wife, and the family without a mistris.

Then in conclusion this falls also burthensom to her, (as it is generally with all things that are too frequently used) then she will be for spurring you up to walk abroad with her, that she may get all sorts of fruits and other fopperies that the season of the year affords; and at the first baiting-place she's for some Cream with sugar, stewd prunes, and a bottle of sider or perry; and thus abroad to spend much, and at home neglect more.

If she have then gone somthing far, she is so excessive weary with it, that if her life must ly at stake, she cannot set one foot further. Herewith is the poor man absolutely put to a stand: ride she may not, or all the fat would be in the fire; and they are so deep in the Country that there is somtimes neither Coach nor boat to be had.

And if you should happen to be where a River is, there's never a boat to be had; but if there should be one, then you must be subject to humour the churlish Ferry man, who seeing the necessity of the occasion, and that you are able to pay for it, will have what price he pleases. And somtimes again you are timorous your self to hazard it, because many women are very fearfull upon the water.

But indeed, if by this unhappy occasion, a good expedient may be found to please your dearly beloved, it is no small joy. Well then make your self jocund herewith, to the end that other troubles may not so much molest and disturb you.

You may also be very well assured, that your wife no sooner comes to be a little big-bellied, but she receives the priviledge to have all what she hath a mind to & that is called Longing. And what husband can be so stern or barbarous that he will deny his wife at such a time what she longs for? especially if it be a true love of a woman, you must never hinder her of her longing; for then certainly the child would have some hindrance by it.

Forasmuch then as is necessary that you alwaies seek to avoid and prevent this, you must observe, that all women when they are with child, do fall commonly from one longing to another: And then the providing and buying of that for them, must be as great a pleasure to you as it is to them in the receiving and use of it; and that not alone for theirs, but your childs sake also. And truly he that will or cannot suit himself to this humour, will be very unhappy, because he shall not then receive the full scope and freedom of this pleasure.

It is also most certain that these longing desires doth transport their imaginations from one finical thing to another: If it be in the summer, then they long for China Oranges, Sivil Lemmons, the largest Asparagus, Strawberries with wine and sugar, Cherries of all sorts, and in like manner of Plums, and these they must have their fill of: And then when they have gotten through the continuance their full satisfaction thereof; then be assured they begin to long for some great Peaches and Apricocks; And though they be never so scarce and dear, yet the woman must not lose her longing, for the child might get a blemish by it.

If then Apples and Pears begin to grow ripe, you have the same tune to sing again; for she is possessed with a new longing desire as bad, as if it were a Quotidian Ague in all the joints of her body; and whatsoever comes new to her sight, creates in her a fresh longing. If she gets one hour curious Catherine Pears, Pippins, or Russetings, the next she hath a mind to Filberds; and then an hour or two later Wall nuts and Grapes fall into her thoughts; do what you will there's no help for it, her longing must be satisfied, let it go as it will, or cost what it will.

And this her longing leads her from one thing to another, of all what the richness of the summer, or liberality of the harvest, out of their superfluities pour down upon us. Insomuch that the good man wishes a thousand times over that he might once be rid of these terrible charges and great expence.

But alas what helps it? there's no season of the year but gives us some or other new fruits that the women have alwaies a new longing desire to. And if it be in the Winter, then they long for juicy Pomgranates, new Wine upon the must, with Chesnuts; then for Colchester Oisters; then again for Pancakes and Fritters; and indeed for a thousand several sorts of such toys and fancies as do but appear before their longing imaginations. And oftentimes it is no real longing, for that were then pardonable, but a liquorish delicate desire that they are sick of; as may be seen by those who simply imagine themselves to be with child, are alwaies talking of this and t'other dainty that they long after. And that which is worst of all, is that both they and those that are really with child, long commonly for that which is scarcest and hardest to be gotten: Yea in the very middle of winter they oftentimes long to have a Greengoose or young Chickens; which in some places are very hard to be got, and not without paying excessive dear for them.

This longing being so satisfied; immediately arises another, and nothing will serve but Meats, and several sorts of Comfits. Yea how often happens it, though it rain, snow, and is very slippery, that both the husband and the maid, if never so dark and late in the night, must trot out and fetch candied Ginger, dried Pears, Gingerbread, or some such sort of liquorish thing. And what is to be imagined, that can be cried about in the streets by day time, but her longing before hath an appetite prepared for it?

Yea through an excessive eating of raw fruits, and feeding upon multiplicities of sweet-meats; to fulfill their longing; it turns to a griping of the guts and overflowing of the Gall, which again occasion Cholick, & manytimes other lamentable pains. Here is then another new work. There the Doctor must be presently fetcht, and according to what he pleases to order, either a Glister must be set, or some other Physick taken for it.

But by reason these things are not so pleasant to the good woman as the foregoing liquorish delicacies; she thinks it best that the Midwife be sent for, because she hath a great deal better knowledge touching the infirmities of women then the Doctors: Then she is fetcht, and having done the first part of her office, she gives her good comfort; and orders her to take only some of the best white Wine, simper'd up with a little Orange-peel, well sweetned with sugar, and so warm drunk up; and then anoint your self here, and you know where, with this salve; and for medicines [that are most to be found in Confectionres or Pasterers shops] you must be sure to make use of those, then your pain will quickly lessen. You must not neglect also ofttimes to eat a piece of bread and butter with either Caroway or Aniseed Comfits; use also Cinnamon; the first expels wind, and the second strengthens the heart; and they are both good for the woman and the child. Be sure also to drink every morning and every evening a glass of the best sack, for that strengthens the fruit of the womb, and occasions you a good quickness, &c.

Who will doubt, but that she obeys the orders of the Midwife, much better then that of the Doctors. And verily there is also a great deal of difference in the suffering, of such or uneasie fumbling at the back part; or the receiving of such pleasant and acceptable ingredients. And so much the more, when she begins to remember that Doctor Drink-fast used to tell her, that Medicins never make so good an operation, when they are at any time taken against the appetite, or with an antipathy, by the Patient.

Thus you may see, approaching Father, how you are now climb'd up to a higher step of glory: Your manly deeds, make your name renowned; and your joy is so much augmented that your wife looks alwaies merrily and pleasantly upon you, for giving her content; and she now also salutes you with the most sweetest and kindest names imaginable; you must also now be her guest upon all sorts of Summer and Winter fruits, & a thousand other kinds of liquorish and most acceptable dainties. Insomuch that although you did not come into the streets in six months, you may by the humour and actions of your wife know perfectly when Strawberries, Cherries, Apples, Pears, Nuts & Grapes, are in season. And there is no greater pleasure for your best beloved, then that she sees you eat as heartily of them as she her self doth.

Confess then unfeignedly, from the very bottom of your heart; are not these great Pleasures of marriage? And be joyfull; for this is only a beginning, the best comes at last. Know likewise, that this is but as a fore-runner of the sixth Pleasure, and will both touch you at heart, and tickle your purse much better: Yea, insomuch that the experience thereof will shew you that there is a whole mountain of pleasures to be found in the bands of Wedlock. Whereby I fear, that you will, perhaps, make a lamentable complaint, of your no sooner arriving at this happiness.

But comfort your self herewith; that the medicaments of the Doctor and Midwife, perhaps have done such a wished for operation, that you thereby may obtain many Sons and Daughters, which you may then timely admonish and instruct to that duty, so long by your self neglected, and in a manner too late to repent of.

Doubt not, but assuredly beleeve, that now you are once gotten into the right road, you may easily every year see a renovation of this unspeakable pleasure; and beholding your wife oftentimes in this state; in like manner you perceive that not only your name and fame is spread abroad, but your generation also grow formidable. And this all to the glory of your relations, and joy of your dearly Beloved.

Folio 102.
Published by the Navarre Society, London.

THE SIXTH PLEASURE.

Care is taking for the Child and Child-bed linnen; and to provide a Midwife and Nurse.

In good truth it is very pleasant to see how the good womans Apron from day to day, how longer the more it rises; now all the World may plainly see you have behaved your self like a man, and every one acknowledge that you are both good for the sport. Verily this is a great pleasure! And it increases abundantly, when your wife comes to be so near her reckoning, that she feels her self quick, and begins to provide and take care for the Childs and Child-bed linnen. Then you need not fear the turning of the tide, or that a mischance will happen; wherewith all people, seeing no other issue, laugh and scoff unmeasurably; and think that the Midwife hath been greased in the fist (as it oftentimes happens) because she should say, that it was a full created child, and no collection of ill humors, or a wind-egg.

And the greatest joy is, that you have now so hoisted your top-sail, that your wife cannot any more call you a *Dry-boots*, or a *John Cannot*; which were for you such disrespectfull names, and yet for quietness sake you were forced to smother them in your breast, because you could have no witnesse for your vindication.

You are now so far exalted, that you will very speedily be saluted with the name of *Dad* & *Pappa*; which is as pleasing and acceptable for you now, as the name of *Bridegroom* was before.

O how happy you are! & what pleasures doth the married estate provide for you! how glad must your wife be now! how strictly she reckons the months, nay the very weeks and days! O what an unexpressible love hath she for you now! and with what imbraces and kisses she entertains you, because you have furnish'd her shop so well! Now you may perceive that the procreating of children, makes the band of wedlock much stronger, and increaseth the affections.

Now were it well time, that by death either of the good woman or the Child, that you did, by a will, seek the mortification of the disadvantagious Contract of marriage; and by that means get all there is to your self, in place of going back to her friends and relations; But, alas, she hath so much in her head at present, that there is no speaking to her about it, without being a great trouble to her: besides her sences cannot now bear it therefore you must let it alone till another time.

Do you your self but observe, & you'l quickly see that a lying-in requireth so much trimming, that she hath really care enough upon her! the Child-bed linnen alone, is a thing that would make ones head full of dizziness, it consists of so many sorts of knick-knacks; I will not so much as name all the other jinkombobs that are dependances to it. Therefore, ought you to be so compassionate with her, as not to speak to her about any other thing; for all her mind and sences are so imploied upon that subject, that she can think upon nothing else but her down-lying. Hear but deliberately to all her lying-in, and of what belongs to it. Tis no wonder neither for there is not one of her acquaintance comes to her, either woman or maid, but they presently ask her, Well, Mistris, when do you reckon? And that is a Text then, so full of matter that there is oftentimes three or four hours preacht upon it, before any of the Auditors be weary. O that all Ministers were so happy, as to have alwaies such earnest and serious hearers. In the mean while there is no body happier than the maids, for they are then free from being the Town-talk; for at other times, the first word is, How do you like your maid? which is another Text that the women generally preach out of, and make longest sermons in.

But methinks, I should happen to fall here from the Mistris upon the Maid.

To go forward then. See how serious your dearest is, with *Jane* the Semstress, contriving how much linnen she must buy to make all her Child-bed linnen as it ought to be! how diligently she measures the Beds, Bellibands, Navel clouts, shirts, and all other trincom, trancoms! and she keeps as exact an account of the ells, half ells, quarters, and lesser measures, as if she had gone seven years to school to learn casting of an account.

Let this measuring and reckoning be pleasant to you, because the charge thereof will fall costly enough for you. To morrow she goes to market, to buy two or three pieces of linnen, one whereof must be very fine, and the other a little courser. And you need not take any notice what quantity of fine small Laces she hath occasion for, by reason it might perhaps overcloud this sixth pleasure of marriage, which you now possess.

Why should you not be merry? you have now above all things a Wife to your mind; who whatsoever she imagines, desires or doth, it is alwaies accompanied with wishes. O, saies she, how glad shall I be; when all things is bought that there ought to be for the making of my Child-bed linnen. And no sooner is it bought, but then she wishes that it were made.

But this requires some time: and then you'l have reason to rejoice; for it is commonly the usual custom of the semstresses to let you go and run after them, and fop you off with lies and stories, till the time be so nigh at hand, that it will admit no longer delay.

Yet before you see that your wife hath accomplisht this desire, you'l find her very much troubled at two several causes, which will make you glad when she hath once obtained them. For these are things of importance, to wit, the making choice of a Midwife and a Nurse, because upon one depends the health and preservation of the life of the Woman; and on the other that of the Child.

Let it no waies molest or trouble you, but rather be pleasing and acceptable, if she be continually chattering at you, and desiring your advice and councell, who she shall make choice of or not; hereby you may observe, that you have a very carefull wife; and if you listen a little more narrowly, you will hear what a special care she hath for all things; then she will every day be relating to you that amongst the number of Midwives which have been recommended to her, there is not one that pleases her; for one is too young and unexperienced, another is too old and doting; a third is too big handed; a fourth hath too much talk; and the fifth drinks too much wine. To be short there is so many deficiencies in every one of them, that the good woman hath need of a learned Counsellors advice to help her to chuse the best.

And the like trouble hath she also concerning the taking of a Nurse, having already spent above a months time in examining among her kindred and relations, and other good acquaintance, how such and such nurses have behaved themselves; & she is informed that there are few to be found but have certainly some faults or other, and somtimes very great ones, for one is too sluttish, another saunters too much, a third too lazy; another too dainty: and then again, one eats too much, and another drinks too much; one keeps company too much with the maid, and another in like manner with the good man: And such a one or such a one are the best, but they were not very handy about the hearth, to make ready some liquorish dainty things for the good woman, which is a matter of no small weight.

Behold! hath she not very great cause to be troubled: and thereout you may very well also observe how happy you are, seeing you have gotten a wife that night and day is busie and taking care of all these concerns and other affairs. Yes verily, although her big-belly be very cumbersom to her, yet she must be abroad, every day from morning till evening, to take care and provide all these important things, that nothing may be wanting. Well what a carefull wife you have! how mightily she is concerned for this above all other things whatsoever!

And scarcely hath the good woman gotten these two main instruments; but she finds her self still involved in so much other business, that she hardly can tell how to do or turn her self in it; for now there wants a Groaning stool, a Screen, and a Cradle, with what belongs to it; and heaven knows what more, which have been so long neglected with the care that was taking to get a Midwife and a Nurse. Then again there wants new Hangings, a Down-bed, a Christening-cloath, silver candle sticks, a Caudle-cup, &c. that of necessity must be bought & used at the lying-in, & Gossips feast; so that the good man need not fear that his mony will grow mouldy for want of being turned too & again.

Oh were your dear wife so happy that she had once made an end of all these ponderous affairs, then all would be well: For then she could begin to give order for the making clean the house from top to bottom; and for the pressing of some curtains, Vallians and Hangings; the rubbing of Stools, Chairs and Cupboard; the scouring of the Warming-pan and Chamber-pot: And 'tis no wonder, for when the good woman lies in, then come so many busie bodies that with their glouring eyes are peeping into every hole and corner.

These things do so excessively trouble her brain; that she can hardly the whole day think upon any thing else, yea goes so near her that it oftentimes totally bereaves her of her nights rest insomuch that she is fain to ly very long abed in the morning. And if by night she happen but only to think of Boobincjo, she hath immediately such an alteration in her very intrals, that she feels here or there some or other deficiency; which comes so vehement upon her that the poor husband, though it be never so cold, must out of bed to fetch some Cinnamon and Annis-seed water, or good sack; or else some other such sort of those liquorish ingredients and then these are the principal keys of Musick that the whole night through are sung and plaid upon. O how happy is the good man, that he hath, from time to time, in her child-bearing, learned all these things with so much patience, which makes him now that he can the better bear with all these finical humours.

But for this again, O compassionate Ninny-hammer, you shall have not only great commendations for your patience; but the pleasure also that some of your nearest relations will come and kiss your hands, and withall tell you how happy you are that y'are almost arrived at that noble degree of being intituled Father. And then, with great respect & reverence, they desire to receive the honour, some of being your first-born childs God-fathers, and others to be God-mothers: Neither will they then be behind hand in presenting the Child with several liberal gifts, as an acknowledgement of the honour they receive, above others, in being favoured with your Gossipship.

Well who would not, for so much honour and respect, but now and then suffer the trouble of his wives quamish stomack with some charges to't? And more then that, you have now the best opportunity in the World, to go with your new chosen Gossips, (as you did before with your Bridemen) & chuse & taste out some of the most delicious Wine, for you must be sure to store your Cellar well, because then both the Bridemen and Bride-maids will certainly come to eat some of the long-look'd for Caudle; besides the great number of friends that will come then also to give you a visit, and with all respect wish you much joy: I will not so much as think any thing of those that will come also to the Christning and Gossips Feast.

Be joyfull with this, till such time as the t'other Pleasure begins to appear.

THE SEVENTH PLEASURE.

The Woman falls in Labour.

Behold, young couple, hitherto a considerable deal of time is spent and passed over, with the aforesaid Mirth and Pleasures; do not you now perceive what a vast difference is between the married or unmarried estate? You have, by provision, made your self Master of these six Pleasures; nay oftentimes before you have gotten the longd-for joy of the fourth Pleasure, appears that of the seventh very unexpectedly; for the good woman begins to look so sour, grumble, grunt and groan, that it seems as if she would go into the Garden and fetch a Babe out of the Parsley-bed.

But Uds-lid this is a great-surprizal; for a little while ago she said that she was but seventh months gone of her reckoning. How then? should she have jested upon it? or has the good woman lost her book, and so made a false account? Yet this being the first time of her reckoning, ought the more favourably to be passed by as long as the Trade goes forwards.

Folio 116.
Published by The Navarre Society, London.

There's now no small alarm in the Watch. Who is there that is but near or by the hand that is not set a work! Oh, was Dorothy the Semstress, and Jane the laundress now here, what a helping hand we might have of them! Where are now the two Chair-women also, they were commonly every day about the house, and now we stand in such terrible need of them, they are not to be found? Herewith must the poor Drone, very unexpectedly, get out of bed, almost stark naked, having hardly time to put on his shoes and stockins; for the labour comes so pressing upon her, that it is nothing but, hast, hast, hast, fetch the Midwife with all possible speed, and alas, there is so many several occasions for help, that she cannot miss her maid the twinkling of an eye; neither dare she trust it to the Maids fetching, for fear she should not find the Midwives house; and she hath not shewed it her, because she made her reckoning that she had yet two months more to go.

Therefore without denial away the good man himself must to fetch the Midwife; for who knows whether or no she would come so quick if the maid went; nay it is a question also, being so late in the night, whether she would come along with the maid alone, because she dwells in a very solitary corner clearly at the t'other end of the City: (for after a ripe deliberation of the good woman, the lot fell so that she made choice of this grave and experienced Midwife).

Away runs the poor man without stop or stay, as if he were running for a wager of some great concern. And though it be never so cold, the sweat trickles down by the hair of his head, for fear he should not find the Midwife at home; or that perhaps she might be fetcht out to some other place, from whence she could not come. And if it should happen so, we are all undone, for the good woman must have this Midwife, or else she dies; neither can or dare she condescend to take any of the other, for the reasons afore mentioned.

But what remedy? if there must come another, then she will so alter, vex, and fret her self at it, that all the provocations of pains in labour, turns against her stomack, and there is no hopes further for that time.

But whilest you are running, and consider in this manner hope the best; rather think with your self, what great joy is approaching unto you, if your wife, thus soon, come to be safely delivered of a hopefull Son or Daughter: In the first place, you will be freed from all that trouble of rising in the night, and from the hearing of the grumbling and mumbling of your wife; two months sooner then you your self did expect you should have been.

Be not discomforted although she doth thus unexpectedly force you out of bed, before you have hardly slept an hour, for you see there's great occasion for't; and now is the time to show that you truly love your wife. This first time will make it more accustomary, the first is also commonly the worst. And if you be so fortunate that at the very first you happen to meet with this prudent and grave Matron Midwife, & do bring her to your longing-for dearly beloved Wife; yet nevertheless you may assure your self, that before you can arrive to have the full scope and heighth of this Pleasure, you'l find something more to do: For the Midwife is not able alone to govern and take care of all things that must be fetcht, brought and carried to and again; therefore of necessity the friends must be fetcht with all the speed imaginable, viz. Sisters, Wives, Aunts, Cousins, and several familiar good acquaintances must have notice of it, and be defraied to come to her quickly, quickly, without any delay; and if you do not invite them very ceremonially, every one according to their degrees and qualities, it is taken to be no small affront.

It hath hapned more then a hundred times that the Sister afterwards would not come to the Christning Feast; because, by chance, she heard, that the Brothers wife had notice given her of the Child-bearing before her self; little considering how few people the young people had in the night to assist them; or that the confusion and unexperiencedness was the occasion that they did not think of such a method or order. Nay oftentimes is this sort of jealousie arisen between the Aunt and Cousin; whereby may most certainly be observed the intelligibility of the most prudent female sex.

'Tis true this running seems both troublesom and tiresom but little doth the good man know that he is now first come into that noble School & herein his patience shall be effectually exercised or that this is but the first year of trying the same! O how happy are they that are well instructed in it.

Do but see how impatient the good expecting Father is. What is there not yet wanting, before he hath his lesson perfect! Behold the poor Drone, how he moves too & fro! see what a loss and tostication he is in! he tramples his hat under his feet, pulls the hair off his head, not knowing what he would do, or which way to help his dear Wife; and the Friends that were sent for do not come so quick as he expected, because the most part of them must first trick and prick themselves up before that they dare come; the one fearing the piercing view of another, though they be all near relations and friends.

Here he stands trembling, not knowing which way to turn himself. Womens assistance is at this present most requisite, and a good Stierman at Stern, or the ship may run upon a sand. She runs first backwards then forwards; seeks here then there. And although he hath the keys of all the Chests, and Trunks, his head runs so much a Wool gathering, that, let him do what he will, he can find no sort of those things he most stands in need of.

Alas all things is thus out of order, by reason the good woman did not think to come so soon in Childbed. Oh what manner of Jinkinbobs are not here wanting that are most useful at this occasion; and the Midwife cries and bawls for them that she's hoarse again! here's both the groaning-stool and the screen yet to be made: And Mistris *Perfect* hath them both, but they are lent out.

Yonder Peg the maid runs her anckle out of joint, and her self out of breath, to desire to borrow them of Mistris *Buy-all*. And she's hardly gotten out of dores, before they perceive that the warming pan is yet to be bought; and that that's worst of all, is, that all the Child-bed linnen is not yet starch'd or iron'd; oftentimes it happens that it is yet upon the Bankside at bleach. What a miserable condition is this!

Here the good man is at no small quandary, with all the women, oh were this the greatest disappointment for him! but presently he sees all the womens countenances looking very dole-fully and mournfully at each other, one beginning to pray; another to cry in; there comes a great alteration in the pangs and pains of her Labour; nay they are so desperate, that the fear is, either the mother or the child, or perhaps both must go to pot. For all whatsoever the Doctor hath prescribed, or that hath been fetcht from the Apothecaries; nay the very girdle of Saint *Francis* can work here no miracle.

Uds bud, this is but a sad spectacle. Oh, says Peg the maid, doth this come by marrying? I'l never venture it as long as I live. I do beleeve that it is very pleasurable to ly with a Gentleman, but the Child-bearing hath no delight at all in it. Oh I am affraid, if there come not a sudden change, that my good Mistris will not be able to undergo it. Oh sweet pretty blossom as she is.

'Tis most true, that here wants crums of comfort both for the husband and the wife; yea for the Midwife and all the rest of the Women beside; for they all cry that the tears run streaming down their cheeks; and neither their Cinamon-water, nor burnt wine, can any waies refresh or strengthen her.

Uds-lid: if there come no other tiding the sweetness of this pleasure will prove but bitter to them.

But hark a little! there comes something of a tiding, that brings us five pounds worth of courage with it. Two or three more such, would make every one of our hearts a hundred pound lighter, and the great Caudle Skellet would begin to quake and tremble.

Pray have a little patience, tarry, and in the twinkling of an eye you shall be presented with a Child, and saluted with the title of Father.

THE EIGHTH PLEASURE.

The Womans brought to bed.

Ha boys! after all the toiling, the happy hour is at last arrived, that the good Woman, finally is delivered & brought to bed: well this is a mirth and pleasure that far surpasseth all the other; for the good man is, by a whole estate, richer than he was before.

Who can imagine or comprehend the jollity of this new Father? O he is so overjoyed that it is inexpressible: Doll and Peg must out immediately to give notice of it to all the friends and acquaintance; thinking to himself that every body else will be as jocund and merry at it as he is. Do but see how busie he is! behold with what earnestness he runs up and down the house to give order that the great Caudle Skillet may be in a readiness!

Folio 127
Published by The Navarre Society, London.

What a pleasure is it for him that he sees Mistris *Do-all* attending the Midwife, and giving her all manner of warmed beds and other Clouts, the number and names whereof are without end; and that Mistris *Swift-hand* & Mistris *Fair-arse* are tumbling all things topsie-turvy forsooth to seek and prepare in a readiness all those things that are most necessary for the Child; but little doth he think that they do it more to be peeping into every hole and corner, and to have a full view of all the Child-bed linnen, then out of needfull assistance? And wo be to the Child-bed woman, if they do but find any where a Clout, Napkin or Towel, that by chance hath either a hole or a rent in it: for one or another of them will with grinning and laughing thrust her finger through it, and then shew it to the rest, taking also the first opportunity she can lay hold of, when they are a little at liberty, to make a whole tittle-tattle about it, and very much admireth the carelessness and negligence of the Child-bed woman; as if she were a greater wast-all, and worse house-wife than any of them else when to the contrary, if you should by accident come into any of their Garrets, when the linnen is just come home from washing you would oftentimes find it in such a condition, that you might very well imagine your self to be in Westminster Hall where the Colours that are Trophies of honour are hung up, one full of holes, another tatter'd & torn, and a third full of mildew.

Yet notwithstanding all this peeping and snuffling in to every nook and corner, they finally get the Child swathled: And then to the great joy of the Father, it must be presented him in state by the Midwife, with this golden expression, a Proverb not above two hundred years old, *Father, see there is your Child, God give you much joy with it, or take it speedily into his bliss.*

Uds bud how doth this tickle him! what a new mirth and pleasure is this again! see him now stand there and look like a Monky with a Cat in his arms. O what a delicate pretty condition he's now in!

Well Midwife look to't, for this joy hath taken such a tyrannical possession of his heart, that doubt not but immediately there will be a good present for you, when he gives it you back again. 'Tis no wonder, for if it be a Son, he is at least a thousand pound richer then he was before: though he may look long enough before he'l find a Bankers Bond in his Chest for the sum.

Now whilest the Child is swadled and drest up, all the other trinkum trankums are laid aside; and the Table is spread neatly to entertain the friends, who not alone for novelties sake, but also out of a sweet tooth'd liquorish appetite, long to see what is prepared for them. And I beleeve that although the Kings Cook had drest it, yet there will be one or another of them that will be discommending something, and brag that she could have made it much delicater, if there be then any one that seems not fully to beleeve her, immediately she cites two or three Ladies for her witnesses, who have given her the greatest praise and commendations for her dressing of such dishes above all others. And who can have better judgement than they? This is then a discourse for at least three hours, for they are all of them so well verst in the Kitchin affairs, that its hard for one to get a turn to speak before the other.

But this is an extraordinary Pleasure for this new Father to hear out of all their prittle pratlings how sweetly they will commend the Quill that hath received all the Colchester Oisters, Cox-combs, Sweetbreads, Lam-stones, and many other such like things, for they have found by experience that such sort of ingredients occasion very much the kindness of men to their wives. Yes, yes, saies M^{rs}. *Luxury* it is very good for my husband, and not amiss for any pallate neither, and I'm sure the better I feed my Pig, the better it is for me in the soucing out. And this discourse then is held up with such an earnestness, and continues so long, that the Child-bed woman almost gets an Ague with it, or at the least falls from one swooning into another, whilest there is not so much as any one that thinks upon her.

Happy is the good man, if he can but act the part of a Ninny, and hath busied himself for the most part in the Kitchin; then he may be now and then admitted to cast in his verdict; otherwise, let them talk as long as they will, he is forced in great misery to afford them audience. But it is much better for him, if, according as the occasion gives opportunity, there be now and then spoken something concerning the Child-bed woman, or about the shaking of the sheets, which is seldom forgotten; because he is now already so far advanced in the Cony-craft of that School, that he is gotten up to the Water Bucket.

In the mean while Peg runs too and again, almost like one out of her sences, to hunt for the Nurse, who dwels in a little street upon a back-Chamber, or in an Ally, or some other by-place; and she is just now no where else to be found but at t'other end of the City, there keeping another Gentle woman in Child-bed.

Here is now again other fish to fry, for one will not be without her, and t'other must needs have her, each pretending to have an equal right to her. And the Nurse, finding that each of them so much desires her, thinks no small matter of her self, but that she is as wise as many a Ladies woman or Salomons Cat, and that her fellow is hardly to be found. But before some few daies are past, there's a great trial to be made of the Nurses experience and understanding; for, let them do what they will or can, the Child will not suck; yea, and what's worse, it hath gotten a lamentable Thrush. Alas a day what bad work is here again, the Nurse is so quamish stomackt that she cannot suck her Mistres, therefore care must be taken to find out some body or other that will come and suck the young womans breasts for twelve pence a time; or else her breasts will grow hard with lumps and fester for want of being drawn. Or else also with the sucking she gets in the tipples.

Now is the right time to fetch the Apothecary to make ready plaisters, and bring Fennel-water to raise the milk, that the lumps may be driven away; and most especially that the cloves in the tipples may be cured. Help now or never good M^r. Doctor, for if this continue much longer, the young woman perhaps gets an Ague that may then cost her her life.

Verily, in this state and condition of the woman is also some pleasure to be found, for you may keep your wife now very cheap; she is not now so liquorish and sweet-tooth'd, as when she was with Child; which in deed is very good at all times, but most especially in this pittifull time for there's now nothing fitter for her to eat then a little good broth, stew'd Prunes, Caudle, Water-gruel, roasted Apples, or new laid Egs.

But now, Father, your Pleasure will immediately be augmented, for it will not be long before you will have some or other Gentlewomen come to give you a visit, who will then also out of their Closets of understanding be very much assistant to you with their advice and counsel for there are very few of them that are not deeply experienced in Sir *Thomas Browns* Mid-wivery, and if any thing do happen more then ordinary, they never want for remedies.

Now there is Doctor *Needhams* wife, who by her own experimenting, hath knowledge of several other things: But upon such an occasion as this, there is nothing better then that the child must be glister'd; and for the lumps you must indevour through a continual chafing to get them out of the young womans breasts. But Mistris *Rattle-pate* relates, how miserably, she was troubled with an humour in her breast, when she lay in; but that she had alwaies cured her self of it, by only taking a Sandwich Carrot, and scraping it hollow in the inside, and then put like a hat upon the tipple, this drew out all ill humour, without any pain, or the least fear of danger.

Yes truly, saith Mrs *Talk-enough*, I do indeed forsooth beleeve that that is very good, but here are very sore nipples, and they begin to be chop'd; and there must be a special care taken for that; therefore it will not be amiss to strengthen the nipples with a little *Aqua vitæ*, and then wash them with some Rosewater that hath kernels of Limons steep'd in it. There's nothing like it, or better, I have lain in of thirteen children, but never tried any thing that did me so much good, or gave me half the ease. Pray, dear Mistris, be sure to make use of that, you will never repent it.

But Mistris *Know-all* saith, that she hath made use of this also, and found some ease by it; and that she hath tried above an hundred other things, that were approved to be good; yet of all things never found nothing under the Sun that was more noble then *Salvator Winter's* Salve, for that cures immediately: And you can have nothing better.

Yet Mistris *Stand to't*, begins to relate wonderfull operations done with oyl of Myrrhe; and of the plaisters that are made by the Gentlewoman in Py-yard.

Now comes the sage Matron Experience, saying that she hath learnt a secret from a prudent Doctor that's worth its weight in Gold, nor can the vertue thereof be too much commended. And she hath already communicated it unto several persons; but there are none that tried it who do not praise it to be incomparable: therefore she hath been very vigilant to note it down in S. *John Pain*, and *Nic-Culpeppers* Works; to the end that her posterity may not only make use of it, but participate it to others: This is, *Lapis Calaminaris* prepared, mingled with a small quantity of May-butter, and then temper them together with the point of a knife upon an earthen plate, just as the Picture Drawers do their Colours upon their Pallet, which will bring it to be a delicate salve; and is also very soft and supple for the chops of the tipples; nay, though the child should suck it in, yet it doth it no harm; and it doth not alone cure them, but prevents the coming of any more.

Yes, saith Mistris *Consent to all*, and my advice is then to take a little horn, with a sheeps udder, & lay that upon the Tipples, for that defends them, and occasions their curing much better and sooner.

O what a pleasure it is to hear all the pretty considerations of so many prudent Doctresses! If *Clement Marot* might but revive, I am sure he would find here as many Doctresses, as ever there were Doctors at Paris. But O how happy will this fortunate new Father be, when he may but once see the back-sides of all these grave and nice Doctresses! But my truth, this may very well be registred for one of the most accomplished Pleasures.

But yet all this doth not help the young woman. Perhaps all these remedies may be good, saith the Grand-Mother but they are not for our turns; for alas a day, the very smell of salve makes her fall into a swoon; neither can she suffer the least motion of sucking, for the very pain bereaves her of her sences. What shall we do then? to keep a Wet-Nurse is both very damageable, and cruel chargeable; for Wet-Nurses are generally very lazy and liquorish, and they are ever chatting and chawing something or other with the Maids; and in their manner they baptize it, with saying it is very necessary & wholesom for the Child. And then again, to put the Child out to Nurse, hath also several considerations; first it estrangeth much from you, and who knows how ill they may keep it. Therefore it is best to keep it at home, and indeavour the bringing of it up with the Spoon, feeding it often with some pure and cordial diets fit for the appetite, and now and then giving it the sucking bottle.

But what remedy now? this is all to no purpose: For though the Grandmother, Nurse, and Ant do what they can, yet all their labour's lost. And the Child is so froward and peevish, that the Nurse is ready to run away from it; nay, though she dandle and play with it alwaies till past midnight, it is but washing the Black-a-more; in so much that a Wet-Nurse must be sought for, or away goes the Child to *Limbo*. For this again is required good advice, and the chusing of a good one hath its consideration: But the tender heartedness and kind love that the Mother hath for her Child can no way suffer this, she will rather suck it her self though the pain be never so great. Yet having tried it again a second time, the pain is so vehement that it is impossible to withstand it; therefore the new Father cannot be at quiet till there be a Wet-Nurse found and brought to them. For it goes to the very heart of both Father and Mother to put the Child out to Nurse.

And do but see after much seeking and diligent inquiring, the new made Grandmother, hath at last found one, who is a very neat cleanly and mighty modest woman, her husband went a little while ago to the *East-Indies*, & her child died lately.

This is no small joy but an extraordinary Pleasure, both for the new Father, and Child-bed woman. Oh now their hearts are at rest. And now all things will go well; for as the Wet-Nurse takes care of the Child; the dry Nurse doth of the Mother, & all this pleases the good Father very well.

Now Child-bed-woman your time is come to make much of your self, that you may recover strength. Now you wont be troubled with the pains of sucking, or disturbed of your natural rest: now you must let the Wet-Nurse take care for every thing, and look after or meddle with nothing your self. Now you must sleep quietly, eat heartily, and groan lustily. And though you be very well and hearty, yet you must seem to be weak and quamish stomackt; for first or last the month of lying-in must be kept full out. Do but think now by your self what you have a mind either to eat, or drink; the first and worst daies are with the tossing and turmoiling passed by; neither can you recover any strength with eating of Water-gruel, sugar-sops, rosted Apples, and new laid Egs; you are not only weary of them, but it is too weak a diet for you. The nine daies are almost past, and now you must have a more strengthening diet; to wit, a dish of fine white Pearch, a roasted Pullet, half a dozen of young Pigeons, some Wigeons or Teal, some Lams-stones, Sweetbreads, a piece of roast Veal, and a delicate young Turky, &c. And whilest you are eating, you must be sure to drink two or three glasses of the best Rhenish wine, very well sweetned with the finest loaf sugar, you must also be very carefull of drinking any French wine, for that will too much inflame you.

O new Father, what a Pleasure must all these things be for you; and especially, because now you begin at the Bed-side to eat and drink again with your Child-bed wife; and you begin also to perceive that if all things advance as they hitherto have done, you may then again in few daies make fresh assaults of hugging and embracing her.

This is that jolly month or six weeks that all women talk so pleasantly of; because it learns them alwaies such a curious remembrance. And really it is almost impossible that the husband at these rates can grow lean with it; because he as well as his wife sits to be cram'd up too: And he can now with his dearest daily contrive and practice what the Nurse shall make ready, that his Child-bed wife may eat with a better appetite, and recover new strength again. I would therefore advise the carefull Nurse as a friend, that she should be sure to provide her self with the *Compleat Cook*, that she might be the more ready to help the Child-bed woman to think upon what she hath a mind to have made ready, for her brains are but very weak yet; so that she cannot so quickly and easily remember at first what is pleasantest and wholesomest to be eaten.

O thrice happy new Father that have gotten such a prudent diligent and carefull Nurse for your Child-bed wife! what great Pleasure is this! And behold, by this delicate eating and drinking, your Dearest begins from day to day to grow stronger and stronger; insomuch that she begins to throw the Pillow at you, to spur you up to be desirous of coming to bed to her: Yea, she promiseth you, that before she is out of Child-bed, she will make you possessor of another principal and main Pleasure.

Folio 141.
Published by the Navarre Society, London.

THE NINTH PLEASURE.

Of the Gossips Feast.

Now, O new Father, you have had the possession of eight pleasures, which undoubtedly have tickled you to some purpose.

But now there is a new one approaching, that will be as full of so many joyfull delights and wishings of prosperity, as ever the first and most famous hath been; for it seems as if your Child-bed wife begins to be a weary of this lazy liquorish life, and to leave off her grunting and groaning; because she now longs to be gadding up and down the street, or standing at the dore with her Babe in her arms.

But before this can be done, you know that there ought to be a Gossips Feast kept. To this end the Nurse must be sent abroad; and a serious Counsel held, as if the Parliament of women were assembled, to consult who shall be invited, and who not. 's Wounds, what a list of relations and strange acquaintance are here sum'd up in a company together, to be invited to the Gossipping Feast. 'Tis impossible, the Nurse can ever do this all in one day; because she would not willingly miss any of them, out of the earnest hopes she hath of the Presents she expects. And then also she must give an account to every one of them that are invited of the state and condition of the Child-bed woman and her Child. I wonder that there is no body that sollicites to have the Office of an Inviter to all such sort of Gossippings, but the women understand these affairs and the ordering of such sort of invitations much better than any one else, therefore 'tis not necessary.

O, new Father, what a sweet Delight and Pleasure you must needs have in reviewing this great List of your Gossips! What multiplicities of wishes of joy and prosperity have you to expect! But if I were to be your Counsellor, I assure you I would order the Nurse to desire Doctor *Toss-bowl*, my Lord *Drinkfirst* and then the other Gentlemen, to wit, Masters *Cleardrinker, Dryliver, Spillnot, Sup-up, Seldom-sober*, and *Shift-gut*, to fetch home their Wives in good time from the Gossipping; because you have other mens Wives, who are your near relations, that you must entertain longer; and they otherwise will never think of rising or going home though it were midnight: And by this means you will have a fit opportunity, with a full Bowl and a Pipe, to wash away that rammish sent of a Child-bed out of your brains; and also after many hopes, once arrive to the height of receiving your full delight and pleasure. And then you may e'en clap it all together upon the account of a Lying-in.

Now Nurse, here you have work by whole hand-fulls: for you shall no sooner have made an end of your other errands, but immediately there's so much tricking and pricking of all things up in neat order against the coming of the sharp-sighted guests; that it's a terror to think on't. Their eys will fly into every nook and corner; nay the very house of Office must be extraordinary neat and clean; for Mistris *Foul-arse*, Gossip *Order-all*, and Goody *Dirty-buttocks*, will be peeping into every crevise and cranny: And because they will do it forsooth, according to their fashion, they make a shew as if they must go to the necessary Chamber, with a Letter to *Gravesend*, only to take an inspection whether it be as cleanly there as it is upon the Gossipping Chamber where all the Guests are. And 'tis a wonder if they do not look into the Seat, to see whether there be no Spyders webs spun in it; or whether the Goldfinders Merchandize be of a good colour, equal-size and thickness.

But come let's pass all this by: for in the middle of these incumbrances, the time will not only fly away; but we shall, at the hour appointed, be surprized by our Guests. Uds life, how busie the Wet and Dry-Nurses are with dressing the Babe neatly. Now Father, look once upon your Child! O pretty thing! O sweet-fac'd dainty darling! 'tis Father's own picture! Well what would not one undergo to be the Mother of so fine an Angel! And who can or dare doubt any thing of it, for the Mother loves it, and the Father beleeves it, nay and all the friends that come tumbling in one upon another to-day, do confirm it: For behold, every one looks earnestly at the Babe; and doth not a little commend his prettiness. One saith it is as like the Father (alias Daddy) as one drop of Water is like another. Another, that the upper part of the face, forehead, eys and nose incline very much to be like the mother; but downwards it is every bit the Father. And who forsooth should not beleeve it, if it be a son. Every one is in an admiration. O me, what a pretty sweet Infant! Nurse, you have drest it up most curiously! And truly there's no cost spar'd for the having very rich laces.

Thus they ly and tamper upon this first string, till the Child-bed woman begins to enter upon the relating what great pain in travell she had to fetch this Child out of the Parsly-bed, what a difference there was between her, and others of her acquaintance, &c. Thereout every one hath so much matter, as would make a long-winded sermon; and the conclusion generally is the relating how and when the good man crept to bed to her again; and how such a one had been a fortnight with Child, before she went to receive her churching. Where upon another comes with a full-mouth'd confession, that her husband was not half so hot.

Do but tarry a little yet, till the Gossipping-bowl hath gone once or twice more about with old Hock; then you'l hear these Parrots tell you other sorts of tales.

In the mean while, do but see the husband, poor *Nicholas None-eys* how he rejoyces, that his wife is so reasonable strong again; and that she is so neatly trickt up sitting in state in the best furnished room, by the bed-side! O what a pleasure this is! O how he treats all the women with delicate Marget Ale, and Sack and Sugar! [unless he begin to bethink himself, and for respects sake or frugality, sets some bottles aside; because he perceives it to be nothing else but a vast expence and womens Apish tricks]. How busie he is in carving for them of his Roast-beef, Capons, Turkey-py, Neats-tongue, or some other savoury bit to make their mouths relish their liquor the better; and then stand fast Bowls and glasses for they resolve not to flinch from it. And indeed why should he not? for he is now a whole estate richer then he was before; and what need he care for it then.

Well behold here! Now the womens mouths are a beginning to be first a little warm; and none of them all can be silent, though they should speak of their own Commodities.

O how happy would you be, O Goodman *Cully*, if you had but as many ears as *Argus* had eys, that you might hear every where, whilest you are carving and serving of them, what pretty sweet stories and discourses, these sorts of Parrats will be talking of? For Mistris *Sharp-set* relates, what a pleasure she oft times received in it, to keep School-time with her husband at noons, as soon as they had feasted their carkasses well: but that conning of her lesson had caused her severall times to make a journy to the Parsly-bed.

At this Mistris *Sincere* wonders extreamly; saying how strangely these things happen to one woman more then another. In our Parish there is a married woman brought to bed, but she was so miserably handled by the Midwife, that no tongue can express it. Insomuch that Master *Peepin* the Man Midwife, was fain to be fetcht, to assist with his Instrument; it was a very great wonder that the woman ever escaped it; which is most lamentable indeed to be related; and too sad indeed to be placed by me among the Pleasures of Marriage.

In the mean time, at the t'other end of the Chamber, Mistris *Fairtail* relates a pretty story how their Maid was very curiously stitcht up by their Tailor; and how she was every foot running thither, then to have a hole finely drawn that she had torn in her Petti-coat, another while to have her Bodice made a little wider, and then again to have her stockins soled.

It is no wonder, (saith Mistres *Paleface*) that this should happen to a poor innocent servant Maid; there was my husbands first wives niece M^rs. *Young-rose* that modest Virgin, she kept such a close conversation & daily communication with Master *Scure*, that at last there appeared a little *Cupid* with little ears, and short hair.

Nay then (saith Mistris *Lookabout*) those two sisters need not twit one another in the teeth with it; for the t'other kept such a sweet compliance and converse with the Spanish Fruiterer, yonder at the corner-house, where she did eat so many China Oranges, and other watrish fruits, that they caused her to get an extraordinary swelling under her stomack; which Doctor *Stultus* judged to proceed from some obstructions, wind, and other watrish humours; but it did not continue so long before her Mother, beginning better to apprehend the nature of her distemper, sent her away to her Country-house at Hackney.

Mistris *Lookabout* was going to begin again; but they heard such rapping and knocking at the dore, that one of them said I beleeve there are our husbands; and indeed she guest very well. This augmented their mirth mightily. And especially of the Nurse; for now she was sure that, if the good Cully her Master treated his Gossips nobly and liberally, her presents would be doubled. But Nurse do not cheat your self, for fear it might happen otherwise; I know once a merry boon Companion, who being at a Gossipping Feast, called the Nurse alone to him; and saies to her, Nurse, I'l swear you are very vigilant and take a great deal of pains, in serving both us and our wives with all things, and also filling of us full glasses and bowls: hark hither, my wife is a little covetous, and oft-times so narrow-soul'd that she doth not keep her credit where she ought to do, so that I beleeve her gift will not be very great, and truly because you are such a good body, see there, that's for you, put it some where privately away; & there-with thrusts her an indifferent great brass Counter, wrapt up in a paper, into her hand. The Nurse certainly beleeving this to be at the least a Crown piece, thanks him very demurely, and puts it in her Pocket; never opening it till they were every one of them gone, but then she saw that she was basely cheated. But Nurse you are warned now by this, another time you may look better to't. Yet methinks I'd fill about lustily, it is the good man of the house his wine; and when the Wine begins to surge crown-high; the men are much more generous than before.

And verily methinks I have a mind to take my portion of it also; but yet not so as the Nurse did at my Neeces, who had toss'd up her bowls so bravely upon the good health of the Child-bed woman her Mistriss, that when she was going to swathe and feed the Child, instead of putting the spoon into the mouth, she thrust it under the chin, & sometimes against the breast; and then when she was about swathing of it; as it is commonly the custom to lay a wollen blanket and linnen bed together, she wrapt the poor Infant with its little naked body only in the blanket alone.

O thrice happy young Father, who have hitherto so nobly treated and entertained all your She Gossips, and had the audience of all their curious relations! Now you will have the honour also of entertaining their husbands your He-Gossips, who will not be backward in doing of you reason out of the greatest bowl you will set before them, and talk as freely of a Py-corner merchandize.

Who is there now that doth not praise, and commend your manfull deeds to the highest? Ha, ha, saith Master *Laugh wel*, that's a Child! who ever saw a braver! there's not the fellow on't! O my dearest, I have such a delight in this Child, that if we were but a little alone together, I'd cast you such another as if it were of the same mould. Stay a little, stay a little, saith *Master Fillup*, it may be you would not run so strong a course. Yet I saw once two Souldiers who were Batchelors, that were sitting in an evening drinking in an Alehouse, and talking lustily of the Bobbinjo trade; whereupon one of them said; Cocksbobs *Jack* if I had but a Wife, as well as another, I'd presently get her with Child of a brave boy. Ho, ho, saith the t'other, it is an easie thing to get a Wife if one seek it. If I would, I dare lay a wager on't, I would be the Bridegroom within the space of two hours. The other not beleeving him, they laid a wager between them for a bottle of Wine. Hereupon one of them went out of dores just upon the striking of the clock; & hardly was gone a streets length, before he met with a bonny bouncing girl, who was going of an errand for her Mistris, and he presently laies her on board. But she seemed to be very much offended, that an honest Maid going about her business in the evening, should be in this manner so encountred by a strange fellow, with a sword by his side. Verily, Sweetheart, said he, you have a great deal of reason in all what you say; but you may certainly beleeve that it is an honest person who speaks to you, and only seeks an occasion to be acquainted with a virtuous good condition'd Maid. My wearing of a sword, is because I am a Souldier, and am very well known by many honest people. And truly, if you please to admit me this favour, you shall see and find me to be an honest man, and none of those that go about to ly and deceive any body; and indeed my intention & desire is to marry, to that end seeking nothing but an honest Maid, and I doubt not but that I have at this time found one to my mind. And went forward with his chat in these sort of terms. But the Maid denied him, saying, that she had no mind at-all to a Souldier, because it was one of the poorest and miserablest sort of levelihoods; their pay being but very little, and they were seldom advanced, &c. He on the other side commending & approving a Souldiers life to be the merriest, resolutest, & absolute easiest of any that was under the Sun; because that neither hungrie care, nor finical pride did any waies take place by them, but that they, on the contrary, were alwaies merry, never admitting sorrow into their thoughts. 'Tis true, said he, our pay is but small; but then again, all what the Country people have, is our own;

for what we want our selves, we get from them: we never take care for to morrow, having alwaies something fresh, & every day new mirth. Riches, Sweetheart, doth not consist in multiplicity of Goods, but in content; & there's no one better satisfied than a Souldier, therefore you shall alwaies see an honest Souldier look plump and fat, just as I do: but Drunkards and Whore-masters fall away miserably, &c.

In short, the Maid begun a little to listen to him (and so much the more, because that very morning she had a falling out with her Mistris) and told him, she would take it into consideration. He answered her again, what a fidle stick, why should we spend time in thinking? we are equally matcht: a Souldier never thinks long upon any thing, but takes hold of all present opportunities, and it generally falls out well with him. But she drawing back a little, he saith, ah my dearest, you must take a quick resolution. Behold there, yonder comes a Cloud driving towards the Moon: I'l give you so much time, till that be past by; therefore be pleased to resolve quick, for otherwise I must go & seek my fortune by another. For a Soldier neither woos nor threatens long.

Upon this she considered a little, but before the Cloud was past by the Moon, she gave him her consent; and he gave her his Tobacco-box for a pledge of marriage; and desired something of her in like manner for a pledge; but she said she had nothing: howsoever he persisted so strongly, that in conclusion she gave him her Garter for a pledge of marriage. He was contented with it, and taking his leave, went unto his Comrades; and told them what had hapned to him, shewing them the Garter. Whereupon he that had laid the wager with him, askt, who it was, what her name was, and where she dwelt, &c. And being told by another, that it was a handsom, neat, and very well complexion'd Maid, By my troth, said he, I wish I were to give four Cans of Wine that I could light upon such another. Well, see there, saith the first, if you will give four Cans of Wine, I will both give you the Garter & the Maid too into the bargain: It was done but by Moonlight; so that she'l hardly know whether it be me or another.

Hereupon the agreement was concluded, the two first Cans of Wine were spent, and the Garter was delivered to him, and every one charged to keep it secret.

This second Souldier goes to the Maid next day in the evening, at the hour and place where they had appointed to meet. And there relating to her several passages that were passed between them the day before, and shewing her the Garter, made her beleeve that he was the person that had contracted with her the day before. To be short, the Maid leaves her service and marries him. And that which is most to be observed, is, that that which the first Souldier vaunted to have done, the second performed; for just nine months after they were married, she was brought to bed of a gallant young boy, and they lived very peaceably and quietly together.

Well, I'l vow, saith Master *Crossgrain*, that's a very notable relation; it is better a great deal that the business happen so, then like another, which is just contrary, that I shall make mention of to you.

Barebeard and *Mally*, who by a sudden accident, without much wooing, were gotten together, and their first Bane of matrimony was published; but falling out, they called one another all the names that they could reap together; nay it run so high, that they would discharge each other of their promises, and resolved to go to the Bishop & crave that they might have liberty to forbid the Banes themselves, which hapned so.

Barebeard coming then with *Mall* before his Grace, complained that he did already perceive his intended marriage would never come to a good event, because he found perfectly that this Maid was a lumpish Jade, a nasty Slut, a Scolding, bawling Carrion, & a restless peece of mortality. Therefore it might go as it would, he did not care for the Maid, neither would he marry her, and for those reasons, he desired his Grace to grant that the Banes might be forbidden; as thinking it much better for him to quit her betimes, before it was too late. She on the t'other side said, that he was one that run gadding along the streets at all hours of the night, a private drunken beast, a Spend-thrift, &c. so that she did not care for him neither. Whereupon his Grace smiling told them, well you fellow and wench; do you think that we do here so give and take away the consent of marriage? perhaps when you are married, it may be much better, for the marriage bed doth for the most part change the ten sences into five. But she answered, may it please your Grace, he is no such man to do that, for all that he can do is only to-follow his own round-head-like stiff-neckedness, and e'en nothing else. Whereupon he again answered, may it please your Grace, I have no mind ever to try it with such a creature as she is; I should be then fast enough bound to her; neither would I willingly go alive headlong to the Devil, to take my habitation in Hell.

The Bishop thus perceiving that no good thread could be spun of such sort of Flax, caused the Banes to be forbidden. Then said *Barebeard*, may it please your Grace, am I not a freeman, & may I not marry with whom I please, or have a mind to? to which his Grace answered, yes. Presently *Barebeard* thrusting his head out at the dore, calls out aloud, *Peg* do you come hither now; and begged that his Grace would be pleased to give him leave to marry with this person. Which Mall seeing she cries out, you Rogue, you have been too cunning for me in this; if I had the least thoughts on't, I would have had my *Hal* to have tarried for me at this dore, instead of tarrying for me at another place. Whereupon his Grace, being in great ire, chid them most shrewdly, giving them such strong reproofs, that at first it might very well be imagined that he would never have admitted of a second consent; yet afterwards upon considerations it was granted. But *Barebeard* being now married with *Peg*, they got no children: And *Mall* being married to *Hal*, they had both a Son and a Daughter at one birth. By which its easie to be observed what acquaintance *Mall* had made with *Barebeard* before hand, & why she would rather marry with Hall then with him.

To this again Mistris *Sweetmouth* relates, that she had been several times invited to Mistris *Braves* labour; and that she had been twice brought to bed very happily of two delicate twins. And in the last encounter, for a recompence of the affection of her Beloved, she presented him with two lustly and gallant boys; but because she would equally balance his great bounty; the Midwife takes the same walk again for another, and finding in what condition things stood, she calls for a bason of warm water, bringing out at last a most delicate pretty daughter, that was yet poor thing wrapt up in the Cawl. Which she immediately laid into the warm water, and shewed unto them all the wonderfull works of nature; for there they could see it move and stir, as if it had been in its Mothers glass Bottle; but the skin being just cut open with a small hole, it begun presently to make a little noise like a weak childish voice, which indeed was very rare & pleasant to be seen. In truth, such a Father, who can cast every time such high doubblets, may very well be called by the name of Brave.

But this Story was hardly told before Mistris *Tittle-tattle* pursued it with another out of the same Text, saying, A little more then two years ago I was at a Gossipping by Mistris *Gay*, who was then brought to bed both of a Son and a Daughter, also at one birth; but indeed the Labour came so violently upon her, that as she was standing upon the stairs, not being able to set one foot further; and having neither Midwife, nor any other women of her neighbors and friends, only the assistance of her husband and the Maid; she was immediately delivered of two gallant Children; but they did not live long.

Upon my word, said Mistris *Bounce-about*, it is an excellent help when men understand their travelling upon such sort of roads. It hapned to me once that some Gentlewomen were merry with me somewhat late in the evening; and because I had had several Symptoms of Labour, said this, Mistris *Bounce-about*, if you would now take a walk to the Parsley bed, we would help you very bravely; but neither wind nor weather was serviceable at that time. But they had hardly been gone an hour, and being in bed with my husband, and he very fast asleep; before there begun such an alteration of the weather; that my husband must up with all speed, who wakened the Maid, and sent her for the Midwife laying on fire himself in all hast; yet do all what they could, within less then a quarter of an hour, and that without any bodies help but my husbands, my journy was performed; but things were done with such a confusion; that he received the child in the Christning cloath instead of the Blanket.

And a thousand more such stories as these are ript up; that would burthen the strongest memory to bear them: and so much the more, because it is impossible to distinguish one from the t'other, when the men and the women that gabble so one among another. And oft-times they spin such course threads of bawdery in their talk, that are enough to spoil a whole web of linnen. And who can tell but that their tattling would last a whole night, for there's hardly one of them who hath not at the least a hundred in their Budgets; but because it is high time that either the Dry or Wet-Nurse must go to swathe the child, they begin to break off and shorten their prittle-prattle.

Now young Father, do but observe what fine airy complements will be presented to you at their parting. Every one thanks you for your kind and cordial entertainment, and not one of them forgets to wish that you may the next year either have a Daughter to your Son, or a Son to your Daughter; imagining then that all things is well, when you receive such a full crop: But I am most apt to beleeve that all their wishes aim at the But of coming next year again to the Gossips Feast, to toss up the Gossips-bowl, and in telling of a bobbinjo story they peep into all nooks and corners.

Well, O new Father, this Pleasure begins to come to a conclusion; but prithee tell me, would not a body wish for the getting of such another, that his Wife might make a journy to the Parsly-bed twice a year?

Now Nurse have at you; you shall now reap the fruit of all your running and going early & late to invite them. Oh thinks she by her self, would but every shilling change it self into a crown-peece. But Nurse you'l hardly be troubled with a fit of that yellow Jaundies sickness, for there's no drug at the Apothecaries, nor any lice among the Beggars that can cure you of it. And I dare say Nurse, that you'l go nigh to perceive that its a very hard time, and mony mighty scarce: because formerly the women used to put their hands more liberally in their purses, and one gave a crown, another half a crown; but the times are now so strangely altered, that they keep little mild-shillings only for that use, nay some of them rub it off with a couple of their Grandams gray groats. But howsoever I hope for your sake, it will not be here according as often happens, fair promises but no performances; for if it should, I protest ye ought to have made your bargain to have had a peece more at the least for your Nurse keeping; or otherwise you must have had the full liberty to toss up the remains of all that was left in the Gossipping Bowls, or else to have carried the key of the Wine Cellar alwaies in your pocket, and then after the feeding and swathing the child, you might in the twinkling of an eye, swinge up a lustly glass upon the good health of the Father, Child-bed mother and the Child; for the Wine was laid in to be made use of to that end and purpose; and it is commonly known that the Nurses are not so mealy mouth'd; for although they don't do it that every one should see it, they'l be sure with the Maid to get their shares in one corner or other. But you must for this again think, that the freer you let them take their swing herein, the more care they will take for the Child.

Now Nurse, don't spare to make good use of your time, for it belongs amongst other things to this Pleasure; and the new Father will nevertheless be turning about to another mirth, and then you may be sure to expect to have a God be w'ye. Therefore make much of your self, and toss up your glasses stoutly at the Wine-Cask; who knows whether you may have the opportunity this twelve month again to meet with such a good Nurse-keeping; a liquorish sweet-tooth'd Child-bed woman, & a plentifull housekeeping, is not every where. And you may certainly beleeve, that the month will be no sooner ended, then that you'l begin to stink here; for the Mistris will begin to consider with her self, that she can make a shift with the Maid and Wet-Nurse; so that then you must expect to get your undesired Pass.

Then you must return back again to your own lodging, that dark, moist and mournfull Cell, and satisfie your self, if you can get it, with a mess of milk and brown George, or some such sort of lean fare. So that you'l have time enough to waste away that fulsomness and fogginess of body, that you have gotten in your Nurse-keeping. For there's no body that will give you any thing, or thinks in the least upon your attendance, unless they want you again.

O new Father, pray for it to come again within a twelve month, that you may have a renewing of this pleasure once more; for it is with the Nurse-taking its leave, and will conduct you to a following.

THE TENTH PLEASURE.

A great Child-bed Feast is kept, and the Child put in Cloaths.

Oh how pleasant is th'estate of married people, above that of Batchelors and Maids? how it distributes Mirths and Pleasures! Verily one may in some measure recogitate or write something of it, but it is impossible to imprint so Sun-like a splendor in Potters clay, or to display it with the most curious Colours. Though the accomplishedst Painter might have drawn it very near the life, yet it would be but a dead draught, in comparison of the reality and experience that is found in it self. You have already seen here nine Parts or Tables but it is not ninety Pictures that can sufficiently shew you the fulness of one of the nine Parts.

Be therefore chearfully merry, O sweet Couple, because you are in so short a time arisen to the height of being possessors of all these Pleasures: And so much the more, the ninth being hardly past, before the tenth follows, as it were treading upon the heels of the t'other.

Folio 188.
Published by The Navarre Society, London

They have scarce wiped their mouths or digested the Child-bed Wine in their stomacks, before there starts up a new day of mirth & jollity; for now there must be a Child-bed feast kept & the child must be put in Cloaths. O what two vast Pleasures are these for the young Father! 'tis indeed too much joy for one person alone to be possessor of.

At first you had the Pleasure for to treat the Women, those pretty pleasing Creatures, and to hear all their sweet and amiable discourses. But now you shall be honoured with treating the Matron like Midwife, and those Men and Women that are your kindest friends and nearest relations; Yea and the God-Fathers and God-Mothers also who will all of them accompany you with courteous discourses and pleasant countenances: They will begin a lusty Bowl or thumping glass, *super naculum* drink it out, upon the health & prosperity of you, your Bedfellow and young Son; and very heartily wish that you may increase and multiply, at least every year with one new Babe; because that they then might the better come to the Child-bed Feast.

Here you'l see now how smartly they'l both lick your dishes, and toss your Cups and Glasses off. Begin you only some good healths, as; pray God bless his Majesty and all the Royal Family: the Prosperity of our Native Country; all the Well wishers of the Cities welfare, &c. And when you have done, they'l begin; and about it goes to invest you with the honour and name, in a full bowl to the Father of the Family; Well is not that a noble title; such a Pleasure alone is worth a thousand pounds at lest.

And whilest the Men are busie this way; the good woman with the other Women are contriving on the other side how the Child ought to be put in Cloaths upon the best and modishest manner: For she is resolved to morrow morning to be Church'd, & in the afternoon she'l go to market.

She accomplishes the first well enough, but is at a damnable doubt in the second part of her resolution; for by the way, in the Church, and in the streets, she hath continually observed severall children, and the most part of them dressed up in severall sorts of fashions: Some of them she hath a great fancy for, but then she doubts whether that be the newest mode or not. One seems too plain and common, which makes her imagine in her thoughts; that's too Clownish. But others stand very neat and handsom. 'Tis true, the Stuf and the Lining is costly and very dear; but then again it is very comly and handsom. And then again she thinks with her self, as long as I am at Market, I'd as good go through stirch with it; and make but one paying for all; it is for our first, and but for a little child, not for a great person; therefore it is better to take that which is curious and neat, the price for making is all one; besides it will be a great Pleasure for my husband when he sees how delicately the child is drest up, and his mony so extraordinarily well husbanded.

Now, my dearest, pray be you merry: if the stuf hath cost somthing much, you have need but of little; and it is for your first. When it grows bigger, or that you get more, you must part with much more mony. Don't grudge at this for once, because then you would spoil all your mirth and Pleasure with it. Rejoice that you have a Wife, who is not only good to fetch children out of the Parsley Bed; but is also very carefull to see them well nourished, and neat and cleanly cloath'd. You your self have the praise and commendation of it. Let her alone a while, for women must have their wills; say but little to her, for her brains are too much busied already; and it may be that in three hours time, you would hardly get three words of answer from her; and suppose you should relate somthing or other to her, this shall be your answer from her at last, that she did not well understand you, because all her thoughts, nay her very sences do as it were glide to & again, one among another continually, to order the dressing up of her child.

I am very well assured, O new invested Husband, that your wits at present run a Wool-gathering, because that both Merchandize and Trade are neither of them so quick as you would fain see them; and by reason of this tedious and destructive War, monies is horrible scarce, nothing near so plentifull as you could wish it to be: But comfort your self herewith, that it hath hapned oft-times to others, & will yet also happen oftner to you. Yet this is one of the least things; but stay a little, to morrow or next day the Nurse goes away. This seems to be a merriment indeed; for then you'l have an Eater, a Stroy-good, a Stuf-gut, a Spoil-all, and Prittle-pratler, less than you had before.

You are yet so happy that you have a Wet-Nurse, that carefully looks after the Child; by which means both you and your Wife are freed from tossing and tumbling with it in the night: whilest others, on the contrary, that have no Wet-Nurses in their houses; begin first to tast, when the Dry-Nurse goes away, what a Pleasure it is that the Child must be set by the Bedside, and the charge thereof left unto both Father & Mother, when it oftentimes happens that the good woman is yet so weak, she can neither lay the Child in, nor take it out of the Cradle; insomuch that the Father here must put a helping hand to't, because he is of a stronger constitution, and hath the greatest share in it.

By my faith such as those are they who have the first and true tast of the Kernel of the Tenth Pleasure; because the husband ought as then, out of a tender affection for his wife to rock continually, that she might take her rest; otherwise she would not get any suck in her breasts for the Child: And happy they are somtimes, if they come off with but rocking the most part of the night; for many times it happens, that the Child is so restless and unquiet, that Father, Mother, & Maid; nay and all whatsoever is in the house must out of their beds to quiet it; and though they use a thousand tricks and stratagems, yet all's to no purpose.

And yet this is but a small matter for them neither; for before a few months are past, the child begins to get teeth; and bawls and cries so night & day, that they can tell the clock all the night long; wishing a thousand thousand times over that they might see day-break; and so by the comfortable assistance of day-light receive a little solace for all their toiling and tumbling too and again.

Yet I would advise such as these, that they must in no manner be discomforted at this; if they intend to demonstrate that they have learnt somthing in the School of Marriage, to exercise their patiences: But, on the contrary, to shew themselves contented with all things; being assured, that hereafter when all this trouble is past, they shall receive the happiness, that the child will return them thanks with its pretty smiles; and in time also will salute them with a slabbering cocurring. And I beleeve now that they clearly find that all things do not go so even in this World, as they well imagined: And that the fairest Sunshine of Marriage, may be somtimes darkned with a Cloudy Storm.

You married people, that have the help of a Wet-Nurse, receive a much greater advantage in participating of the Pleasures of Marriage, neither need you to be troubled with tossing & dandling of the child in the night.

O, young House-Father, this is a most incomparable Pleasure for you! For now you may most certainly see the approach of a Daughter to your Son; and by that means reap the possession again of all those former Pleasures; & by every one be saluted with the Title that you are an excellent good Artist.

treasure of old books; may you find an ancestor; may you be blessed by Mr. Hitchcock's good intentions; may you better understand from whence you come as an American.

Teresa Nyquist Tucker

Acknowledgements

My thanks to my mom, Mary Marx Nyquist, who purchased the box of books containing the journal. No doubt, I owe my interest in history and genealogy to her. Thanks to Indiana University Professor David Nord, colporteur expert, who shared his writings with me. Also, I greatly appreciate Melinda McIntosh of the University of Massachusetts' W. E. B. Du Bois Library who quickly and efficiently provided Hitchcock family documentation. I thank American Tract Society archivist, Kristin Mitrisin for allowing me to view the library and for enthusiastically providing background information. Thanks to Shanna Nelson Tucker, my daughter-in-law and partner in genealogy, who contributed many hours of handwriting deciphering and indexing, helping me immensely. And I am always thankful for my considerate husband, Larry, who will occasionally opine that I'm spending way too much time in front of the computer.

Preface

Rummaging through a box of old books is like panning for gold. The sensation of water and sand on the eye and hand is replaced with the visual pleasure of somber-colored covers and artful dust jackets and the kinesthetic pleasure of the texture of embossed covers, of cloth, leather, and paper. But a bibliophile and genealogiophile like me considers the nuggets sifted from books more exquisite and valuable than gold, for books contain the treasure of knowledge, wisdom, and experience.

As I dug and sifted through one box of ordinary books bought at an auction, the feel of a soft leather spine delighted my fingertips. Pulling out the slim volume, I found that the worn leather binding held together hand-stitched pages between marbled paper covers. Excitedly, I skimmed through a handwritten journal dated from 1844 to 1847, its once black iron-gall ink faded to a mellow but distinct sepia. Inside the front, a pasted-in label indicated that Jansen & Bell, a stationer in New York, originally sold the blank book.

Cryptic notations on the first two pages were attached to dates and money amounts. Thereafter, spread over the top of every two pages detailing money transactions is the notation, "The American Tract Society in Account with Amos Hitchcock." I smiled; this is my kind of treasure!

Mr. Amos Hitchcock, the author of the journal, I would later discover, was a young man of twenty-six when he first began keeping this journal. His chosen profession was that of colporteur, a term totally unfamiliar to me. Upon researching, I found that colporteurs distributed religious books and Bibles, or as Amos referred to his material, "good literature." His journal was primarily a business journal, although he might take exception to that description for, although he was paid for his work, he considered his job a calling, a ministry, done for the glory of God and the betterment of mankind.

He left his home and family in Brimfield, Hampden County, Massachusetts in 1844 and traveled to the American Tract Society's headquarters in New York where he acquired supplies. In

November he bought a memorandum book, which is probably the now 160-year-old journal I discovered in the box of books.

He sailed to Savannah, Georgia and proceeded cross-country to his mission field, East Tennessee. For almost two years, he dutifully traversed the rough, hilly terrain of Knox County, Sevier County, Anderson County, and Blount County by foot and horseback distributing Bibles, pamphlets, tracts, and books. As he traveled he would sometimes lodge with a family sympathetic to his mission, visit other families in the vicinity, and then move on. If he found himself away from his boarding house at nightfall, he would sometimes take meals and spend the night with hospitable strangers. Amos found East Tennessee rough and unrefined compared to his home state. He describes poverty, illiteracy, and rampant drunkenness.

While performing his job, Amos recorded business expenses such as the purchase of literature and subsequent literature sales. When those he solicited were too poor to buy his material, he freely gave it to them. He also documented his personal accounts, recording his daily expenditures from crackers to contributions at camp meetings.

Best of all for family history researchers, he lists names and addresses of people to whom he mailed literature or letters. He made a list entitled "Names of Persons in Tennessee, a few of the many visits by me as Colporteur" and another, untitled, listing names and their local post offices. Occasionally he mentions a name within his journaling or business sections. For example, January 19, 1846 he wrote a letter to Mr. Joseph Meek, Esq. of Academia, Knox County, East Tennessee. In all, he lists or mentions over 300 people, most in Tennessee, but also some New England business associates, and hometown family and friends.

By January 25, 1846, Amos expressed uncertainty about his life among the hills of Tennessee. It was a demanding endeavor for this New England man, physically, spiritually, and emotionally. Fording creeks, walking when the terrain was too rough for his horse, he would move from county to county and area to area within counties. He suffered illness, verbal abuse and ridicule, and homesickness. In November of 1846 he returned to Massachusetts where he continued to conduct American Tract Society business through most of 1847.

Why did this little treasure wind up in a box of books at an auction? I've often wondered. Perhaps it simply got lost, was misplaced. Perhaps its owner considered it unimportant; not everyone is interested in family history or history in general - they just don't know gold when they see it.

It is my wish that others will extract enjoyment and benefit from this small window on history. As you read and study *Tennessee Travels 1844-1847, Journal of Amos Hitchcock,* may you appreciate the

Part I

Introduction

Part I
Introduction

Overview

This book, *Tennessee Travels 1844 – 1847, Journal of Amos Hitchcock*, is a reproduction and a transcription of an old journal written by Amos Hitchcock (1818 – 1876) with additional research on the people and publications mentioned in the original.

From Brimfield, Hampden County, Massachusetts, Amos Hitchcock began keeping this journal in 1844 when he became employed with the American Tract Society as a colporteur, a traveling distributor of Christian literature. After working two years in East Tennessee, he returned to his home in Brimfield where he continued keeping his journal through October of 1847.

Tennessee Travels 1844 – 1847, Journal of Amos Hitchcock explores his journal and related subjects in five main parts, appendixes, references, and index.

Part I: Introduction gives an overview, describes a brief history of the American Tract Society's colporteurs, explains how the transcription was accomplished, and gives a physical description of the journal.

Part II: A Chronological Journal is a transcription of the original journal, but, in order, beginning with the earliest date, October 30, 1844, and ending with the latest date, October 28, 1847.

Part III: Visitation and Mailing Lists are lists of people and their associated places which served as Mr. Hitchcock's address book. There are no dates associated with these lists.

Part IV: The Original Journal is a photo copy of each journal page in the order it appears in the original journal.

Part V: The Hitchcock Family is a brief history of Amos Hitchcock's ancestors, contemporary relatives, and children.

Appendix 1: Publications explores every publication that Amos mentions in his journal.

Appendix 2: Resources is a short list of research sources for those wanting to explore further.

References lists sources of information used.

Index lists every publication, organization, place, and personal name in this book.

The Colporteur's Mission

To better understand the context of Amos's journal an understanding of his employer and the position of colporteur is helpful.

From 1844 through 1847, the journal's author, Amos Hitchcock, worked for the American Tract Society. Still existing today, the American Tract Society became a national institution in 1825 when several regional societies, including the American Tract Society of Boston and the New York Religious Tract Society, consolidated. These regional societies were offspring of the Religious Tract Society of London, founded 1799. From its beginning, the American Tract Society's purpose has been Christian literature distribution to the masses.

The methods developed for distributing literature were so successful that the American Tract Society and other 19th century religious literature publishers became business administration innovators of their time[1]. Their efficient and effective organization, communication, and distribution methods had such a marketplace impact that secular publishers railed against the unfair advantages that "the Church" had when engaging in literature sales.

In the late 1820s, the American Tract Society paid "agents" who provided publications to volunteers. These volunteers canvassed areas primarily in the north and northeast United States. Wishing to expand the distribution into the poorer southern and western rural areas, the Society eventually abandoned the agent-volunteer distribution system and, in 1841, developed a more efficient, centrally controlled distribution system. "They set about to build a national distribution system based on salaried employees, geographical administrative divisions, and a hierarchy of salaried managers. This was the beginning of the American Tract Society's famous system of colportage."[2] This was the system that Amos worked within.

These colporteurs transported trunks and boxes of books, pamphlets, and tracts to areas in need of Christian literature. Then, traveling by ship, horseback, horse and wagon, and foot, they visited the population in a particular area, selling and giving away the printed material.

In 1844, colporteur Amos Hitchcock left his home in Brimfield, Massachusetts to begin his service in Tennessee. He was a manager responsible for at least two associate colporteurs, Thomas H. Aikman, working in Roane County, Tennessee and William H. Smith, working in Anderson County,

Part I: Introduction

Tennessee. It is estimated that there were about 175 colporteurs in the service of the Society during Amos Hitchcock's tenure[2]. The number of people that they succeeded in visiting on foot and horseback is remarkable. Amos visited 1, 272 families in his first year alone[3].

The work of colporteur was not without its critics. While working in East Tennessee, one of the most stinging criticisms that Amos Hitchcock encountered was the accusation that he was "engaged in speculation." Amos gives an account of this experience. "He said he viewed the work in which I was engaged as a speculation. I asked him in what respect? He answered that he thought those who wrote the books and those who were circulating them were speculating. I asked him if he would like to engage in such a speculation, for the sake of the gain? He would not consent. I then told him plainly the principles of the Society and how the works were furnished and told him the salary of this Colporteur, etc. Well, says he, if it is a good work, go ahead. I'll keep my hands clean from it. Says I, you will not oppose it then, will you? He said he wouldn't. I told him that in the sincerity of my heart I believed it to be a good work, or I should not have been there, for if I was after gain, I should have been in some other business, but the object of the Society was to do good, and if my heart deceived me not, it was my desire also…"

And indeed, the American Tract Society was noble in its intentions, and monetary gain was secondary to putting "good books" into the hands of the public. Colporteurs were instructed and encouraged to provide free materials to those who couldn't afford to buy. Amos would sometimes give a quick summary of a situation in which he would give books, pamphlets, and tracts: "Poverty to the extreme. No professors. No books but the Bible. Gave *Anxious Inquirer*. Next, no Bible and no books, gave Allein's *Alarm* - next no books but Bible – gave a book. Next, a poor family – gave a book. Next, a wicked family- sold Baxter's *Call*."

At the time Amos Hitchcock was in its employ, the Society was headquartered at 150 Nassau Street, New York, New York. He wrote reports and letters to secretaries of the organization there. He also kept in close contact with Seth Bliss, Secretary of the American Tract Society at 28 Cornhill, Boston. Today the American Tract Society is headquartered in Garland, Texas and is still in the business of spreading the gospel of Jesus Christ through pamphlets, books, and tracts.

The Transcription

Transcribing the Journal

I have kept the transcription very close to the original. Any additions or changes are made for clarification or interpretation based on other parts of the journal.

Suggestions and explanations about the transcription:

- Important note to family history researchers: In the original journal, several letters and words look similar. When looking for a specific name, remember that the following letters look similar: capitals K and R and the capitals J and L. When hurriedly or imprecisely written, a frequent occurrence, vowels and the letters r, n, m, and v within words appear the same. This means that words, such as Harvey and Henry sometimes look quite similar.

  I suggest that if you are researching a name with, for example, an initial letter K, you also look at the names beginning with R. Try to imagine what other words a name might look like if its vowels and other letters were slurred together carelessly. Examine both the original text and the transcription. Use other primary sources, such as censuses, to cross reference names.

- Capitalization has been edited, and punctuation has been added for reading consistency and ease.

- Some spelling has been corrected, since his misspelling mistakes might be thought of as unintentional "typos." Some archaic spelling has been left, because it was the accepted spelling of that time and is still recognizable to us. Example: neighbor/neighbour.

- Abbreviations have been expanded when they can be interpreted based on other areas of the journal. Example: Sabbath School is sometimes abbreviated "S.S." and the American Tract Society is found abbreviated "A.T. Society."

- Where the same entry has been made in the journal more than once, I have recorded it only once in the Chronological Journal.

- Italicized words or letters in square brackets are words or letters I have added for clarity.

- All names and personal expenses are transcribed. Business records relating to the American Tract Society are not transcribed completely. These records can be found in *Part IV: The Original Journal* on pages 88, 90-91, 94-99, 101-103, 105, 111, 119, 149, 151, 158-161, 164-165, 167-175.

The Journal

Journal Description

The original 8 ¼" x 6 ¾" journal's cover is blue and brown hand-marbled paper (reproduced on the cover of *Tennessee Travels 1844-1847*) with brown leather spine and corners. Inside the front cover, a small pasted-in label identifies the store where Mr. Hitchcock bought the journal: "Jansen & Bell Dealers in BOOKS and STATIONERY, Law Blanks, and Blank Books, 158 Nassau-street, N.Y.," just a few doors away from the American Tract Society, which was at 150 Nassau-street.

Amos Hitchcock kept several types of records in this little journal: wages, banking transactions, living expenses, payments for literature, letters written, number of families visited, mailing lists, newspaper and magazine subscribers, and narratives of his daily experiences.

Among his first entries are the purchases of a pencil and memorandum book. It is likely that penciled entries are written with the pencil he purchased for ninety-two cents on October 30, 1844 and this journal is the memorandum book he purchased on November 11, 1844 for nine cents.

Especially interesting to family historians, are Amos Hitchcock's mailing lists, which provide names and addresses for individuals who have purchased periodicals. Occasionally individuals are also listed in his journal narratives or accounting sections. Over 300 individuals are listed in the journal.

There are a few pages missing from the original journal. Four leaves have been neatly cut out of the very center of the journal, between the blank pages. It looks as if nothing was ever written on these pages. Five leaves immediately preceding the back cover are missing, scraps of writing are seen on the ragged stubs.

Inside Front Cover

The inside of the front cover, left page, is written in pencil and consists mainly of deposits by month and day, however, no year is associated with the month and day. These probably correspond to the year 1845 or 1846 since it is the journal's very first page.

Written vertically on top of the penciled records, in the middle of the right side of the page is "April. 1847 Received of the Tract Society $3.62 ½..." The addition for this sum is shown.

As well as deposits of silver, gold, specie, and bills made with Cowan & Dickinson, he also records money stored in a trunk.

The following names are mentioned without specific dates:
- Thomas H. Aikman. Other records in this journal and at the current American Tract Society headquarters indicate that he was an associate colporteur, under Amos Hitchcock. Mr. Aikman served for six months as a colporteur in Roane County, Tennessee.
- Wm. Harvey (or Henry) Smith. He also was an associate colporteur serving in Anderson County, Tennessee under Amos.
- Mr. Cowan. Several entries indicate that Amos entrusted money to Mr. Cowan for safekeeping.
- Cowan & Dickinson. This might have been a bank of some sort since money was deposited with them.

Tennessee Travels 1844-1847, Journal of Amos Hitchcock

On the right page inside the front cover, entries are written in both pen and pencil. The following entries have a month and day but no year associated with them. They are most likely from the year 1845.

- February 4th B. *[Boston]* Recorder, containing "Necessity of Colporteurs," sent to Maria, also to J. C. M.
- March 1 Moved to P. Nances self and Horse staid *[stayed]* till *[March 6]*
- March 6 Took breakfast and left
- March 19 Eve*[vening]* put up horse & *[illegible word]*
- *[March]* 20 Took breakfast, left *[March]* 21 b*[efore]* din*[ner]*
- March 27 Had dinner by self of *[next word faded]*
- March 29 Came and took dinner and boarded here till Monday *[March]* 31, p.m.
- April 2 Came in p.m. took supper and staid till the 4th after dinner
- Due for money recd for 4 copies of Nelson $1.76

THE DEPARTURE FROM EDEN.

Illustration from the 1838 edition of *Scripture Biography for the Young with Critical Illustrations and Practical Remarks* compiled by Gallaudet; organized and edited by Thomas Hooker. *Courtesy of The American Tract Society.*

---

1. Nord, David Paul. "Systematic Benevolence: Religious Publishing and the Marketplace in Early Nineteenth-Century America" *Communication and Change in American Religious History.* Edited by Leonard I. Sweet. William B. Eerdmans Publishing Company, Grand Rapids, Michigan. P. 258.
2. Ibid. P. 254.
3. *Twenty-first Annual Report of the American Tract Society* Presented at New York, May 13, 1846.

Part II

A Chronological Journal

Part II
A Chronological Journal

A Daily Accounting of Travel and Expenditures

Amos Hitchcock was a man with a mission: to bring godly literature and religious instruction to the inhabitants of East Tennessee. Working as a colporteur, for the American Tract Society, he left his home in Brimfield, Massachusetts and traveled to New York where he picked up his "kit," supplies for his work. In New York, he boarded the brig *Clint* and sailed to Savannah, Georgia. From Savannah, he traveled through Macon, Griffin, and Marietta, Georgia. On he went to Maryville, Tennessee and to Knoxville, where he began the work of distributing free literature to those unable to pay, and selling books and periodical subscriptions to those willing to obtain the literature for a price. His salary was $150 a year.

He recorded his living expenses, the number of families he visited, the amount of literature he sold and gave freely, names of some of those visited, and listed subscribers to the publications he sold. Following are these transactions and his impressions of those people and places he visited, transcribed in the sequence he lived and experienced them.

October 1844

October 30 — Cash paid for silver pencil .... .92

October 31 — For blacking boots .... .12

November 1844

November 1	Cash paid for passage, etc. 4.06			For 1 paper......................06
November 8	One clothes brush..........................50		*November 21*	Cash paid for passage to depot............................. .50
	Mrs. Maver for board.................9.00			Cash paid for passage to Macon [*Georgia*]..........................8.00
	Cash received to pay for board 9.00			Cash paid for breakfast and dinner 1.00
November 11	Memorandum book 09			Cash paid for passage from depot to hotel .... .50
	Temperance report 10			
November 12	Postage on letter sent .... .20		*November 22*	Cash paid for crackers and raisins 25
	Refreshments.................................09			
November 13	[*In New York*] cash received as outfit [*from the American Tract Society*] 20.00			Cash paid for board at hotel 2.25
			November 23	For freight on boxes from S[*avannah*] to M[*acon*] 3.35
	Cash received to defray expenses in reaching New York...4.06			Cash paid for passage in omnibus to depot.......................... .50
	Postage on 60 papers sent to Brimfield, Massachusetts 90			Cash paid from Macon to Griffin, Georgia 3.00
	Donation to the American Tract Society, New York 5.00		*November 28*	Cash paid for passage from Griffin to Marietta [*Georgia*].... 5.00
	Cash paid Thomas Lyon, Master of the brig *Clint*; for passage [*from New York*] to Savannah 20.00			Cash paid for board at Griffin, 5 ½ days......................... 3.50
			November 29	Cash paid for freight on boxes from Macon to Griffin [*Georgia*]..........................2.22
November 19	Cash paid for transporting trunk...25			
November 20	Cash paid for transporting boxes to depot................................25			Cash paid for breakfast & dinner 58

December 1844

December 4	For supper, lodging, and breakfast.....................................37 ¾			Cash paid to Mr. Harris for supper, lodging, and breakfast...25
December 5	For supper, lodging, and breakfast...40			For dinner .... .10
December 9	To Mr. Legg for transporting self and boxes to Maryville [*Tennessee*] 18.00		*December 10*	For ferriage, meal, and lodging .... .39
	To Mr. Cockran for hauling books and trunks 5.00			For passage from Athens [*Georgia*] to Maryville [*Tennessee*] 3.75

December 11	For supper and lodging	.40
December 12	For passage from M[aryville] to Knoxville	.75
	For postage on letter and papers, etc. from Brimfield, [Massachusetts]	.37 ½
December 13	For postage on letter from New York	.25
December 14&17	Ferriage	.12 ½
December 16	Received box of publications	
December 17	[See December 14, 1845]	
December 21	For one horse 5 years old per J.M. Toole	30.00
	For saddle	12.00
	Stirrups & blanket	1.75
	Bridle & Martingale	1.75
	Saddle bags	5.00
December 28	For shoeing horse	.50
December	Total cash paid for per passage, freight, meals, lodging, etc. from S. [Savannah] to Knoxville	62.06

January 1845

January 2	Cash paid for hauling books From Maryville to Knoxville [Tennessee] on December 20	1.50
	For 1 pair saddle bags	5.50
January 4	For 1 bottle of ink	.12 ½
	Sold 4 pamphlets and 11 volumes	
January 6	For 1 pair of leggings or wrappers	.37 ½
January 7	Visited 10 families. Granted 12 tracts and 40 pamphlet tracts. Sold 27 volumes	
January 8	Visited 19 families. Sold 12 tracts and 17 volumes. Granted 1 volume and volumes. 349 pamphlet tracts	
January 9	Visited 13 families. Sold 14 tracts and 11 volumes. Granted 2 volumes and 216 pamphlet tracts	
January 10	Visited 2 families. Sold 4 tracts and 7 volumes. Granted 1 volume and 48 pamphlet tracts	
January 11	Visited 16 families. Sold 15 tracts and 8 volumes. Granted 196 pamphlet tracts	
January 13	Visited 8 families. Sold 12 tracts and 2 volumes. Granted 3 volumes and 144 tracts	
January 14	Visited 12 families. Sold 15 tracts and 13 volumes. Granted 3 volumes and 144 tracts	
January 15	Visited 12 families. Sold 18 tracts and 6 volumes. Granted 18 tract and 4 volumes	
January 16	Received of Miss Temple, Treasurer of the Female Tract Society, Knoxville, for tracts bought of A. T. Society, N. Y. [New York]	10.00
	Committed to Mr. Cowan the above sum with money received for pub[lications] to the amount of $150 to be remitted by him [duplicate	

	entry states amount remitted is $160.00] 150.00		Cowan & Dickinson.................2.40
	Received of Bible Society, Knoxville 6 Bibles to be sold at 37 ½ cents and 12 Testaments at 12 ½ cents 3.75	*January 27*	Visited 13 families. Sold 13 tracts and 21 volumes. Granted 74 pamphlet tracts and 4 volumes....................
January 17	Sold 16 volumes............................	*January 28*	Visited 4 families. Sold 4 tracts and 4 volumes. Granted 24 tracts.........................
January 18	Visited 12 families. Sold 15 tracts and 1 volume. Granted 204 tracts and 1 volume	*January 29*	Visited 2 families. Sold 2 tracts and 1 volume. Granted 8 tracts ....
	For ferriage ....12 ½		
January 20	For postage on letter to Athens [*Georgia*]..........................10	*January 30*	Visited 28 families. Sold 2 tracts and 1 volume. Granted 8 tracts ....
	Postage on letter............................25		
	Postage on papers..........................08		
	Sold 7 volumes.............................	*January 31*	Sold 25 pamphlet tracts and 19 volumes. Granted 256 pamphlet tracts.............................
January 25	For premium on $160.00 to		

February 1845

February 3	For postage on letter from [*American Tract*] Society 25		Received of the Bible Society, Knoxville, 6 Bibles 37 ½ cents [*each*] 2.25
	Postage on 2 letters........................35		
	Received of Bible Society, Knoxville 12 Testaments 12 ½ cents 1.50	*February 13*	The Society acknowledges the receipt of the above [*January 16th entries*].......................
February 6	For keeping horse several nights Dr. W. 57	*February 18*	Saddle cover 1.75
		February 24	For shoeing horse..........................50
February 12	For ferriage 10		

March 1845

March 1	Dr. [*Draw*] for four months service from November 1st to March 1st 50.00	*March 2*	Monthly concert............................ .20
		March 3	Postage on letter from [*American Tract*] Society .... .25
	Cash received for sales up to date..262.81		Cash paid for horsekeeping, shoeing, ferriage, postage, premium, etc., since arriving 4.94
	Cash received for *Messenger* 1.00		
	Cash received of Tract Society, Knoxville 10.00	*March 4*	Total cash remitted by draft from John T. King 60.00

Date	Description	Amount	Date	Description	Amount
	Cash proved counterfeit	1.10		Shoeing horse	.25
March 5	Received 6 Bibles and 12 Testaments	3.35		Postage on letter	.25
March 6	Committed to Mr. Cowan money for safekeeping: $25. in paper, $15. in gold, and $2. in silver			Total cash remitted by draft to John T. King	40.00
				Cash received of Tract Society, Knoxville	9.42
March 20	Premium on $40.	.60	March 27	For 2 books presented	.25

April 1845

Date	Description	Amount	Date	Description	Amount
April 1	Cash paid for premium from Mar 1st to Apr 1st and cash paid for shoeing horse	.85		.18]	.18 ¾
			April 18	Postage	.25
	Cash received for publications March 1st	7.41		Washing clothes	.50
				1 pound of salts	.25
April 2	Postage on letter from [American Tract] Society	.25	April 23	4 sheets of paper	.05
	Freight on two boxes of books, 312 lbs., 5 cts. [cartons]	15.60	April 24	Freight on 2 boxes of books From N. Y. [New York]	19.25
April 4	Postage on papers up to date	.18 ¾	April 25	Postage on letter from [American Tract] Society	.25
April 6	Contribution at 3rd Creek to buy Mr. Sears a horse	.20		Received from Thomas H. Aikman, associate colporteur, for 1 box of publications	89.62
April 10	Postage on letter from the [American Tract] Society	.25			
April 14	Postage on letter from Griffin	.18 ¾	April 26	1 box of publications [purchased by Wm. H. Smith, associate colporteur]	87.75
	1 box of wafers	.05			
April 16	For shoeing horse [duplicate entry states amount paid is			Also to 4 German books [purchased by Wm. H. Smith, associate colporteur]	1.22

April 28, 1845

Bought a check of H. White cashier of the Bank in Knoxville, which runs thus: Bank of Cape Fear, No. 385, Branch at Asheville, April 28th 1845. Cashier of the Bank of America, N.Y. Pay to the order of M. M. Gaines seventy-four dollars. J. F. E. Hardy, Cashier.

The above check wrote on the back, M. M. Gaines, H. White, cash. *[cashier]* Mr. White signed his name in my presence. I paid him $60. in bills and $14. in silver, for discount I paid him 2 qtr. ct. on paper, 1 ½ on specie, in all $1.40. Amos Hitchcock.

[Note: across this entry is written "Settled Sept 1st"]

April 29	Total cash remitted by drafts		from John T. King 44.00

May 1845

May 1	Cash received for publications from April 1st to May 1st 80.15	*May 4*	Monthly concert........................... .40
		May 5	Silk handkerchief as cravat........1.00

May 5, 1845

On my way from K. to Esq. M's--- where my books are deposited, was led to call at Deacon S---s in consequence of rain. He told me that a young man from G--- County had left his house that morning for K. and would be back soon, and he knew he wanted to obtain some of my books. I waited until he came back and sold him 9 volumes amounting to $3. He had recently been hopefully converted, and I requested him to loan the books to his neighbors that they also might be benefitted by them. They were expecting soon to organize a church in the neighbourhood. Who can tell how much good may result from the seed thus sown?

May 6   Cash paid for shoeing horse..........50

May 10, 1845

I have been labouring this week among a destitute people, both as to books and money. In passing a family where I had previously visited and left a tract, I saw the woman out and asked her if she had got ready to purchase some books? She replied that she had one I might have if I wanted; she didn't thank anyone for leaving such books with them. If she couldn't have a good book she didn't want any. It was a temperance tract, and she owned that she liked a dram when she could get it. In conversation with her, she owned that they had kept a distillery and them had been terrible times about there, and she had wished the whole concern burnt. She knew that intemperance was a bad thing, but she had sense enough to drink without drinking intemperately. It seemed by what she said that both herself and her husband were much displeased with the tract, yet that woman is a member of the Church. I called at a distillers and tried to sell him some books but, after examining them a long while, he refused to buy pleading that he had no money for that purpose. I gave him *Debates of Conscience with a Distiller*. He thought I was trying to pack it on him pretty close, and he was not at all pleased. He said he didn't wish to do anything that was wrong. I questioned him if it was not wrong to sell his liquor to those that he was satisfied would make a bad use of it and get drunk and destroy the peace and happiness of their families and the community. He didn't see how he could sell to one and not another. If they would make bad use of it, he could not help it. We had considerable conversation, and I doubt not but there will be some debates of Conscience with that distiller.

I have visited 50 families, only 8 of which have purchased books, and 22 have been supplied gratuitously. Some seemed truly grateful for what was given them, and others had no thanks to offer. But for all the trials and labours to furnish the people of this section with good religious books, I rejoice that I have been able to do so much. May the blessing of God attend the truth scattered abroad.

May 11	For services from March 1st to June 1st	37.50		Kingston .10
				6 sheets of paper .10
	Received 2 boxes of publications		May 16	Received 2 boxes of publications
May 12	1 lb. of sulphur	.25		Shoeing horse .50
May 15	Postage on letter from			

May 17, 1845

Saturday evening. During the week I have visited but few families being hindered from various causes, yet I have sold one sett of the *Evangelical Family Library* of 15 volumes for $6.50, 1 *Christian Library* of 45 volumes for $20., 1 sett *Gallaudet's Scripture Biography* for $2.20, and about 70 other books. I have received about $55.

Thursday evening was the anniversary of the Female Tract Society, Knoxville. There was not very many present, but the meeting was thought to be quite interesting. The pastor of the 2nd Presbyterian New School Church opened the meeting with prayer. The reports of the secretary and treasurer were read and a few statements and a letter from the American Tract Society by myself, after which Rev. Mr. McMullen delivered a spirited address, apparently much interested in the cause. He pledged himself to aid in the work of distributing the publications to the extent of 200 volumes if he could be furnished with them. He referred to several instances of the usefulness of these works. Rev. H. Sears of the

Baptist Church closed with prayer. There was also singing adapted to the occasion. Yesterday I supplied Mr. McMullen with 227 books to the value of $64.55. I trust he will do much good by this means. I am encouraged to persevere in the work believing it to be one, which God will bless. O for wisdom to direct in all my ways.

May 23, 1845

Spent 4 days in visiting in a broken portion of the county. Some appeared rejoiced to get good books to read, while others manifested no desire to obtain them. I have found a kinder reception in the portion of the county recently visited than what I anticipated from what I had heard previously. I feel as though the Lord had been favourable unto me. I ascribe it to the goodness and mercy of God that I have succeeded as well as I have thus far. To some families I have sold the second time, and they would still be glad of more if they had the means to spare. Some, I believe, expend the last bit of money they have for books, and many say they have not any money about them. There is truly great destitution of money and books and, I fear, of pure religion. May the Lord bless the publications circulated to the good of many souls.

May 23	Received of Thomas H. Aikman, associate colporteur, for 8 packets of tracts 2.00		A. T. S. [American Tract Society], N. Y. [New York]............. .25
May 24	Postage on letter from the	*May 25*	Donation for lib. at Beaver Dam .... .37 ½

May 25, 1845

Yesterday I visited a few families and made sale of books to the amount of 35 cents. I found that several visited had read or heard various publications, which I had before circulated amongst others. In some instances they were much pleased with them, etc. In one family I found 3 or 4 tracts, which one of them had given to him in New Orleans. They *[were]* these of the American Tract Society. They thought they were about the best reading they ever saw. But, although the works are read with interest, yet I find no evidence of conversion through their influence.

May 30	Postage on letter from T.H. .... Aikman, Roane County ....06 ½		For publications *[purchased by* *Wm. H. Smith, associate*

	colporteur] 5.20	
May 30 & 31	Ferriage............................ .11	
May 31	Cash paid Brabson & Toole for freight on 5 boxes of books from New York to Maryville, Tennessee, 924 pounds 41.58	
	Cash paid for transporting 4 boxes from M. [Maryville, Tennessee] to K. [Knoxville] 1.42	
	Cash received for publications, from May 1st to May 31st 88.13	
	For services from March 1 to June 1 .... 37.50	

June 1845

June 1, 1845

Sabbath. During the past week I have sold about 10 dollars worth of books and granted some. I find that my visit at a certain place sometimes previous has caused a great disturbance throughout the neighbourhood. The distiller spoken of under date of May 10, I understand, has been very much displeased with me, as also are his relatives, which are numerous. I was informed by a brother-in-law of his that he had not read the tract until last Sabbath 25th, although it had been read by several. But last Sabbath he read it, and some of it he liked very well, and some he did not. It was rumoured that I was a going to publish him in the paper. I found that that visit and the tract have been the means of much conversation for considerable distance, and I can but hope that good will result from it. That man is a professor of religion, and I since learn that one of the men present at that interview was a person of the very character that I spoke of, viz one who gets drunk habitually and abuses his family in a most shocking manner, driving them from the house and compelling them to spend the night in the open air, unless the neighbours take them in. He drove one of his daughters from home because she professed religion. I visited his family during the week and gave his wife a Baxter's *Call*, which she said she should have to hide from her husband.

There is a great deal of whisky made and drunk, I think, in the county and from the reports of Brothers Aikman and Smith it appears that there is also in Roane and Anderson Counties. Their sales have been small, yet considering the field, I think they have done well, and I hope and pray that they may be the means of great good in those benighted and destitute places.

June	For services from March 1st to June 1st 37.50		June 3	Box of publications 109.42
June 2	Postage on letter from Brimfield [Massachusetts] 25		June 7	Freight on books from K. [Knoxville] to Esquire Hillsman's.................................... .50

[Note: Mr. Hitchcock lived with the Hillmans for almost four months, until late September 1845.]

June 7, 1845

I have recently heard of quite an attention to religion in a settlement where I have circulated books and tracts. I know not that they were the immediate cause of the revival, but I doubt not but they have had an influence. I granted Baxter's *Call* and Harlan Page in families where I learn there has been conversions or attention to religion since. May the Lord bless them to the good of souls there. I frequently find people engaged in reading the works obtained when I have occasion to pass afterward. I, however, have but very feeble hopes of doing much good in the neighbourhood where I am now located. I have no faith, but I will still pray and try to do something that shall be for the good of this people, and may the Lord open the hearts of the people to receive these truths which I am permitted to bear to their dwellings and to profit thereby.

June 11	Postage on letter from T. H. A. [Thomas H. Aikman], Roane County............................06 ¼			Aikman, associate colporteur, for 1 box of publications sent by stage 82.74
June 12	For clothing, trimming, and hat...9.56 Received of Thomas H.		June 13	Postage on letter from A.T. S. [American Tract Society], New York.. .25

June 14, 1845

Saturday evening. My visits during the week have been but very few owing in part to the weather and partly to receiving a call from my associate in Roane County to send him more books as he was nearly out of a suitable assortment. I rejoice that he is able to circulate such good books in that county.

I sent him a box yesterday by stage to the value of $72.59. His health has been bad but was much better when he wrote. I met a gentleman in Knoxville who hailed me, but I did not recognize him. He spoke of getting the *History of the Great Reformation* from me and said he had read it with a great deal of interest, and he had two children which he wanted to have a sett each, and he wanted to get two more setts. I met another gentleman Esquire B – who had purchased the *Spirit of Popery* and 8 other books to the value of $1.75. He said he had read some in the *Spirit of Popery* and thought it worth as much as he gave for all. I frequently hear of the people speaking of the books as being about the best books they ever read. I sometimes sell a book where at first there is no encouragement at all, but after reading some from it, they are induced to buy. But, I have as yet heard of no conversions resulting from the reading of those works, but I labour in hope that some of the good seed sown will bring forth fruit to eternal life by the blessing of God.

June 18	Shoeing horse	.25		pantaloons 3.00
June 19	Postage on letter from T.H.A. [Thomas H. Aikman], Roane County	.06 ¼	*June 25*	Postage on letter from A. T. S. [American Tract Society], New York ..... .25
June 20	For making coat and			

June 29, 1845

Sabbath. During my visits the past week, I found one man who would not receive any of the publications. He seemed opposed to anything of the kind and did not often go to meeting because those who pretended to preach would not preach the gospel. I understand from good authority that he afterward swore awfully about the books and tracts. An intelligent Christian <u>Slave</u>, who was a near neighbour to him, tried to have him read a tract which I gave him, but he would not, and he asked him if he would hear it read, at the same time turning to a woman present asking her to read it, which she did. The tract was <u>The Sinner's Prayer</u>. He listened with attention and made some remarks at the close indicating that his feelings were touched. Thus truth has been presented to his mind, which may be the means of good. I sold the servant <u>B. S. Rest</u>. At one house at which I called, a neighbour was present who was quite a wealthy gentleman, it was supposed(or had been), but his appearance showed that he was a friend of strong drink. After a while, I proposed the subject in which I was engaged and asked if he would not like to examine and purchase some of the books? He promptly answered <u>no</u>; he had seen books a plenty of that kind. I asked him if he was familiar with the history of the Reformation? He seemed to wish for no conversation with me. After awhile, I mentioned the name of Nelson and asked him if he ever was acquainted with Dr. David Nelson of East Tennessee. He seemed to have some knowledge of him. I told him I had a book written by him on the cause and cure of infidelity, at the same time getting the book. He borrowed some spectacles and read a while when he asked the price. I told him the price, which he immediately paid. Some of his acquaintances thought it was the very book he ought to have.

A few days ago I called at a house where the man was absent considerable distance in the field, but as I had had some encouragement that a young man, a relative, who was at work with him would purchase some books, I resolved to visit the field, which I did. But such swearing and vile, profane language and cursing about the books and tracts etc. etc. I have not met with in any travels since engaging in the work. I endeavored to deal plainly with him and gave him a tract, and sold his nephew a dollar's worth of books. I am enabled to scatter good books often among bad persons and cherish the hope that the efforts of the Society for East Tennessee will not be in vain.

A week yesterday I visited a neighbourhood about 7 miles from this and sold them a *Library* for their Sabbath School, which had been in operation but 2 or 3 Sabbaths. They purchased $10. worth, and I think there was some interest in the work.

June 30	Shoeing horses paid to Levi McCloud 60	*June*	Discount on gold purporting to be $5.00 25

July 1845

July 1	[Entries labeled:] 1844 & 1845: Total sales since commencing agency, to date, by self..............................492.00		to date...33
	[Sales] by Tho. H. Aikman 87.95		Postage on papers for quarter ending this date............................20
	[Sales] by Wm. H. Smith...........61.95		Postage on letter from Roane [County], T. H. Aikman 10
	Grants since commence of agency by self 26.25		1 box of publications 71.23
	[Grants] by Tho. H. Aikman 14.46		Cash received for pub. from June 1st to July 1st 53.34
	[Grants] by Wm. H. Smith..........5.61		Cash received of Wm. H. Smith, colporteur 35.00
	Postage on letter, paper, up		

July 3, 1845

Knoxville. *[On this date, Amos documents a check written in April. See April 28, 1845.]*

July 3	Cash remitted by check in letter date July 3, addressed 150 Nassau Street, New York.. 74.00 Cash paid for discount on the above... 1.41 Reverend William Rogers,		to the Secretaries of the American Tract Society, No. Dr. for 31 books to be forwarded him by Joseph Hillsman, he wishing to distribute as a volunteer 7.12
		July 4	1 quire of paper.............................30

July 5, 1845

Saturday. The pastor of the church where they purchased the *[Christian] Library* spoken of above attended meeting in this neighbourhood, 3rd Creek, today, and in speaking of the enterprise, said he had never known so much "said about books in so short a time before." The youths and the adults seemed much pleased with the works. Said one Brother (Esquire M----) , "they are some of the most spiritual works I ever saw. " Said a Sister, "I wouldn't grudge the amount paid for all," for one book she had read. A general interest was manifest in the reading of the works.

Deacon Johnson, who had purchased the *History of the Reformation [actually says "Redemption"]*, told me he was much pleased with the work. Mr. B., who had bought Nevin's *Thoughts on Popery* and 1 other work, told me he had read them with much interest. They were powerful works, and he wanted to get some more, but had not the means. I constantly receive testimony of the approval of the books.

July 10	Cash received of Tho. A.	Aikman, colporteur 88.00

July 13, 1845

Sabbath morning. During the past week I have visited and supplied about 60 families with religious reading, and generally conversing with them according to my ability on the all important subject of religion and frequently reading from the works I had to the Christian and impenitent. I visited a neigbourhood properly called the Great Bend, but from some cause had acquired the name of Sodom. From what was told me before entering the place, I had no anticipation of selling any books, but I succeeded in selling about $2.60 worth and in some instances where vice, ignorance, and poverty reigned. I endeavored to be faithful and do them good; I was kindly received and treated with usual respect.

My sales during the week have been rising of $12. I am sometimes told by the people that there is no use in visiting such [illegible word] families they are so wicked, but I tell them they are the ones I want to visit if by any means I may do them good, and in several such places I have reasoned with them and deposited those truths which have been blessed of God in other places to the conversion of souls. O that the labours of the past week may prove a rich blessing to many a fellow traveler to eternity. Brother Aikman from Roane County was up on Thursday after more books. He has been very diligent and successful in the work, and, I trust, will prove a rich blessing to that county together with the books and tracts he <u>circulates</u>. I <u>think</u> him well <u>calculated to be useful in the work</u>.

One evening I rode up to a little cabin where was a free coloured woman and several children, some white and some coloured. I asked them if they would like to get some good

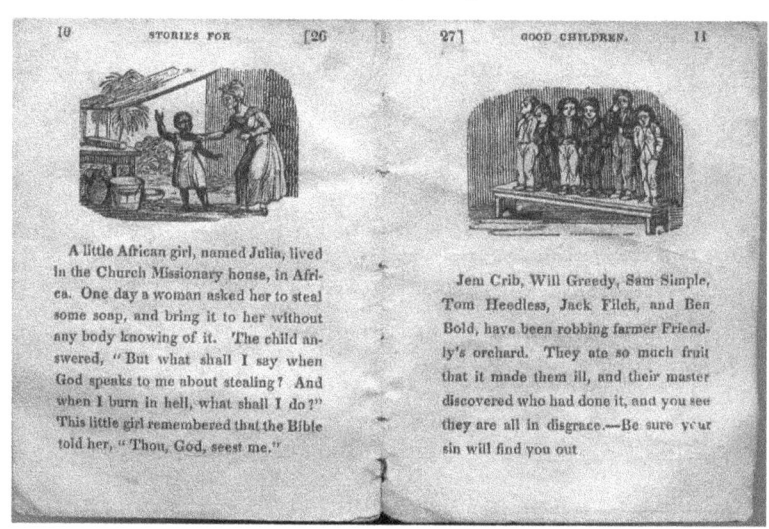

Pages from a children's tract, circa 1840s.
Closed tract size is 2 ½" x 3 ½".

books? She said they had no money to pay for them. I thought by the appearance she might have told the truth. I therefore, after conversing with them and reading some from a tract, gave them the tract and a children's tract and went on. I stayed within half a mile that night, and before I got ready to start in the morning one of the girls came over, to tell me they wanted I should call there, for they wanted to get some books. As I was going by that way, I called, and they purchased two books to the amount of fifty cents.

Frequently when I introduce my books they tell me they have no money to buy books with, but after my reading some from the works, they will search untill they find money to buy two or three books. Sometimes persons will borrow of their neighbours in order to purchase. At one house, where neither the man or his wife were professors, they seemed quite eager to get books, but had only 25 cents, which they expended and still wanted more. And so anxious was the woman to have Nelson on Infidelity that she set off to a neighbour's some distance to borrow. She borrowed one dollar, which they expended for books. I feel that it is a good work to sow the good seed. May the Lord bless it and make it fruitful, is my prayer.

July 18	1 book presented to Mr. and	Mrs. Murray .... .19

July 18, 1845

Of the 56 families reached this week, but six have supplied themselves by purchasing books. The amount received for them: $1.00. I have furnished 16 by grants to the amount of $1.79 and granted 106 tracts. I am sometimes almost discouraged, but when I remember that God often uses apparently feeble means to carry on his work, I am prompted to go on in my efforts to do good, and if I cannot sell the bound volumes I can give the little tract and frequently call the attention of the impenitent to the subject of religion. May God bless the labours of this week for great good.

July 24, 1845

Have visited in the neighbourhood where I sold them a *[Christian] Library* in June and learn that the people are very much interested in reading the books. One person remembers that she had no doubt but there had been more reading in the neighbourhood since I was there, than there had been for five years. I observed to others that I thought she must be mistaken. They thought she had judged pretty correctly. There is another school near that, which is anxious to get a *[Christian] Library*, but money is so hard to get, I fear they will not be able.

July 28	Cash paid for postage on	letter from Roane County .... .05

August 1845

August 1	Cash paid for postage on one letter from N. Y. [*New York*] and also one from Roane [*County*] .... .15	Cash received for Publications from July 1st to August 1st .... 41.03 Total sales by self &

	associates to August 1st 688.62		sent by Mr. - .... .25
	Total grants by self & associates to August 1st 122.79	August 8	Postage on letter from Brimfield .... .10
	.... 17.60		In part for shoeing horse .... .62 ½
	Publications on hand to Balance 829.01		Cash paid Cowan and Dickenson for an order on a
	.... 537.55		firm in N. Y. [New York] 100.00
	.... 1366.56		Deposited in specie money
	Total cash remitted as per Dates 150.00		with Cowan and Dickenson for an order on a firm in
	.... 60.00		New York 75.00
	.... 40.00		Cash paid for premium on
	.... 44.00		the above at 2 pr carton 2.00
	.... 74.00		Postage on 2 letters 15
	Total cash retained on acct. of services esq? Soc? Etc. of		Freight on books .... .56
		August 16	For repairing shoes .... .25
	self & associates 387.95	August 17	Contribution at Concord
	Total cash on hand to balance 39.16		campmeeting .... .25
		August 21	Donation for S. S.
	.... 795.11		(Sabbath School) library at Dr.
August 4	Received of Thomas H. Aikman, associate colporteur,		Westerfield's .... .75
		August 22	Postage on letter .... .05
	1 packet of temperance tracts		

August 22, 1845

From various causes, I have visited but few families since my last date. I have scattered some religious works, however, which may God bless. I have attended some religious meetings. At two of them I presented some statements relative to the function of the Society, its object and aim, the plan and extent of its operations, and some of the results. I found that it was a means of awakening considerable interest and of leading many to desire the most powerful books I had; I was encouraged and led to hope that good would be the result. I have the cooperation of the pastors generally. My small books are now about all gone, and I need a new supply. My associates, I think, are faithful and devoted to the work, and I rejoice that they engaged in the work. Several instances of an interesting nature are reported, which I will omit inserting here, as I have spoken of them already. There have been several revivals in this vicinity, and I doubt not but the books and tracts have had an influence. Wherever I hear from them they are much liked. O may the Lord bless.

August 24	Contribution at campmeeting .12 ½		(paid)..2.00
August 26	Ferriage..05		Settled above receiving $6.75
August 28	Left with Reverend William Rogers for sale: eight books		and one book..............................7.12
		August 29	Postage..05

September 1845

September 1	Postage......................................12 ½		*September 3*	Postage..10
	Moving books...............................40		*September 5*	Postage..05
	By cash received for publications from August 1st to September 1st 43.78		*September 7*	Contribution at campmeeting......20
	Received of Thomas H. Aikman, associate colporteur, for 1 box of publications to be sent by stage to *[illegible word]* 26.05		*September 10*	1 volume German and 500 pps. tracts *[purchased by Wm. H. Smith, associate colporteur]* ....64 Paid to Wm. H. Smith for 3 month's service ending July 31st 1845 ....37.50

September 11, 1845

I have just ordered a new supply of publications, which I know not as I will ever circulate, but I feel unwilling to abandon the field without trying to do more for the cause of Christ and the good of my fellow man in this region. There is great wickedness in this region. Murder. Robberies. Theft etc. is very common. It is considered unsafe to travel without being armed, and I have been advised by ministers and others to go armed, so that I might defend myself in case of necessity, yet I am reluctant to take that course and for the present think I shall not, but I intend to have with me the sword of the spirit, and I desire to have a good shield, and that, by the blessing of God, will, I trust, protect me. I feel that the Lord has been good to me, and I desire to love him more and serve him better.

There is considerable rumor of war, and I feel that it is very likely there will be, for we are a sinful nation and deserve chastisements. But, O God, deal with us as thou seest best. Hear the prayer of thy people and extend the Kingdom of the Redeemer visibly, and may the kingdom of Satan be overthrown. Bless all societies that exist for to aid in this glorious work. Bless the American Tract Society, its officers, and agents in their labours, and bless the publications wherever circulated. O that many may be brought to the Savior in this region by these means, and may the hearts of the people here and elsewhere be opened to come up to the support of this noble and glorious enterprise. The Lord has blessed at other times and in other places; may He bless here also is the desire of my heart. O for a spirit of prayer.

September 12	Postage on letter from R. H. Moore	10		And Dickinson in specie 75.00
	Postage	.02		Received of Thomas H. Aikman, associate colporteur, for books and tracts 7.85
	Received from James Park for publications	6.75	*September 14*	Contribution .... .25
September 13	Deposited with Cowan			

September 17, 1845

Received two boxes of publications, which upon comparing with the invoices, I find contain six books charged $.18 ¾ which are but $.12 ½: *Dying Thoughts, B. Life, H. on Meekness*, two of each making $.37 ½ less than the bill. The above publications are included in the account of publications on hand August 1st.

September 18	Postage	.05	*September 20*	Freight on 2 boxes books, 467 lbs., 4 ½ per lb. 21.00
September 19	1 box of publications [purchased by Wm. H. Smith, associate colporteur]	68.14	*September 24*	Contribution .... .12 ½

September 25, 1845

D'Aubigne's *History* is highly prized by those who read it. Brother Aikman sold a sett to a gentleman who was so much pleased with them that he valued them worth at least $6.00. A gentleman overtook me as I was traveling one day, whom I did not recognize, but he soon spoke of my having sold him D'Aubigne's *History* and says he, "If there was no probability of my being able to obtain another set, I would not take $10 silver dollars for it. It is a work that ought to be in every man's library. Several who have called upon me and have taken up the works when called away to dinner or for any purpose would be sure to mark the place where they left off as they were so much interested with it they wanted *[to]* pursue it. " Says he, "It matters not where they open and commence reading they find it interesting."

A minister of the gospel who had purchased the *Evangelical Family Library* and several other works, recently he obtained D'Aubigne's *History* (an aged brother buying it and presenting it to him). He told me recently that he thought it the most interesting of all. He hardly knew how to leave it when he was reading, it was so interesting. Another Minister told me that he has read Mosheim's *History* and others but when he read D'Aubigne's, he found them the best of all. He recommended them highly and aided in selling several setts. Another Minister told me that he would hardly be without them at any price. This was at a M. *[possibly Methodist]* campmeeting. I had but one sett with me, which I sold, and several other persons would have been glad to have obtained a sett. Many others who have obtained them have spoken of them with much interest. Bunyan's *Pilgrim's Progress* is received with delight by many. A person told me that one of his relatives was so entertained that he never left the book until he read it through.

September 26	For shoeing horse .... .62 ½		Selected publications *[purchased by Wm. H. Smith, associate colporteur]* 7.14
September 28	Contribution .... .10		
September 29	Received of Thomas H. Aikman, associate colporteur, for books and tracts 4.26		Received 1 box of publications, found 10 cts. more than is charged..
September 30	Postage .... .05		

October 1845

October 1	Cash received for publications since September 1st .... 35.17 1 quire of paper .... .25	*October 3*	Received of Thomas H. Aikman, associate colporteur, 1 *Family Library* sent by stage 6.50

October 4, 1845

At Archibald Walker's. I left Esquire Hillsman's last week after making it my home for near 4 months. When I asked for my bill to be made out he replied that it was already made out. He charged nothing: himself and family accept as payment the gratitude of self and *[the]*

Society. For their kindness, I felt constrained to grant him D'Aubigne's *History* and 5 other volumes amounting to $2.81 ½. I trust, in this respect, I have done no more than I ought. I am now to visit in a neighbourhood where I have attended some of their meetings and have sold to several of the people. How I will succeed hereafter I know not. O, for wisdom and grace to discharge my duty.

October 14	Postage on letter and paper for qr. [quarter]..........27 ½		Postage on papers, pamphlets, etc. pr. quarter..........40
	Postage on letter from [American Tract] Society................10		Received of Cowan, Capt. [?] of Bible Society 12 Bibles 4.00

October 15, 1845

Visited Mr. B.; sold D'Aubigne's *History* and *Memoir of Mrs. Graham* thence to Mrs. Angela [Gist?]. Poverty to the extreme. No professors. No books but Bible. Gave *Anxious Inquirer*. Next, no Bible and no books, gave Allein's *Alarm* - next no books but Bible – gave a book. Next, a poor family – gave book. Next, a wicked family- sold Baxter's *Call*.

October 16, 1845

Visited several very poor families seemingly as destitute of the decent comforts of life as I about ever saw. Granted several books. Converse with nearly all; visited on the subject of religion. Visited one family where a young lady had been sick for several weeks and was much deranged. It was truly grievous to see and hear the poor creature. It is a family afflicted indeed. The mother had recently died and another of the daughters was sick. Gave the sister who was able to be about Flavel on *Keeping the Heart*. I trust she is a Christian, but she is greatly tried. O, may the Lord bless the poor efforts of his unworthy servant and the publications circulated.

October 25	Cash received of Tho. A. Aikman, asst. colporteur..........38.03	October 30	Shoeing horse..........1.00 Cash paid for freight on 1 box of books, 200 lbs., [4 ½ cent per] lbs..........9.00
October 29	One phial of oil of spike............12 ½ Postage on letter from [American Tract] Society................10 4 volumes [purchased by Wm. H. Smith, associate colporteur] 1.44	October 31	Postage on letter..........10 Cash paid for freight on 2 boxes of books, 708 lbs., 4

[cents per lb.] 28.32
Cash received of Wm. H. Smith, asst. colporteur 61.82
1 volume [purchased by Wm. H. Smith, associate colporteur] .... .40
Paid Wm. H. Smith, associate colporteur, for service ending October 31st 37.50
Publications returned by Wm. H. Smith, associate colporteur 28.00

Publications granted by Wm. H. Smith, associate colporteur 31.70
Cash retained by Wm. H. Smith, associate colporteur, for expenses 6.71
Cash received of Wm. H. Smith, associate colporteur 61.82
Discount on sales of Wm. H. Smith, associate colporteur 4.59

November 1845

November 1   Cash received for publications since October 1st. 42.97

November 8   Donation to the American Tract Society 20.00

November 11, 1845

One year has passed away since I entered upon the service of this Society as a colporteur. I feel that I have been an unprofitable servant, yet by the blessing of God, I have been the means of sowing some good seed. But, whether any of it has fallen into good ground where it will yield fruit, I know not.

During the year, I have put in circulation by sales about $1070.00 worth of publications and about $120. by grants, with the aid which I have had. We have visited about 3,760 families with many of whom we held religious conversation and, almost without exception, left something of a religious character for them to read. Several who were destitute have been supplied with the Bible.

November 16   Pencil points .... .05
November 22   For vest pattern and

trimmings 1.50
For silk handkerchief .... .75

December 1845

December 1   Postage on letter from Miss --- .... .10
December 16   Cleaning watch .... .50
                  Qrt. of chestnuts .... .06 ¼

Received of J. H. Cowan 12 Bibles and 12 Testaments 5.20
December 26   One pair of boots 2.50

January 1846

January 2	Postage on 2 letters from Mass[achusetts] 20		*January 9*	One Bible, a present to ---- .... .33
			January 15	For cleaning boots .... .05

January 25, 1846

Sabbath. Since my last date, I have been able to prosecute my work but slowly. Yet, I have been pressing forward. Many interesting scenes have I witnessed, and many interviews enjoyed which tend to strengthen my attachment to this country and the people and the work in which I am engaged. But while this has been the case, I have experienced trials of various kinds, which have at times depressed my spirits, and led me to feel that, perhaps, duty required me to occupy some other field of labour in my sojourn in this world. Recent letters from my kindred have stirred up my mind on the subject of withdrawing from my present field of labour and returning to the home of my childhood and youth, to engage in my former occupations. But I know not what to do. I did feel that it was a clear case, that it was the Lord, that I was led to come forth to this region. Is it his will that I should tarry or return? May I be guided aright in this matter is my prayer.

January 28	For one copy of the *American Messenger* to Esq[uire] John		Campbell .... .17

February 1846

February 1	~~Messenger to William Creswell, Ellijoy, Blount Co. Messenger sent to John Henry Sr., Maryville~~		*February 5*	Added to trunk paper [money] 25.00
	[These entries are crossed out.]		*February 9*	For one letter from home .... .10
	Deposited in trunk $80 in paper [*money*] $50 in specie		*February 14*	For repairing bridle and for medicine, etc. .... .75
February 4	For shoeing horse per Henry Huffaker, Esq. 10		*February 21*	For buttons .... .06 ¼
			February 23	Postage on letter from M. Hitchcock .... .10

March 1846

March 2	For one inkstand 25		*March 3*	Balance due me as per
	One comb 25			Annual Report 66.87

	By error in bill of publications credited to Society in Annual Report of date .... 1.50 Publications on hand as per	March 5	annual report .... 404.10 Discount on uncurrent money ....09 Ferriage..10

March 6, 1846

My time has been principally occupied since the month came in with making out my Annual Report and with other duties connected with my station, besides visiting. Yesterday I visited a few families and made sales to the amount of $4.40. I endeavored to be faithful in my conversation with those visited. Several were not religious, but acknowledged its importance and necessity. I hope that the truth presented in conversation and on the printed page will exact an influence for good. I found one family with no Bible or other religious book. I had no Bible with me but gave them "<u>Book of Proverbs</u>." Gave the <u>Backslider</u> to an old man who had been in the church but was not now. Had no religious book but the *New Testament* and *Hymn Book*, could not read, but wife could. Gave Book of Proverbs to a family who had no Bible or religious books. The man had been a member of the church but was not now. Gave *Dying Thoughts* to a poor family destitute of religious books and of money to buy. The man could not read, but his wife could.

March 7	Deposited in trunk, in gold .... 52.50 Deposited in trunk, in silver .... 7.50 Total amount now deposited with James H. Cowan in		specie .... 109.80 Due for money recd. for 4 Copies of Nelson......................... 1.76

March 8, 1846

Sabbath. Sales during the week 20 volumes amounting to $5.40. Families visited twenty. Con *[conversation]* eighteen. Destitute of Bible: 4. Of religious books: 8. May it be found at least that the labours of the week were not in vain.

March 9, 1846

Proceeded to my work. First house, family had no Bible or other good books and no money to buy. Gave Baxter's *Dying Thoughts*. To next family gave *Christian Almanack*, children's tracts, etc. The next was a place represented by the neighbours as being next to nowhere. I found it, however. The woman said that herself and husband were both members of the church; but from what I had learned, I was induced to leave Beechers on *Intemperance* and the reading also. At the next house was a woman and her children destitute of religious books. I asked if she was professor of religion? She said her daughter was. I told her that would not answer her turn. She said she had been a professor but was not now. I asked her why? She said she didn't know, unless it was her own meanness. I warned her of her danger and exhorted her to examine herself, whether she was in the road to heaven or hell. Gave her Flavel on *Keeping the Heart* with such advice as I was able.

At the next cabin, lived a couple of women of reputed lewd character. They had several children. They could both read but had no books. I gave them *Village in the Mountains* and a tract and warned them to prepare for <u>death</u>, <u>judgment</u>, and <u>eternity</u>. At two or three of the next families I made small sales. At one of these I spent the night and although professors of religion and belonging to a sect very strenuous (Preeders) *[Unclear spelling]*, yet, I was asked if I wouldn't have a <u>dram</u>. It seemed that old and young partook of the poisonous liquid. May their eyes be opened to see their folly and danger.

March 10, 1846

Visited 18 families, 9 of whom were destitute of religious books and 5 of the Bible. To 6 families I granted a bound volume and to others the *Christian Almanack* and tracts. Yesterday and today I have visited 30 families – found 16 destitute of religious books. My grants amounted to $2.18, my sales to $3.24. Thus, I have left light and knowledge behind me and I pray God to make it the means of promoting righteousness - peace and joy in the Holy Ghost, but my faith is weak.

Astonishing wickedness prevails. Sabbath breaking, profane swearing, intemperance, gambling, and lewdness appear to be very common. Professors of religion take their dram of liquor and in more than one instance have asked me if I would have one too? One time I took occasion to testify against the use of whiskey. The parents seemed to think that it was good to use a little. They said they had but one child that was a drunkard. I asked them if that was not enough? They thought that somebody else was to blame in making him a drunkard. I asked them if they had any assurance that some of the others would not become drunkards too? They thought there was no danger at all. For my own part I thought there was danger. Several in the neighbourhood have recently been so loaded with whiskey as to lay out at night. Fighting is common in the neighbourhood especially at public gatherings. <u>I would sow the good but it seems almost like casting pearls before swine.</u>

March 11	Cash paid for meals, lodging, house [or horse] keeping, etc..........27			1 pencil..06 ¼
March 13	Making vest 25		*March 16*	One saddle blanket of Mrs. J. Campbell 1.50
March 14	Shoeing horse ....87 ½			

March 16, 1846

<u>Sevier County</u>. Saw a young man in a field and hailed him. He came to the fence, and I commenced talking with him and showing my books. He concluded not to purchase. He said he had formerly belonged to the church but had neglected duty and was now a wild young man. I said what I could to persuade him to break off his sins and return to duty. He finally bought *Persuasives to E. [Early] Piety*.

The next house was a family of Blacks. Some of them could read. They had a Testament and several other books, but no Bible. I sold them one and gave them such tracts as I judged suitable to them. Some of them were professors but others were not.

At the next house found a widow and her children. She would be very glad of the books, but had no money to buy with.

The next I sold to amount of $1.50. At the next house I found a woman and children, but they could not read. She was a wicked person. I read some of the works and warned her to flee from the wrath to come.

March 18, 1846

In the three past days I have visited 37 families, 25 of whom were destitute of religious books if we except the Bible and Hymn Book and in nearly every instance I had to grant them a book or leave them destitute still. There seemed a very good desire to obtain them, but the means to do so were out of hand. I judge that nearly one half of the heads of families were unable to read. In 3 or 4 cases there was not a reader in the family. I read considerable and endeavored to be faithful in conversation. I sold to the amount of $3.64

and granted $2.87. In several instances the people expressed their hearty thanks for the gift bestowed.

The county is very hilly and the people very poor. The Friends of the Bible recently supplied them with the scriptures so that I found but 3 destitute, 2 of which had a Testament. I supplied 2 of them, and the other, I think, will get one soon although not a member of the family can read. I had no Bible with me but sold them a good book. The head of the family was a professor and said he liked to hear reading if he could not read himself.

I sold Baxter's *Call* to a young man who was not religious and said he could not read any of account. I told him I believed he might learn if he would. His wife could read some. I saw his father afterwards who said that his son sat down and studied his book a good while and remarked that he meant to read it through and through. In consequence of reading from Alleine's *Alarm*, an impenitent young woman persuaded her husband to purchase the book. I think the books will be read with interest, and I hope they may be with profit.

March 21, 1846

Yesterday visited 9 families, sold 10 books, had conversation with most. At the first house, the man was not a professor, but owned the importance of religion. I sold him *Religion and Eternal Life* and a young woman present bought Baxter's *Call*. At the next house found a young man who had been very vicious. His whole frame shook and trembled, as I suppose, from the effect of his dissipation. He had a wife and children but no <u>religious books</u>. Mr. H---, a young man who was riding with me, bought a Bible and gave them, and the woman gave me 10 cents for a good book. I conversed freely and thought I discovered some evidence of feeling and reflection on his part. At another house we found a widow and several children, <u>young men</u>; I think none of them were religious. They bought Nelson on *Infidelity* and it was said by some afterward that it was a very suitable book for them, for if there was any place where that work was needed it was there, One of the sons remarked to his mother after he had been reading it sometime, that it entertained more value than any book she had set her eyes on for a long while. At the last place we found a member of two different families and sold one of them Nelson and the other Pike's *Persuasives*. They were both nonprofessors. (Today attended a meeting at Boyd's Creek Church B. S. The pastor,

Reverend William Billen, spoke a few words to the point with reference to my business and recommended people to purchase. I sold a few and distributed several tracts. I feel as though the way was prepared for a more intensive circulation of the works by attendance at that meeting.) It is a needy region. The people need just such reading as this Society furnishes.

March 21	Cash paid for freight on Books per Mr. Thomas 1.00		Postage on letter from New York .... .10
	Deposited in trunk, in silver ... 10.00		Postage on letter from S.
March 28	Cash paid for ferriage to Esquire Henry Huffaker .... .50		Hitchcock .... .10

March 28, 1846

Saturday. During the week I have been able to prosecute the work to some extent, but my sales have been few. Of 33 families visited in 2 days, 18 were destitute of religious books except the Bible, and, in almost every instance, I found an expression of poverty and the appearance of it. Of the 33 only 4 purchased books. In one of these instances I found six women at one house, representatives of six different families. I made known my business. The woman of the house said they did not wish to purchase. I commenced reading form Baxter's *Call*. When I paused, one of them remarked that, that was a good book. I took occasion to make some remarks and the woman of the house told one of her visitors if she had the money, if she would pay for it, she would pay her again. She said she would have to go home for it, which she did. In the meantime, I commenced reading from *Religion and Eternal Life* having learned that but one of the six was a professor of religion. When the woman came back with the money, they concluded to take it instead of the *Call*. I said what I could to persuade them to seek the one thing needful. The people are mostly very poor having but little of what is considered in some places of the comforts of life.

April 1846

April	One pair of shoes for self .... .87		March 1st 41.29
April 1	Publications granted from March 1st to April 1st 13.34	*April 4*	Postage .... .15
			Postage per quarter .... .45
	Cash received for sales since		Shoeing horse .... .50

Ferriage 05

April 4, 1846

Saturday. During the week have visited 35 families, sold 42 books amounting to $11.28 and granted to the amount of $2.22. At one house the people wished for one of the books but did not know how to pay for it at the time. As I was to be back that way Sunday, I let him have Baxter's *Call* at 15 cents. When I returned, he brought out the money and paid me but wanted to know if I just took the books about to sell? He said several persons had been there since I was along which told him he was a fool for buying the book – that I was bound to give the books – that money was contributed a good while ago for this very purpose, and they thought I was selling what I could and pocketing the money. I told him plainly the principles of the Society and read a letter of explanation and recommendation given by a Minister in Knoxville. He said he had no reason to find fault, as he did not contribute any thing. He wanted a Bible for a friend, and as I had none with me, he wanted I should send him one, which I did, and he sent the pay for it. I endeavor to tell the truth plainly and to prove it to be so by my works but I suppose some will not believe.

I found one family destitute of Bible or religious books. I conversed with them and gave them a Bible and other religious reading. They were poor indeed, if we might judge from testimony and appearance. Not a chair in the house, but children plenty.

Esquire Johnson, who purchased some $3.00 worth of books and subscribed for the *[American] Messenger,* saw me passing and hailed me. In the course of our conversation he said he had read his papers and the books he had purchased with a great deal of pleasure. He admired their character and viewed them as eminently calculated to do good. His children also were much interested in reading them. He considered the *Messenger* as one of the most valuable religious papers he ever saw. Others have expressed their delight in the works and a desire to have more if they had the means to purchase.

| *April 5* | Deposited in trunk, in silver ....5.00 | *April 10* | Deposited in trunk, in silver ...10.00 |

April 12, 1846

During the past week I have visited but 43 families, but my sales have been greater than I have effected some previous weeks when more families were reached, being to the amount of $15.81. My grants amount to $2.63.

At one house I found a widow and her children. Had no religious books but Bible and *Hymn Book*. She was a professor, and one of her daughters was in the church as a seeker. I conversed with them and judged that the *Anxious Inquirer* would be a very suitable book for the daughter, which I gave her.

At another found a widow without Bible or any reading of consequence. Gave her a Bible and other religious reading for which she seemed very grateful.

Another cabin visited contained a numerous family but no books. It appeared to be the abode of poverty. I had no Bible but gave them *Scripture Promises* and tracts.

I frequently find publications, which I distributed several weeks ago, have been ahead of me several miles. At a house said to be a place of wickedness, after conversing awhile, the woman said she had an excellent good book, which she brought forth to show me. I knew the book at first sight and told her that I sold the book to a man at – naming the place – for 15 cents and changed a $5.00 dollar bill to do it. She blushed and said it was so. The book was Baxter's *Call*. She said she knew she was doing wrong, living as she was, but she hoped to do better some day. I told her God's time for her to repent was now, but the devil would persuade her that by and by would do as well. I warned and exhorted her to break off her sins, and turn to God and left some reading with her to stir up her mind when I was gone. I might speak of other instances, but I forbear. I still feel that it is a blessed work, to live and labour for the cause of Christ and the good of souls. May the Lord follow with his rich blessing.

| *April 13* | Postage on letter .... .10 | *April 16* | Deposited in trunk, in bills ..... 35.00 |

April 19, 1846

During the past week my sales have amounted to about $16. and my grants to about $5., besides Bibles.

At one house, there was a family without books and if I mistake not, without ability to read. I gave them a Bible. One of the young ladies said she intended to learn to read. I think she was a member of the B. *[probably Baptist]* church. At another place I found a man who had been in the church, but was addicted to intemperance. He was very friendly and proposed to ride with me through his neighbourhood, which he did. He was very full of his talk and friendship. "I must take dinner with him and come back and spend the night with him. " He spoke freely of his dissipation – he knew it was ruining him, and he had determined never to get drunk again. But he had promised so many times before that his friend's have but little confidence in him. He is a young man of talent and education and possessed a handsome property. Liquor has quite a different effect upon him from what it has upon many. Instead of prostrating him into the gutter <u>dead</u> <u>drunk</u> it makes a <u>fool</u> and a <u>mad</u> <u>man</u> of him. According to his own testimony and that of his acquaintance, a very little will make him raving distracted – reason leaves the throne while the evil spirit seems to take entire possession. I conversed plainly and earnestly with him if he would avoid drunkenness and its consequences, never to let the first drop pass his lips – that there was no safety on any other plan than entire abstinence. I told him he had occasion to be thankful that he was alive and had not been ushered into eternity in his drunken sprees. I told him to look at the injury he had done to the cause of Christ – to his family – his friends, and himself. That he had occasion to exercise deep repentance for the past and seek forgiveness, and to implore divine assistance to withstand temptation and to overcome in future. During the evening, he commenced reading the tract *Fool's Pence* but could not well proceed. I took it and finished it. We conversed and read till after 11 o'clock. He felt a confidence that his folks would never have to weep on account of his drinking again. May it be even so.

At another place, family had no books save Bible. The woman brought forth all the money she had as she said: 6 ¼ cents, and I gave her a book at 12 ½ cents and other readings. One of the neighbours said she thought that she had better have bought some meat with the money, as they had none. I hope the book will prove more beneficial to the soul than the meat would have been to the body. There seems to be more care for the body than for the soul.

April 20	Deposited in trunk , in silver 5.00	*April 24*	Cash given to an Indian .... .05
April 23	Deposited in trunk, in silver 5.00		Ferriage .... .05
	Shoeing horse 50	*April 25*	1 bottle expectorant 1.00

	3 blank books .... .25	April 1st 64.89
April 29	Deposited in trunk, in silver .. 10.00	Cash on hand as per report
April 30	Publications granted from	date 36.60
	April 1st to April 30th 13.12	
	Cash received for sales since	

April 30, 1846

During the last 10 days, I have made but little progress in the work of visiting, having visited but 69 families. I found 11 of these destitute of the Bible, 5 of whom I supplied. My sales have amounted to $32.79 and my grants to $5.75, besides Bibles.

At a mill, I found a poor man, who purchased $1. worth of books, among which was Baxter's *Call*. He let a neighbour have it, and he called at my deposit and bought another; this he disposed of also, and when he saw me he bought the 3rd. He seemed to be some interested in giving the works circulation.

At another house, I could neither sell nor give them anything.

At another place, found a family of free blacks. Sold them two books. They seemed desirous of obtaining knowledge and of doing what was right.

At another place found a house where the children were quite reluctant about taking tracts. The parents were away from home. They however took two or three small tracts. I since learn that they were afraid that the folks would burn them. I found the parents at a neighbour's house. When I made known my business, the man commenced abusing the Society, their publications, and their agents, according to his ability of using language – if we except profanity. He was very wise in his own conceit, as well as righteous in his own eyes. All those societies which were abroad in the land and all the denominations but the one to which he belonged, for he was a professor and a preacher, he thought, were not aiming at the glory of God, or the good of their fellowman but at self aggrandizement and exaltation. He said the Bible was not light, or a means of grace, and that the spread of the Bible was not a means of spreading light. I tried in calmness to tell him the truth, but he seemed to be devoid of reason. I have since been informed that he drinks to excess, and I know not but he was under the influence of strong drink at that time, for I found him on the bed. I since learn that he had determined to insult me as bad as he could, when I should come along. I think I have not met with such ill treatment since I have been engaged in the work as from this same (Reverend Samuel Pate) preacher.

The next day I saw one of his sons at a mill where I was distributing some of the works. He selected a tract, which he seemed to want, and I told him if he wished it, he might take it. He did so. I was pleased to be able to bring any of the works to bear upon any of the family. May he see his error and be converted there from.

Several purchased works from the fact that conscience was on the side of truth, as set forth in the books and brought before their mind by my reading to them.

Today visited but 4 families, supplied them with something valuable, it clouding over and commencing raining, put together with loosing my way, prevented my doing as much as I wished, but thanks be to God I was enabled to sow some truth where greatly needed. May it even prove so.

May 1846

May 1	Deposited in trunk, in gold 52.50		May 2	Ted and St. Paul and Mimsa........ .20
	Deposited in trunk, in silver......7.50		May 3	Contribution to ....
	Deposited in trunk, in bills......35.00			S. S. [Sabbath School] .... .32 ½

May 6, 1846

Have as yet visited but 36 families this month: conversed with 27, found 21 destitute of religious books, except the Bible, and 6 destitute of that, 3 of whom I supplied. My sales amount to $9.72 and my grants to $4.09, besides the Bibles. One day I found 18 families, 6 destitute of Bibles, and 17 destitute of religious books, 15 of whom I supplied with religious books – tracts, *Almanack*, etc, and the other 3 with a Bible. My sales amounted to $.10 cents. I should judge that there was not much money left. The people generally seemed favourable but were destitute of means to purchase.

I gave Baxter's *Call* to an old man who seemed to be on the verge of eternity and was living without a well-founded hope of heaven. I said what I could to persuade him to attend to the concerns of his soul. In nearly every instance I laboured to bring some important Bible truth before the mind, and I can but hope that good will result from my labour in that neighbourhood.

I sometimes am disheartened and almost feel resolved to let the work alone for others to perform, but when I consider, I can but view it as a good work and that God has blessed me in it, and although I may not be permitted to behold the fruit of my labours, I doubt not but many will bless God in eternity for the visit of the colporteur in this region, and when I remember now that I have an urgent call from man at least, if not from God, to labour on, I am prompted to go forward and do what I can for the advancement of the cause of Christ and the good of my fellowman. O, that I could do more in this blessed work, for as such I view it, and I trust I ever shall.

May 7, 1846

Visited 18 families, found 5 destitute of the Bible – supplied 2. Distributed 37 tracts and sold publications amounting to $2.12 ½ and granted to the amount of $.56 – besides Bibles and tracts. I endeavored in connection with the distribution of the works to add a word or two, as opportunity occurred.

At one place I called at the house – the man was in the field but was sent for. He declined coming as he was busy at work, although not far from the house. His wife seemed desirous to obtain a book, but for reasons best known to herself, did not. As I started from the house I went so as to see the man, and, after some conversation and examination, he called to his wife to bring his money, which she did, when he purchased the *Persuasives to Early Piety*. May it prove a rich blessing.

Cover of a publication that Amos Hitchcock sold as a colporteur. *Courtesy of the American Tract Society.*

May 8, 1846

Visited 15 families, sold 1 Bible and 33 books and a packet of tracts – amount of sale $7.69. Granted 2 books and 39 tracts. Colonel Compton rode with me this day. We found the people generally able and willing to purchase one or more books. Found but one family destitute of Bible and 3 destitute of religious books, all of which I supplied. The work was looked upon as a good work.

May 9	Deposited in trunk, in sliver .. 10.00		*May 11&15*	Postage and dressing boots..........15
May 10	Contribution at Shiloh..............57 ½			

Tennessee Travels 1844-1847, Journal of Amos Hitchcock

May 13   Deposited in trunk, in silver .....8.00 | Deposited in trunk, in bills 25.00

May 13. 1846

During the last three days have been travelling in the 10 District or, as is frequently and truly called, Knob District. I have visited about 40 families, with whom I had some conversation on the subject of religion. It was a very difficult section to visit but a very needy one. There were those that told me they thought there was no use in visiting a certain neighbourhood, as the people couldn't read and wouldn't try to do as they ought. I told them my business was to visit them and see if I could not do them some good. I was generally kindly received, and the people expressed an interest in the subject of education and religion, although many of them could not read.

Found 11 families destitute of the Bible. Supplied 4. 26 families reported themselves as destitute of religious books except Bible. 26 of the 40 visited were supplied with one or more books and the others with tracts. My sales amounted to $7.32 and my grants to about $4., besides 4 Bibles. I called on one man to whom I had previously sold Doddridge's *Rise and Progress*. He said Doddridge had given him a pretty good rub. He thought it an excellent book. He purchased 12 volumes to the amount of $3.32 remarking that he thought by the time he read them all through he ought to be a pretty good man. I told him I had no doubt but he would be if he practiced according to the instructions which they contained. He was an competent man, and I think will read his books.

Another man said he didn't wish to look at the works. I asked him if he did not like to read good books? He had the Bible and that was good enough. He said he viewed the work in which I was engaged as a speculation. I asked him in what respect? He answered that he thought those who wrote the books and those who were circulating them were speculating. I asked him if he would like to engage in such a speculation, for the sake of the gain? He would not consent. I then told him plainly the principles of the Society and how the works were furnished and told him the salary of this Colporteur, etc. Well, says he, if it is a good work, go ahead. I'll keep my hands clean from it. Says I, you will not oppose it then, will you? He said he wouldn't. I told him that in the sincerity of my heart I believed it to be a good work, or I should not have been there, for if I was after gain, I should have been in some other business, but the object of the Society was to do good, and if my heart deceived me not, it was my desire also, and I believed that the enterprise in which I was engaged was eminently calculated to effect the object.

At another place, I found a family out in the fields, another on the side of a mountain planting corn where in was too steep to stand or walk without difficulty. They had no Bible and no religious book, and none of them could read. I conversed with them and gave them a Bible and tracts; they promised that they would have it read, and they were calculating to send their children to school.

At another place, was a family, which I was told, might not treat me very civilly. I found the man at home. I entered into conversation with him on the subject of religion and found that he was ready to admit his guilt and change and [ready to admit] the importance of religion. I gave him the treatise on *Keeping the Heart.* He got his specks and immediately commenced reading. Soon he remarked that he faulted it already. I asked him what objection he had to it? He said it was too good a book for him. I told him I knew it was addressed to Christians, but if he was not one, I wanted him to become one and then it would just suit. He thought it would be a fine thing if he was one.

Another young man rode with me a part of one day to aid me in getting about, as it was very difficult there being nothing but paths and many times not even that without letting down fences. In the course of conversation, he said that he had formerly been trying to live as he ought, but he had mixed with bad company, and it seemed now that he was worse than ever. I talked plainly and faithfully with him, and he seemed to feel the importance of abandoning his sinful habits. As the Lord enabled me, I endeavored to speak a word for his cause and the good of the people, and my hope and prayer is that good may result from my visit here.

May 14	Postage on letter .... .05	Order from C. Wallace, Knoxville, remitted to O. R., Kingsbury, N.Y. 150.00
May 16	Publications received as per bill 134.71	
May 16 & 18	Buttons and linnen .... .62 ½	Premium on above, 2 per cent 3.00
May 19	Collars, pins, and postage .... .35	
May 21	Cloth, trimming etc. for pantaloons 4.69	Cash paid Cowan & Dickinson for freight on box of publications from N. Y., weight 261 lbs., 4 cents
	Now deposited with Cowan & Dickinson in year 101.11	

per lb. 10.44

May 21 1846

Went to Knoxville to attend a meeting of the Female Tract Society. Sold some few books in Knoxville. Had a good meeting. Exercises of the meeting were prayer, singing, reading of their report – report and statements by self, respecting my labours – addresses by Reverend Messrs. Sears, McMullen, and Myers- singing and prayer. It was thought by some that the meeting would do good.

May 23, 1846

Spent last night with a gentleman who was thought by some to be tinctured with infidelity. He purchased Nelson's work of me last winter and afterward told me he was much pleased with it. He recommended it to others also. He afterwards purchased other books – and this morning himself and wife purchased 4 more. They had several books borrowed from their neigbours, which I had sold. One was Doddridge's *Rise and Progress,* which the wife said she thought had considerable impression on his mind. I read with them and prayed for them and hope the Lord will have mercy upon their souls.

May 24 & 25   Shoeing horses 50   1 pair of shoes for self.............. .87 ½

May 30, 1846

During the last 4 days have visited 70 families. Conversed with 62 – found 21 destitute of the Bible – supplied 7 – granted 36 books and 180 tracts, besides *Almanacks*; value of grants $7.16. My sales were 100 volumes amounting to $33.11 ½.

At one place, the man was quite advanced in life, but was not a professor. One of his daughters selected Baxter's *Call* for him to buy remarking that he needed something to lead him to do differently. He bought the book.

At another place, found the family destitute of the Bible and of money to buy. I offered to give them one. The woman said she hated to take it without paying for it. She said they were able to pay for it but had not the money then. I told her she might leave the pay if she chose with one of the merchants of Sevierville. She said that she would do so. They lived several miles from town, but I soon found the money for the Bible there. I believe that most of the destitute might pay for them if they had a disposition and could be waited upon a while.

May 30, 1846

Mr. Sears spoke in his address of one young man when giving in his experience previous to baptism stating that it was Doddridge's *Rise and Progress*, which I had circulated, that was the means of leading him to the Savior.

At another place, the man instantly charged me with being engaged in a speculating business. I told him he was entirely mistaken, and if he was at all acquainted with the value of books, he would not pronounce it a speculation. He acknowledged his ignorance respecting them and said he could not read. I told him the principles and object of the Society and read to him from some of the works. He finally bought Baxter's *Call*. He had a large family.

May 30, 1846 continued

At another place, I met in my way representatives from 3 or 4 different families. I conversed with them freely and noticed that one of them was considerably affected. I furnished them with books, tracts, etc. and hope that the interview may be blessed.

Much of the route was very bad travelling and caused me much fatigue. The people were very poor and destitute of books and money. But they are now supplied with something that is calculated to do them good. May the Lord bless it unto them.

My labours for the month have exceeded my expectations. My receipts for sales exceed those of any month since commencing my agency, if we except the first when I laboured in Knoxville. They amount to $89.38 and my grants to about $19., besides Bibles. I visited about 200 families, 46 of whom reported themselves destitute of the Bible, only 18 of which I supplied. I have not the convenience for supplying the county in full, yet I rejoice that I am able to bear some humble part in the great and glorious work of circulating the Bible and Bible truth as presented in the works of the American Tract Society. O that it may prove a rich blessing to many souls.

June 1846

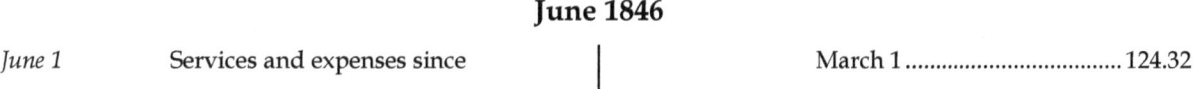

June 1   Services and expenses since | March 1 .... 124.32

	Shoeing horse 60		Loss of publications since March 1st as per date of inventory 4.21
	Cash received for sales since May 1st................ 89.38		Balance on hand as per quarterly report of date..........293.27
	Cash paid self as retained on account of services and use of horse 41.25		Balance due me as per quarterly report of date 78.76
	Publications granted from May 1st to June 1st 19.06	June 5	Deposited gold in trunk...........52.50
	Error in bill of publications received May 16th 25		Deposited silver in trunk 32.50

June 6, 1846

During the past week, my visits have been but few owing to various causes, being but 36. I found 8 destitute of the Bible, 4 of which I supplied. My sales amounted to $19.25 and my grants to $3.18.

Some of the time, my health has been so feeble that I have been constrained to solicit a resting place in the day time, yet from day to day I have been engaged in the prosecution of the work, though in much weakness of faith as well as body.

I have been a portion of the time in Weir's Cove some part of which was very difficult to get at the people. There was generally a very good disposition manifest towards the enterprise. Esquire Mullendore and Major Cunningham rode with me, and my success thus far in that section may be attributed in some degree to their influence. We called upon one man who had no Bible, but after a long and trying effort, we succeeded in selling him $2.50 worth of books, a thing at which all who heard of it seemed astonished, but when the subject was fully explained they are not so much surprised. The man was a deliverer of silver and having a $10. bill, which he feared was not good, he wished to exchange it for specie for which I made arrangements to do so, although I did not do it wholly at the time. At another place I found a family retired from the main road and far aside [?] in the mountains. The woman had been a cripple for years, her joints being displaced by the power of her disease; neither she nor any of the family were professors. I conversed freely with them and sold them Baxter's *Call,* although they had not means to pay in full.

June 9	Ferriage 05		Postage on report, papers, etc. .12 ½

June 10	Postage............13			Deposited bills in trunk............8.00
	Postage on circular and papers............09	June 13		Deposited silver in trunk............40.00
		June 20		Deposited silver in trunk............5.00
June 11	Cloth for pockets and making pants............54			Deposited bills in trunk............8.00

June 13, 1846

During the past week have completed one district and commenced another. Found the people generally poor. But there were exceptions. Some of those who had the means to purchase lacked the disposition. One instance where the man seemed somewhat desirous for some of the books, his wife was so much opposed, that he did not purchase. She seemed to be a <u>hard shell in reality</u>.

Another man I saw away from home and conversed with him and read to him from Doddridge's *Rise and Progress*, which he seemed pleased with. He was not a professor and could not read but said he would care to take a book if he was at home. I was going by his house in the course of my route, but when I got there he had been talking with the women about it, and they did not want any of the books. It seems as though some of the people did not wish for any aid in religious instructing except it be from their own notion. They reject the different benevolent enterprises <u>of the day and have no Christian fellowship with those who engage in them.</u>

I sold one man who said he could not read $2.00 worth of books; some of his children could read some. He carried on a distillery, and from the <u>indications I would think that he took freely of the liquid poison</u>.

Another, to whom <u>I had sold $4. worth before, afterward bought *The Fountain of Life and Method of Grace*</u>.

In my last tour, I had to travel several miles to reach the first house and to ford the Pigeon River, I think, some 6 or 8 times, in some places the ford being very bad on account of large stones and rock. Yet, I succeeded in reaching the neighbourhood in safety and selling more books than I expected. If money had been as plenty as honey, I think the people would have supplied themselves with a good assortment of books, but, as it was, many that wished for the works were unable to purchase a single book even at 10 cents. I found 3 families out of 17 destitute of the Bible and of means to purchase, which I supplied.

One man on whom I called, wanted some of the books but had no money by him. He had money due him and thought probably he could borrow from his next neighbour until he could get his money. He accordingly went on with me. But his neighbour was in pretty much the same situation. He had no money on hand but a neighbour of his living about 3 miles out in the mountains was owing him, and he thought he could get some of it. It was a place very difficult to get at, there being no road excepting a kind of trail over logs, rocks, and mountains and a place which I had been advised by several to omit visiting as it was so bad and so far beyound the settlement, being about two miles. I resolved, however, to go if this man would go with me, which he consented to do. As it was a rainy evening and getting too late to undertake such a trip, I concluded to spend the night where I was.

In the morning we started, and although difficult and dangerous in some places, we arrived in safety. The man is a kind of herdman employed in keeping cattle in the mountains. He was apparently a man of good natural abilities and disposition and abilities but was not a professor of religion. He stated that he had seen some of my books in an adjoining county and would have been glad to have got some of them there. He said his means were now but small, yet he would buy $2. worth, which he did, and also let my guide have a dollar, which he then expended for books.

There was another family about half a mile farther on which we were compelled to visit on foot, if at all, as the way was impossible for a horse. We found a little cabin with the ground for a floor. There were two families living here, the father and son with their wives. There was none but the young woman in. She said they had no Bible or other religious books. She was a professor of religion and could read some and would be very glad of a Bible but had nothing to pay for it. I gave her one and some tracts with such advice as I was able.

I had been informed that the old man was a very wicked opposer to religion and that he would not allow the Bible in the house nor religious singing. With how much truth this information was clothed I know not. The woman appeared grateful for the gift and said she would keep it and read it. May the blessing of God attend the tracts circulated in those families.

In returning, we called upon another family. The man I had seen some days before in another district when he was at work. He urged us to stay to dinner, which we did and during our stay they seemed anxious that I should read from the books, which I did. He said that the folks where he was at work were very much pleased with their books, and he wanted to get some of the same kind. The woman said they had collected a little money to pay their taxes with, but the good Lord had sent the good man with his books first, and she was glad of it. They said if they had $5. they would be glad to spend it for good books.

I have been cheered to witness the manifest desire of some to obtain the works, yet I would not wish to convey the idea that the desire is general and strong as I could wish, for many seem to care for none of these things.

June 19   Shoeing horse .... .60

June 20, 1846

During the week, my visits have been few and my sales small. Nothing of special interest brought to view. To one family living far out in the mountains I sold $5. worth of books. The parents could read but little and the children none. I think there were 14 children at home and 3 absent. They solicited and obtained the promise that, if no providential hindrance prevented me, that I would visit them again and help them read the books. I said what I could to encourage them to obtain a teacher for their children and, by some means or other, be sure to give them education sufficient to enable them to read.

I found some of the tracts, which I had given to a minister near S. *[probably Sevierville]* – 20 miles distant in the mountains. One old man, which got one of them, said that he gave it to a son of his which had been neglecting duty, and it seemed to do him a great deal of good. I found 9 families destitute of the Bible and supplied 4. I found 21 destitute of religious books except the New Testament and Hymn Book. My sales amount to $11.43 and my grants to $3.41. Some of the people had no wish for the books but generally there seemed a desire to obtain them. Some seed has been sown. May it yield fruit.

June 30   Cash paid for stirrups .... 1.00   tracts, Mrs. Gist .... .25
               Cash paid for one packet of

June 30, 1846

Since the 20th, I have visited 79 families found 21 destitute of Bible, supplied 13. Made sale of publications to the amount of $20.53 and granted to the amount of $7.04. A good degree of interest manifested by many. Not uncommon for persons who have purchased previously to buy again. Some, however, have no use for such things.

I called at one place where the man did not wish to purchase. I asked him if he ever read tracts? He said no. I asked him if he would like to have some of them? He said no he didn't want any. I told him that there was as good preaching in some of them as he probably ever heard. I took the one from the writings of Harlan Page, *Motives to Early Piety* and read most of it to him. He said that was very good, but he had seen some that he did not believe was true, and he had decided to have nothing to do with any of them. I told him that although he might never have witnessed any thing like what was stated in these he had seen, yet it might be nonetheless true. He said there was so many different kinds of books about, he didn't know what were good, only the Bible and Hymn Book. I told him these were not denominational; the Society which published them being different branches of the Christian Church. I read from different works to none of which he could find any fault, but as he had determined not to read such things, he would not receive any.

Another place where I called, the man had a distillery and appeared to be quite too much addicted to the use of whiskey. I showed him the books and told him their object and their price. He got hold of Beecher on *Intemperance* and after looking at it awhile he remarked that the doctors ought to read that (Dr. H--- was with me) and asked me if it was not a medicine book; I told him that it might be and that doctors were much pleased with it. He, after some hesitation, bought it, which very much pleased the gentleman who was with me, as he was anxious to have him have it but did not wish to let him know it.

I called upon an old man who was a cripple. Had no religious books but Bible and Hymn Book. Neither he nor his wife, I think, were professors. I conversed with them on the importance of religion and gave him Baxter's *Call*.

Another place the folks were very poor. The man was teaching school. He had no Bible. I supplied him with a copy, charging him to make good use of it. He is, I afterward learned, a great drunkard, although his appearance was that of a sober temperate man. May the Lord bless the labors of this month.

July 1846

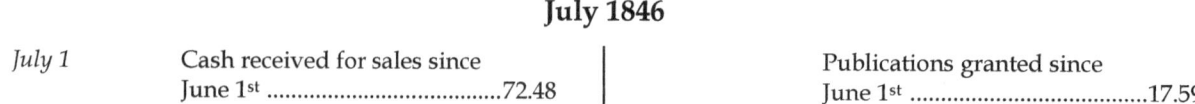

July 3-7   Postage on letters from Society 22

July 4, 1846

Since the month came in, I have received for sales $10.15.

At one place, a man had borrowed a book which one of his neighbours had bought several weeks before, of me. He thought it was one of the greatest books that could be purchased. It told all that a person needs to know and do. The book was *Religion and Eternal Life*. The man had formerly been unfavorable to missionary and tract operations and other things of a kindred notion, but through the preaching of the work by a highly esteemed minister, his views were somewhat changed. He wished for information and for some of the books but had no money.

At another place, I found a family destitute of the Bible. I asked the woman if they ever had one? She said no. I asked her how long they had been married? She said about 40 years. They had raised a large family of children. I gave them a Bible enjoining it upon one of the daughters who could read, to read it attentively, not only for herself but for her parents. I sold to some who were formerly said to be opposed to every thing of the kind. The work is onward, and I trust it will not be in vain.

July 4	Deposited gold in trunk.......... 52.50		Postage on report, papers, etc. .12 ½
	Deposited silver in trunk 22.50		Ferriage..05
	Deposited bills in trunk........... 50.00	July 10	1 pair of pantaloons of Mrs.
July 8	Bought book, presented to		Drennins......................................1.08
	Mrs. John Campbell...................12 ½	July 13	*Messenger* for Mrs. Gist...........16 2/3
July 9	Deposited gold in trunk........... 25.00	July 25	Deposited silver in trunk........ 10.00
	Deposited bills in trunk........... 30.00		

July 21, 1846

Of the last 50 families visited, 13 were destitute of the Bible, 8 of whom I supplied. 32 were destitute of religious books except the Bible and Hymn Book. My sales small – grants liberal amounting to $7.37, besides Bibles.

When I first came into the neighbourhood, some of the people were very much opposed to the publications and thought also that when I left any, the folks would have to pay for them. I took occasion to visit a monthly meeting in the neigbourhood and had opportunity to speak. I endeavoured to show them the character of the work and of the enterprise and to remove their prejudices. From what I since learn, I judge that the views of some are changed from what they were.

July 26, 1846

Of the last 66 families visited, 22 were destitute of the Bible and about 40 destitute of religious books except the Bible. My sales have been very small, amounting to only $5.85 and my grants have amounted to $5.44. In one little neighbourhood, I think, there is some 8 or 10 destitute.

In most cases, I met with apparent kind reception and a desire to obtain some of the works but the means to purchase were lacking.

At one place, I found several men present who were the head of different families. I sold to three of them a book a piece. While there, the man of the next house was passing and was called in. I told him my business upon which he began to pile ridicule upon me and the works. He thought if those who were going about living on the people and getting every fourpence there was in the country would take the mattock or the trowel and get to work, it might be as well. I told him the object of this enterprise was not to swindle the people out of their fourpences, but it was to teach them with religious truth that was calculated to do them good. After considerable conversation, he invited me to call at his house at dinner. I did so. And I learned there and from other means what, I think, was the cause of his being so full of his laugh and ridicule in the morning.

He is a distiller and a dram drinker, and before dinner the bottle must be passed around for children and all who would to partake of. I tried in vain to sell him some of the books, but gave his daughter several tracts. I left several of Beecher's *Sermons* in the neighbourhood, which I hope will do some good, but my faith is weak.

At another place, I found the man drunk. I asked the daughter if they had religious books besides the Bible? She said they had not. I asked her if they would be glad to purchase, she said she would be glad to have some but her father was not in a situation to purchase as he was drinking. Although they had money to purchase if they would, yet I was constrained to give the girl the *Dairyman's Daughter* and such advice and counsel as I could.

I have had conversation with several aged sinners and endeavoured to deal plainly and faithfully with them. I have often felt that it was truly good to go from place to place and converse on the all important subject to those who there is but little, if any, reason to believe or think much of it. I read and furnish them with reading suitable for them and leave them expecting to see them no more until the judgment of the great day. O, may it be found there that my labours have not been in vain.

About the middle of this month was the coldest weather ever known at this time of year, it was said by some. It was colder than I was accustomed to witness at the north, I think. There has been some very warm weather since. First ripe peaches that I had was July 20th, since which I have had several times. Ripe apples are abundant. My health is improving, I think. I am now at Mr. Samuel B. Hammer, a Methodist brother. I find himself and family very agreeable.

August 1846

August 1, 1846

Have just completed Sevier County, having been engaged about 4 ½ months. It is a very rough, broken, mountainous section of country. The people are settled among the knobs and hills without much regard to roads or conveniences. The path to many of their dwellings lies through fields, which renders it necessary to lay down bars and fences. In other instances, it is unsafe to ride a horse, and it becomes necessary to walk.

There are, I would judge, about 1,000 families in the county. I have visited 952; of this number, 220 were destitute of the Bible and about half destitute of religious books, except the Bible. A large portion of the people cannot read. Common schools are very scarce, and, I would judge, inferior to what they should be. I have supplied 87 destitute families with the Bible and granted about 35 volumes, mostly to the destitute of religious books, besides more than 1,900 tracts or waive payment. The value of sales is about $300., value of grants about $87.

The people generally seemed to view it as a good work, although there were some exceptions. I have endeavored to sow the good seed as extensively as I could consistently. I am happily disappointed in being able to put in the hands of the people of this county so much valuable reading. May it be the means of rich blessing.

August 1	Cash received for sales since July 1st 40.68			part to Horatio Butler................. .09
				Postage 10
	Cash received for 14 copies of *Messenger* to commence with July 1846.........................2.33			Cloth, trimming, etc., and making 1.10
			August 5	For shoeing horse (Samuel Hammer).................. .31 ¼
	Publications granted since July 1st 26.58			Postage on papers....................... .05
	Cash on hand as per report of date 36.24		*August 6*	Postage on letter........................... .10
			August 14	Shoeing horse .... .10
August 2	Contribution at Middle Creek campmeeting................25		*August 15*	To Patrick kindness in moving books..............................25
August 3	Presiding elder at Middle Creek 25			Dr. Birdwell one bottle extract sarsaparilla 1.00
August 4	For *American Messenger* in			One ___ (illegible) in part............. .13

August 23, 1846

Blount County. Commenced labouring in this county on the 17th. Have visited 78 families, found 9 destitute of the Bible and 24 of other religious books. I had company most of the time, which made my labours more pleasant. Found a general desire to obtain the books but little means to purchase. Sales amounted to $26.96, grants $5.47. Endeavored to speak a few words in most of the families on the subject [of] religion. The conscience seems to be on the side of vital godliness, but, alas, the life of too many is manifestly on the side of the world, the flesh, and the devil. May the spirit of the Lord be poured out, the truth set forth in the works of this Society be as a server of life unto life.

August 24	Shoeing horse (Mr. Williams) 75	*August 28*	Postage on letters......................... .15
August 24	Deposited gold in trunk 77.50	*August 29*	Hugh Bogle for making deposit at his house two weeks 2.45
	Deposited silver in trunk.........32.50		
	Deposited paper in trunk 100.00		
August 27	Deposited silver in trunk 5.00	*August 31*	Deposited silver in trunk...........5.00

September 1846

September 1	Sales since June 1st 163.58		and use of horse since June 1st.......................................41.25
	Cash received for sales since August 1st 50.42		
	Cash paid self for services		Publications on hand as per quarterly report of date 73.79

Cash on hand as per report of date (quarterly report) 42.79	New York, (quarterly report)...... Publications granted since August 1st 9.48
Rev. R. S. Cook, New York (quarterly report)..........................	Loss of which I can give no account 2.25
1 letter written to R. S. Cook,	

September 1, 1846

Visited 19 families. Sold publications to the amount of $1.20. People poor – money scarce. Visited 3 families of free blacks. Two of them purchased. At one of the places a little boy 10 years could read well. Gave him the ten commandments to commit to memory. At another place, a free black woman bought a book for her son. Was well received in general and left something good with all. Mr. John Henry, with whom I am staying, rode with me.

September 3	For linnen for bosoms,	collars, etc. .... .75	

September 5, 1846

Saturday evening. Have visited during the week 76 families. Sales have been small, amounting to only $8.79 and my grants to $4.17. Found nine families without the Bible. A portion of the week has been spent among a poor destitute people. One day in visiting 22 families my sales amounted to only 57 ½ cents. Many things render it discouraging, yet when I remember the object of the enterprise and its adaptation to prove useful, I am prompted to hold on. I am permitted to bestow a precious gift to many families who need such as the American Tract Society sends forth. May the God of blessing bestow his favour upon the favours of this Society that they may prove a rich and lasting blessing to the people –

September 5	Deposited silver in trunk 10.00	*September 11*	One letter from Reverend Shepherd Wells, Jonesborough, dated September 8 .... .05
September 7	Postage on letter .... .10		
	One letter from Lucy H. Bliss, Warren, date: July 26 .... .10		
	One circular and letter from the American Tract Society .... .07		Publications received as per bill 333.27
September 8	1 letter to Lucy H. Bliss, Warren, Massachusetts, date: July 26....................................		Error in bill of publications .... 1.51 There was two books less than charged at 23 cents each & 2 ½

	cents charged on 60 books over price............1.50			Hitchcock, Brimfield, (dated August 27)............10
	Cash paid Brabson & Toole for freight on boxes of publications............20.20			One letter from Ruth C. Bliss, Warren [Massachusetts]............10 Postage on two letters............20
September 12	One letter from Sarah			

September 15, 1846

During the two past days, have been visiting in Miller's Cove and visited 31 families. Granted 17 books and 37 tracts. Sold twelve books amounting to $205. People generally very poor and destitute. I conversed with some of them on the subject of religion and the salvation of the soul. I fear but still hope. May the Lord add his blessing to my feeble efforts. O, for more faith and a deeper work of good in my own soul.

At one place the man, who was very old and decrepit, after hearing me read awhile from Baxter's *Call,* thought it was the best kind of preaching. He bought the book. At another house the people said that they had heard me and the books spoken of in another—

September 17	Bill at Hotel Maryville, self and Henry............75 Miss Margaret Henry ___ [illegible]............05			For *American Messenger,* Henderson and Toomey............33 ½
September 18	Repairing watch at Maryville...1.00		September 26	One letter to Ruth C. Bliss, Warren [Massachusetts]............
September 24	For three maps............2.00 For four books presented............85		September 30	Shoeing horse, John Myers, Tuckaleechy............62 ½

October 1846

October 1	Publications granted since September 1st............12.46 Cash received for sales since September 1st............41.90			Shepherd Wells............10 Deposited gold in trunk............10.00 Deposited silver in trunk............8.00
October 2	1 letter to Reverend R. S. Cook, New York (monthly report)............ 2 letters from Reverend		October 4 October 5	Contribution at campmeeting.....25 Postage on one letter from Reverend O. Eastman and J. Ackley............10 Postage on paper............05

October 6	Sent one letter to Reverend Shepherd Wells, Collumbia, Tennessee	
	1 letter to Abner Hitchcock, Brimfield *[Massachusetts]*	
	Repairing pencil	.17 ½
	5 yards of cloth	.87 ½
	To Mr. Lamb for repairs, etc. ...	.16 ¼
	Deposited gold in trunk	7.00
October 19	1 book presented to Mr. Dickinson	.50
October 20	Ferriage	.11
October 21	Two books presented	.40
October 27	3 books presented	1.00
	Postage and pencil leads	.07
	One packet of tracts	.25
	1 letter to Sarah Hitchcock, Brimfield *[Massachusetts]*	
October 28	Services since October 1st	25.00
	Use of horse	2.50
	Cash received for sales since October 1st	37.07
	Cash on hand due Society	48.13

Publications granted since October 1st	13.51
Publications sold since September 1st	78.97
Publications invoiced and left at Brabson & Toole from Boston *well [?] [next word illegible]*	296.90
Loss of which I can give no account	3.71
1 letter to Reverend R. S. Cook, New York	
1 letter to Reverend Shepherd Wells, Gen. qqt Collumbia, Tennessee	
1 letter to James H. Cowan, Esquire, Knoxville, Tennessee	
1 letter to Messrs. Craig, Pope, & Anderson	
Cash received of Col. J. M. Toole for horse, saddle, and saddle bags, etc.	50.00

November 1846

November 4	Cash paid the American Tract Society to constitute myself a life director in full ($20. paid previously)	30.00
November 6	Passage home from Maryville, Tennessee to Brimfield, Massachusetts	33.00

Cash received of S. & N. S. Hubbard's note	36.00
Total one pair of boots $2. and one pair of slippers .50	2.50
Cash on hand as per inventory errors excepted	316.37 ½

November 9, 1846

Papers sent out:

Boston Recorder to Wesley Huffaker, Boyd's Creek, East Tennessee.

American Messenger for November, Miss Caroline Wills, Louisville, East Tennessee.

Youth's Companion to Deacon John Smith, Knoxville, Tennessee.

Youth's Companion to John Mullendore, Esquire, Sevierville, East Tennessee.

Youth's Companion to Samuel Henry, care of John Henry, Senior, Maryville.

Youth's Companion to St. Paul Gist, Sevierville, East Tennessee.

Day Spring to Mr. David McCroskey, Sevierville, East Tennessee.

November 10	Wrote one letter to Mr. James C. Porter, Sevierville, East Tennessee...........................	*November 17*	Ten sheets of letter paper and one box of wafers......................... .16
November 11	One silk neck handkerchief.......... .83	*November 18*	To C. R. Brown for Mrs. Lyman for medicines................... .25
	Five yards red flannel .30 a yard 1.50	*November 19*	Sent one letter to Mr. John Mullendore, Esquire, Sevierville, East Tennessee..........
	1 vest.............................. 1.50		
	1 hat 2.75	*November 21*	Sent one letter to Mr. John Mynatt, Esquire, Church Grove, Knox County, East Tennessee.......................
	To Abner Hitchcock for taxes paid for me 38.20		
November 12	Cash received as interest on S. and N. S. Hubbard's note 36.00		
November 14	Wrote one letter to Mr. John Henry, Senior, Maryville, East Tennessee	*November 22*	To John C. Callahan in behalf of Wd. [probably widow] Eton....... .25
			~~Cash received of L. H. B. for two books.................................... .25~~

November 24, 1846

Papers sent out:

2 *Youth's Companion* to Mr. J. C. Porter, Sevierville, East Tennessee.

2 *Youth's Companion* to Reverend Gideon S. White, Academia, Knox County, East Tennessee.

November 26	Sent one letter to James Moses, Esquire, Knox County, East Tennessee		York, New York ....
	Sent two letters to the American Tract Society, New	*November 30*	One letter to Samuel Bowman, Gap Creek P.O., Knox County, East Tennessee.............................

November 30, 1846

Mailings sent out:

Youth's Companion to Andrew Bogle, Ellijoy P.O., Blount County.

December 1846

December 1	For twelve sheets of paper 10		One pair of woollen gloves, lined 33
December 2	Sent one letter to Reverend Seth Bliss, Secretary, American Tract Society, 28 Cornhill, Boston, Massachusetts.............................	*December 7*	~~Cash received of Deacon Bishop..........................25~~
December 5	One letter to Martin Moore, Proprietor of the *Boston Recorder*, Boston, Massachusetts..............................05	*December 10*	Postage on two *Almanacks* sent 05
		December 10	1 letter received from Seth Bliss, Secretary, American Tract Society, Boston...................

December 10, 1846

1 *Christian Almanack* to Mrs. Angelina F. Gist, Sevierville, East Tennessee

1 *Christian Almanack* to Mr. William Thomas, Boyd's Creek, Sevier County, East Tennessee

December 11	Paid for freight on one box of publication from Boston to Warren, Massachusetts depot......44		[pamphlets?] value ....2.10 $^{2/5}$
	1 letter received from Seth Bliss, Secretary, American Tract Society....................		Also 76 copies of Messenger; all grants ....
	1 case of publications as per bill..............................91.42	*December 12*	Donation to the American Education Society 25
	Error in bill 25		Postage on circular.......................02
	399 tracts = 3160 pps		Cash received for sale up to date..........................7.72 ½

December 14, 1846

Papers sent out:

1 *American Messenger* to Colonel Jm. *[James]* M. Toole, Maryville, East Tennessee

1 *American Messenger* to Mr. William H. Smith, Maryville, East Tennessee

1 *American Messenger* to Mr. James Black, Ellijoy P.O., Blount County, East Tennessee

1 *American Messenger* Reverend Gordon Mynatt, Church Grove P. O., Knox County

1 *American Messenger* to Mr. David Wills, Greenville, Green County, East Tennessee

December 15	One letter written to Mr. David Wills, Greenville, East Tennessee..		Reverend John S. Craig, Maryville, East Tennessee............
	Cash paid to D. F. McGilvray for overcoat, dress coat, and pants..34.00	*December 17*	One letter written to Reverend Seth Bliss, Secretary, American Tract Society, Boston (remittance
December 16	One letter written to		and request)................................10.00

December 17, 1846

Papers sent out:

1 *American Messenger* to Reverend John S. Craig, Maryville, East Tennessee

December 17	Cash remitted in letter to Reverend Seth Bliss, American Tract Society, No. 28 Cornhill, Boston, Massachusetts 10.00		Cash received for sales since December 12th 6.83
		December 20	One letter from Reverend Seth Bliss, Secretary, American Tract Society, Boston...
December 18	Cash paid for two books (presented)................................ .28 ¼	*December 24*	1 letter from Reverend Seth Bliss, Secretary, American Tract Society, Boston.....................
	Cash paid for one bottle of Hungarian Balsam 1.00		
December 19	Cash paid Sarah Hitchcock for one bottle Ex[tract] sample 75		1 letter from Reverend O. Eastman and circular, New York..

Papers sent out December 24:

1 *Boston Recorder* to John Hillsman, Esquire, Knoxville, Tennessee

1 *Springfield Gazette* to Eliza Wills, Louisville, Knox County, East Tennessee

American Messenger to Reverend Robert Kimbrough or Arhcibald Walker

December 25	Cash paid for one umbrella		(J. F. Hitchcock) 1.33

Cash paid for freight on one box from Boston to Warren.......... .25	*Colportage*, all grants to be distributed 42.41
452 tracts, 2,582 pps. *[pamphlets?]*, also received 82 copies of *American Messenger* and *Facts Respecting*	*December 26* Cash received for sales since December 19th................................ 6.35 ½

December 30, 1846

Papers sent:

1 *Dayspring* to Reverend H. Sears, Knoxville, East Tennessee

December 30	One letter written to Mr. Thomas Smith, Academia,	Knox County, East Tennessee.....

[See page 149 for records of December American Tract Society business.]

January 1847

January 1	Received letter from James C. Porter, Sevier County, East Tennessee		*January 2*	Cash received for sales since December 26th 2.63

January 2, 1847

Papers sent:

January *Messenger* to Mr. Thomas Boyd, Louisville, Knox County, East Tennessee

January *Messenger* to Thomas Rogers, Esquire, Knoxville, East Tennessee

January 2	Sent letter to Mr. Thomas Boyd, Louisville, Knox County, East Tennessee..................		written to Reverend Seth Bliss, 28 Cornhill, Boston 15.00
			Cash received of Abner
January 3	Received letter from Reverend Seth Bliss, Boston..........		Hitchcock on note balance 15.00
			Cash received of Abner
	Monthly concert .... .25		Hitchcock balance on
January 4	Twelve sheets of letter paper....... .10		settlement .... .25
January 7	Cash remitted in letter		

January 7, 1847

Papers sent:

[Christian] Almanack to Dr. Birdwell, Sevierville, East Tennessee

[Christian] Almanack to Dr. J. M. Hammer, Sevierville, East Tennessee

[Christian] Almanack to David McCroskey, Sevierville, East Tennessee

[Christian] Almanack to Reverend Eli Roberts, Sevierville, East Tennessee

[American] Messenger to John Jornagin, Esquire, Clinton, East Tennessee

January No. *[issue], American Messenger*, to John Henry, Senior, Maryville, East Tennessee

January No. *[issue] American Messenger* to Reverend Johnson Adams, Weir's Cove, East Tennessee

January 8	Postage on letter and 4 *Almanacks* 20	January 15	Letter written to Reverend Seth Bliss, 28 Cornhill, Boston (remittance) 10.00
	One pair combs 21		Paid ninety-four *Family Christian Almanacks* returned 2.35
	Received 1 letter from John Henry, Sen *[Senior]*, Blount County, East Tennessee	January 19	Letter written to Mr. Joseph Meek, Esquire, Academia, Knox County, East Tennessee ....
January 9	Cash received from sales since January 2nd 4.98	January 20	Letter written to Colonel James M. Toole, Maryville, East Tennessee ....
January 12	Received Register – Baptist and Episcopalian from Porter, Gist, & Co. Received *Christian Mirror,* Portland, Letter on Colportage	January 22	For 5 books bought of William E. Hitchcock 2.00
	Received one circular and Baptist minutes of Association, Knoxville	January 23	Letter from Seth Bliss, Boston Cash received for sales since January 14th 2.07
	Letter written to Mr. John Hillsman, Esquire, Knoxville, East Tennessee	January 24	Four copies of *American Messenger* and postage 1.00
	Postage on four papers received ....06 ¼	January 26	Letter written to *Boston Recorder,* Martin Moore, Proprietor ....
January 13	1 letter from Reverend Seth Bliss		Letter written to Mr. Wesley Huffaker Esq., Boyd's Creek, Sevier County, East Tennessee ....
January 14	Cash received for sales since January 9th ....8.36 ½		

| January 28 | Received letter from Reverend Homer Sear, | | Knoxville, East Tennessee, dated January 7............................ |

January 28, 1847

Paper sent:

1 January *Dayspring* to Mr. Swan, Louisville, Knox County, East Tennessee

January 28	Cash received of S. Homer [or Homer] in part of note 400.00	January 29	1 letter from Reverend H. Sears, Knoxville, East Tennessee.......................................
	Received letter from James C. Porter, Sevier County, East Tennessee	January 30	Cash received for sales since January 23rd .... 1.50 ¾
	Postage on two letters from Tennessee .... .20		
	Postage on two letters sent......... .15		

February 1847

February 1, 1847

Mailings sent:

American Messenger to Deacon John Smith, Knoxville

American Messenger to John Henry, Senior, Maryville

American Messenger to William E. Creswell, Ellijoy, Blount County

Boston Recorder to Hugh Blair, Sevierville

| February 1 | Two, Emily, Maria 10.................... .20 | | Knoxville, East Tennessee .... |
| February 2 | Sent letter to Joseph Estabrook, president, East Tennessee University, | February 3 | Sent letter to David McCroskey, Sevierville, East Tennessee .... |

February 5, 1847

Mailings sent:

Three *Youth's Companion* to James C. Porter, Sevierville (up to January 28)

One *Youth's Companion* and *Dayspring* to Mrs. Angelina F. Gist, Sevierville, Feb. no.

February 6	Postage on letter from John Mullendore, Sevier County, Tennessee..........................10	February 8	Sent letter to Pinckney H. Toomey, Esquire, Sevierville, Tennessee.......................................
	½ quire of paper............................10		

February 9, 1847

Mailings sent:

American Messenger to Dr. J. M. Ramsey, Mecklenberg, East Tennessee

Two *Youth's Companion* to John M. A. Ramsey, Mecklenberg, East Tennessee

February 11	Cash received for sales since January 30th 5.09		Letter to Rev. Seth Bliss, Boston, Massachusetts
	Cash remitted to Reverend Seth Bliss in letter 10.00		Postage on papers from Knoxville........................ .04

February 12, 1847

Sent *Boston Recorder* to James C. Moses, Esquire, Knoxville

February 16	One bottle Wistor's Balsam 1.00		February 11th............................. 3.40
	1 pair of rubbers..........................1.00	February 17	Letter to Reverend James Cumming, Walden's Creek P.O., Sevier County, East Tennessee..............................
	1 concordance................................33		
	Book presented to black boy with 12 ½ cents cash (Mrs. Webster)........................22 ½	February 18	Letter to Deacon John Smith, Knoxville, East Tennessee............
	Postage..............................01		
	Letter from Reverend Seth Bliss, Boston..................................	February 27	Cash received for sales since February 16, [illegible word/s] 3.00
	Cash received for sales since		

March 1847

March 3	Cash remitted to Reverend Seth		Bliss, 28 Cornhill 5.00

March 3, 1847

Families visited up to date, 50; volumes sold, 196; packets of tracts sold, 8; children's tracts, 4.

March 4, 1847

One *Boston Recorder* and one *Christian Citizen* to James C. Porter, Sevierville

March 4	Letter to Reverend Seth Bliss, Boston (report and remittance) .... Letter to Mr. John Henry, Senior, Maryville, East Tennessee Letter to Little Pigeon Sabbath School, and James, Maria, and Elizabeth Porter, Sevierville	March 7	Cash contributed at monthly concert .... .25 Cash for 1 book presented to Mrs. Whitney's boy, <u>To Edward</u> .... .01&.10
March 9	Letter from Reverend Seth Bliss, Boston (receipt)	March 8	2 papers from Tennessee .... .03
		March 9	Letter from Colonel James M. Toole, Maryville, East Tennessee (written at New York) ....

March 10, 1847

Mailings sent:

American Messenger to John Myers, Tuckaleechee Cove, Blount County, East Tennessee

American Messenger to Joshua Gist, Sevierville, East Tennessee

American Messenger to Caroline Wills, Louisville, Knox County, East Tennessee

American Messenger to William Bryon, Esquire, Henry's Cross Roads, Sevier County

One *Dayspring* to Alexander Gamble, Esquire, Maryville, East Tennessee

March 10	Letter to John Mullendore, Esquire, Sevierville, East Tennessee .... (Since above *[entry on March 3, 1847])*: families visited, 17; volumes, sold 44; p. tracts, 5; children's tracts, 1, cash received .... 11.46 Postage on letters, papers, etc. (up to date) .... .08	March 13	Donation to the American Tract Society .... 2.00 Two books presented to Mr. and Mrs. Partrige *[partially legible]* .... 1.00 Postage on paper .... .01 Postage on 4 *Messengers* sent .... .12
March 12	Postage on letter from Tennessee .... .70	March 15	1 bottle of Wistor's Balsam of Wild Cherry .... 1.00 1 pair of spectacles .... 1.37 ½ Postage on paper .... .02
		March 16	Postage on letter sent to

	Springfield..........................05
March 17	Postage on letter from Joseph Meek, Esquire, Knox County, East Tennessee 10
	½ quire of letter paper..................10
	1 bottle of Burns Sarsaparilla & Tomato Bitters 1.00
	Two oranges ....06 ¼
	Three *Youth's Companions* to Mrs. Hannah Porter, Sevierville, East Tennessee ....
	Letter sent to Reverend Mr. Sanford, Holland, Massachusetts ....
	Letter from Wesley Huffaker, Esquire, Sevier County, East Tennessee......................
March 19	Mother's wafers ....06 ¼
	Postage on letter from D. McCroskey, Sevier County, Tennessee 10
March 20	Since 10th: families visited, 5; volumes sold 13, p. tracts, 0; children's tracts,1 ....4.17 ½
March 24	Book presented my mother..........10
	Paid for Linus Homer to be refunded for Tract Society, postage.......................... .50
	Repairing of watch 50
March 26	Postage on letter from

	Greenville and *Boston Recorder* to Joseph Meek, Esquire, Academia, Knox County, East Tennessee.............................13
	American Messenger to Deacon John Smith, Knoxville, East Tennessee.............
	Letter to Reverend Seth Bliss, Secretary, American Tract Society, 28 Cornhill, Boston, Massachusetts, containing $15. on account and $20. to constitute Miss Sarah Hitchcock a life member ....
	Letter from David Wills, Tusculum College, Green County, East Tennessee................
	One *Boston Recorder* to Joseph Meek, Esq., Academia, Knox County, East Tennessee................
March 27	Letter to Mr. Archibald Walker, Louisville P.O., East Tennessee......................................
	Letter sent to Mr. Hugh Bogle, Ellijoy P.O., Blount County, East Tennessee..............................

April 1847

April 1	2 bottles of Wistor's Balsam of Wild Cherry 2.00
	Perforated paper......................... .08
	Two lemons................................. .04
April 3	Loaned William E. Hitchcock $2. for a week or

	two ....
	~~Received of the above 75 cents~~, May 10, paid ....
	Letter from Rev. Seth Bliss, Boston...
April 5	For the relief of the Irish.............1.00

April 8	For 2 papers from Tennessee..... .03		*April 9*	Letter sent to Mr. Joseph Meek, Academia P.O., Knox County, *East Tennessee* ....
	To make donations up to $40. Letter to Reverend Seth Bliss, Secretary, American Tract Society, 28 Cornhill, Boston Massachusetts, enclosing $4 donations from Brimfield..............		*April 10*	Cash received of S. and N. S. Hubbard as interest 54.00
			April 11	Letter from Deacon John Smith, Knoxville, East Tennessee ....
	Letter to Mr. William Thomas, Boyd's Creek, Sevier County, East Tennessee.............................		*April 12*	Postage on letter from Tennessee .... .70

April 12, 1847

Mailings sent:

American Messenger to Deacon Elijah Johnson, Knoxville, East Tennessee

American Messenger to Reverend Ashley Winn, Sevierville, East Tennessee

American Messenger to Mr. Hugh Blair, Sevierville, East Tennessee

April 13	Postage on 4 *American Messengers* .... .12			McCroskey, Sevier County, Tennessee .... .10
	Letter from the Tract Society, Boston, Massachusetts...................			Received of the Tract Society $3.62 ½ - .47=3.15 ½ - 2.25 = ...90 ½
April 15	Postage on paper from J. C. Moses, Knoxville, East Tennessee .... .02			Received letter from Tract Society, Boston.............................
April 16	Postage on letter sent to Mr. William Stowe, Springfield, Massachusetts............................... .05			Received letter from David McCroskey, Sevier County, East Tennessee ....
			April 20	Letter from David McCook, Sevier County, East Tennessee...
April 16	Letter to Reverend Seth Bliss, Boston, request for books............			
April 17	1 bottle of Burn's Sarsaparilla and Tomato Bitters.................... 1.00		*April 22*	Letter to Colonel James M. Toole, Maryville, East Tennessee...
	2 oranges ....06 ¼			
April 19	Letter to Mr. David Wills, Campbell's Station, Knox County, East Tennessee		*April 23*	Letter to Colonel Thomas Rogers, Esquire, Knoxville, East Tennessee ....
	For mother, wafers................... .06 ¼		*April 24*	1 package of publications 13.90
	Postage on letter from D.			292 pps of tracts, gratis 20 ....

	Reports from Knoxville		tracts, 1, cash received .... 3.46 ½
	Received Baptist Report from		1 Register from Knoxville............
	D. McCroskey...................................	April 26	To make donations up to $6.
	Paid for freight on package 25		for Tract Society .... .23
	Postage on letter from D.		4 books presented and one
	McCroskey, Sevier County,		sheet of paper used....................... .07
	Tennessee...10		Letter to James C. Moses,
	1 book presented my Mother 10		Esquire, Knoxville, East
	Paid for Linus Homer		Tennessee..
	]partially legible], for Tract		Letter to Reverend Seth Bliss,
	Society, postage to be		Boston, order for books,
	refunded 50		remittance 6.00
	Repairing of watch 60	April 29	Postage for tract sent to
	Since above *[entry on March*		Lieutenant S. C. Gist,
	10th] : families visited, 6;		Sevierville, East Tennessee 03
	volumes sold, 18; children's		

May 1847

May 2	Monthly concert..............................25		Deducted tract volumes, 11,
May 3	Received letter from Seth		amounting to 4.84
	Bliss, 28 Cornhill, Boston	May 5	Since the above *[April 24th*
	Two oranges...................................04		*entry]*: families visited 1;
	1 package of books, 1,232 pps. of		volumes sold 15, cash
	tracts, 82 cents, gratis 11.86		received 3.90
	Paid for freight on package 25		1 set of D'Aubigne's *History*
May 4	Twenty-nine volumes drawn		*of the Reformation*......................... 1.50
	by Miss Sarah Hitchcock to	May 6	Letter from Thomas Smith,
	which she is entitled in		Knox County................................
	consideration of life	May 7	Postage on five *American*
	membership...............................10.00		*Messengers* sent to five
	Letter to Mr. Aaron Bliss,		Sabbath Schools............................ .15
	Warren, Massachusetts		

May 7, 1847

Mail sent:

American Messenger to Calvin Mynatt, Church Grove, East Tennessee

American Messenger to Thomas Smith, Academia, East Tennessee

American Messenger to Jordan Houck *[or Hawck?]*, Boyd's Creek, East Tennessee

American Messenger to James C. Porter, Sevierville, East Tennessee

American Messenger to Dr. J. M. Hammer, Sevierville, East Tennessee

May 8	Letter to secretary, American Tract Society, 150 Nassau St., N.Y.	May 9	Cash received for 1 bottle of Wasters Balsam 1.00

May 13, 1847

Boston Recorder to David McCroskey, Sevierville, East Tennessee

Springfield Gazette, to Mrs. Dickinson, Knoxville, East Tennessee

Knoxville Register of April 28 from the office

May 13	Postage on papers sent and received .... .07		Hammer, Sevierville *[enclosed]* for 6 *Messengers* 1.00
May 16	Postage on letter and paper from Tennessee............................. .11		*Register* of May 12 from office .... Sent letter to Reverend James
	Knoxville Register of May 5 from office		N. S. Huffaker, Jonesborough, East Tennessee ....
	Letter from Reverend James Huffaker, Jonesborough, East Tennessee		Postage on paper.......................... .02 For 6 *American Messengers* 1.00
May 20	Sent *Boston Recorder* to Reverend R. B. McMullen, Knoxville, East Tennessee	May 27	Cash remitted to Reverend Seth Bliss 5.00
May 26	Letter from Dr. J. M.		

June 1847

June 1	Postage on letter from J. C. and Maria Porter, Sevierville ..... .10		Porter, bookmark enclosed to Elizabeth and Maria,
	Letter from Reverend Seth Bliss, Boston	June 5	Sevierville, East Tennessee............ Postage on papers received........... .03
	Letter from Reverend O. Eastman, New York, (circular)	June 10	Postage on 2 letters from Tennessee and 1 paper sent .... .23 1 box of blacking............................ .10
June 4	Letter to J. C. and Maria		Letter received from

President Joseph Estabrook, Knoxville..

Letter received from Colonel J. S. Compton, Sevierville, East Tennessee..............................

Sent one *Boston Recorder* to Reverend Isaac Anderson, D. D., Maryville, Tennessee..........

June 14, 1847

Papers sent:

1 to Secretary, American Tract Society, New York, enclosed $1. for *American Messenger*

Youth's Companion to John Mullendore, Esquire, Sevierville

Youth's Companion to J. C. Porter, Sevierville

Youth's Companion to Lieutenant S. C. Gist, U. S. N., Sevierville

American Messenger to David Wills, Campbell's Station, East Tennessee

American Messenger to John Henry, Maryville, Tennessee

American Messenger to Deacon John Smith, Knoxville, East Tennessee

American Messenger to John Jornagin, Esquire, Clinton, East Tennessee

June 14	Postage on 8 papers sent to East Tennessee 24	*June 24*	Postage on letter and paper..........13
	1 tract volume No. 1st 44		½ quire of letter paper.................10
	2 volumes, David Moulton............25		Letter from William Thomas, Sevierville, East Tennessee ....
	Letter sent to the Secretary of the American Tract Society, New York for Messenger enclosed 1.00	*June 26*	Letter to Thomas Smith, Academia, Tennessee ....
		June 28	Postage 02
			Ink 06
June 19	One quart of strawberries to Strawberries to Geo. 05	*June 30*	Letter to Reverend G. [or J.] S. Waded [partially legible], and George Hardin [or Hadin], Knoxville..
	Letter received from William Thomas, Sevier County, East Tennessee...		

July 1847

July 1	Sent letter to James Cowan, Esquire		P. O., Blount County [this entry was with January listings, but then crossed out] ....
	American Messenger to William E. Creswell, Ellijoy	*July 4*	Monthly concert...........................20

July 8	Postage on letter, New York 05		*July 18*	Contribution sent to Fer. Evangelical Society........................25

July 22, 1847

Papers sent:

American Messenger to John Hillsman, Esquire, Knoxville

American Messenger to Geo. Hardin, Knoxville

American Messenger to Reverend John S. Coram *[partially illegible]*, Academia

American Messenger to Samuel Hammer, Sevierville

July 31	Since above 1– postage on letters,		papers, etc........................50

August 1814

August 9, 1847

Mail sent:

American Messenger to Andrew Bogle, Ellijoy, Blount County

American Messenger to John Henry, Senior, Maryville, East Tennessee

American Messenger to Deacon John Smith, Knoxville

American Messenger to Joseph Meek, Esquire, Academia *August*

August 9	Postage on paper sent..................12			Hair brush 04
August 14	Since the above *[since May 5th entry]* volumes sold, 16; children's tracts, 62, *[cash received]* 3.73		*August 27*	Umbrella........................1.33
				2 ¾ yards lossimen *[?]* 2.29
				Silk and twist................................17
				Dwilling *[?]* and buttons 10
August 18	Taxes for 1847 .... 13.42			6 yards cotton.................................75
	Postage on letter and two papers 13			Pack cards *[or cords]* 15
				1 ½ yards linen............................1.12
August 20	Postage on letter, paper, and children's tracts 05			Thread..05
				Gloves 67
August 20&21	Families visited, 23; dist cts 14; volumes, 28, children's tracts, 5...6.29			Silk pocket half 75
				Penknife...54
				Two pairs suspenders...................30
August 25	Wallet..12 ½			½ quire of letter paper 06

September 1847

September 3	Donation to the American Bible Society 50		linnen .... .37 ½
	Postage on three books given 06	*September 20*	Passage to Boston 2.05
	Postage 10	*September 21*	Library fifty volumes 2.50
	Families visited 55, disp. cts. 14, vols. sold 69 .... 16.27		Two books .... .06
September 7	1 scripture manual .... 87 ½		Blank book 75
	Two baskets .... 37 ½		Subscription to *American Sunday School Journal* to be sent to Tennessee 1.00
September 8	Postage 10		*Youth's Companion* to be sent to J. C. Porter 1.00
	Books presented 11		
	Families visited, 32; dis cts. 42 ½; volumes sold, 36 .... 7.38 ½		Passage from and to the depot, Boston .... .50
September 9	Postage 01		Bunker Hill, etc. .... .11 ½
September 13	On note of N. S. and S. Hubbard 500.00		1 Bible .... .94
September 16	Postage 02		Refreshment, etc. .... .06
	Books bought 18		Fare from Boston to Warren [*Massachusetts*] 2.05
	Cloth 21		Admittance to lecture on physiology .... .25
	Total publications on hand 31.13		
	Discount on silver 2.00	*September 22*	Three daguerreotype likenesses 3.75
	Cash on hand 45.00		
	Families visited, 45; volumes sold, 33 .... 10.01		3 blank books .... .46
	Not paid, 1 39		Postage on setts .... .10
	Drawn by Sarah Hitchcock, 29 volumes 10.00	*September 23*	Deposited in the Savings Bank, Springfield 600.00
	1 volume .... 12 ½	*September 25*	Fare from Tolmer to Lenox and back 4.55
September 17	Cash on hand 43.81		Newspaper .... .03
September 18	For cutting pants 25	*September 28*	Fare from C_l_tville [*partly illegible*] to Springfield .... .20
	Cash received of N. S. Hubbard 116.68		Postage on letter sent Philadelphia 05
	Cash received for ½ yard		

October 1847

October 3	Postage on papers 03		Cash received for twelve books .... .12
October 4	Cash paid Abner Hitchcock for book of Savings Bank 102.25		Cash received from Abner

	Hitchcock for note 293.03		Total 303.67
	Cash received from Abner		*October, no date* Cash received from Linus
	Hitchcock for work 50.00		Homer 119.55
October 28	In trunk gold 253.67 and $50.		

[Note: the following were not associated with a specific year.]
September *[1846?]* Families visited, 55; dis cts. ; volumes, 69.........16.27

Report to Society: Families visited 234; volumes sold 487 amounting to $125. Tracts distributed gratis 7266, value $4.45. Also 150 number of Am. *[American]* Mess. *[Messenger]*. About 150 days labour. *[Follows entry on June 14, 1847, so may relate to this time period.]*

Part III

Visitation and Mailing Lists

Part III
Visitation and Mailing Lists

Names of Persons in Tennessee, a few of the many visits by me as a Colporteur

Knox County
Samuel H. Love
Addison Armstrong
Dr. Wm. H. Montgomery
Obadiah Tinker
Robert Blair
Wm. Reeder
Amos Carter
Martin B. Carter
Alex Shipe
Gaines McMillen
John McMillen
Wm. Tinker
David Brewer
Mr. Rawhoof
Wm. Lovelace
John S. Waters
David Childs
Francis Bounds

Gen. Joseph A. Brooks
Robert Armstrong
Preston Lee
Geo. Shinneberry
Baxter or Beseter
　　Edmundson
Isaac McCampbell
Jacob Gibbs
Esq. Crispin
Andrew C. Copeland
Wm. W. Salmon
Wm. Gibbs
Joseph Mynatt
Andrew Roberts
Eli Skaggs
Martyn L. Mynatt Esq.
Philip Smith
Ham. Scott
Geo. Graves Esq.

Mr. Brigs
Levi McCloud Esq.
Samuel McKinley
Reese [?] Bayless Esq.
Esq. Bell
Wilson J. Norman
Archibald Doulon
Mr. Childers
Rev. Robert Kimbrough
Jessee Groner
Aaron Gentry
John Muny Esq.
Andrew Keith
Dea. John Weaver
James McLain
Robert McBath Esq.
Widow Colliers
Rev. John Nicholson
Elijah Walker

Tennessee Travels 1844-1847, Journal of Amos Hitchcock

Walter Kennedy
Wm. Morris Esq.
James Lithgo
Maj. Samuel Lowe
Patterson Russell
Rev. Samuel B. West
Rev. James Blair
Parker Gant
Col Craig
Esq. Seaton
Henry Temple
Widow Young
Jackson Temple
Harvey or Henry Johnson
Dr. Wright
Gibson Hardin
John Hardin
Geo. Gallaher
Rev. Archibald A. Mathes
Nelson Ladd

Roane County
Lawson Low or Love
Esq. Rogers
John Campbell
Rev. Henry Dake
Widow Reynolds

Knoxville
Andrew J. Hown or Nown
Archibald Collen or Cullen
J. Johnson Esq.
Rev. Jacob Huffaker
Rev. Christian [?] Huffaker

Henry Huffaker Esq.

Gap Creek
James H. Greene
Jonathan Johnson
Col. Geo. Mabery
Jacob Pickle
Rev. Robert Young

Cades Cove
Blount County
John Caldwell Esq.
Robert Birchfield
Widow Layman
C ----n Layman
Green Hill

Samuel B. Hammer
Geo. Loveday
Widow Hill
Solomen Williams
Rev. Wm. Ogle
Maj. John Howard
Wm. Huskey
Rev. James Edwards
Rev. Andrew Conatser
George Henderson
Joshua Gist
Widow Jones
Adam Houck
Col. Wilson Duggen
Asa Derrick

Henry's Cross Road
W. M. Bryon Esquire
Thomas Cote Esq.
John Brabson Esq.
Joseph Shaddon
Widow Malcom
Wm. Wayland
Jordan Houck
James Sharp
Daniel L. Trundle
Rev. Wm. Hodge
John Trundle
Maj. Jeptha Davis
Col. Lawson
Asa Layman
Philip Shults
Daniel Ernest
Wm. Trotter
John A. Poindexter
John C. Yett Esq.
Esq. Bogert
Joseph Snapp
John Baily or Boily
Sam Pate

Anderson Woods
Dr. Wm. Ford or Ferel
Hugh Blair
Rev. Wm. Ellis
Morgan Davis Esq.

Walden's Creek
Maj. David Cunningham

Sevier County

John Nichols
John Andes
Rev. Johnson Adams
Rev. James Cummings
Widow Montgomery
Rev. Ashley Winn
Archibald Scruggs
James Brock or Bruck
Rev. Isaac Kimbrough
Wm. Cannon
John Cannon
James Ellis
John Kindles
Lewis Rennear or Kennear Esq.
Rev. Gamaliel Bryant

Blount County

Wm. E. Creswell
Rev. Campbell Boyd
Joseph Bogle
James Black
Esq. Cummings
Albert Bogle
Col. Matthew Bogle
Rev. John Russum
Richard Williams
Andrew Bogle
Marion W. Rogers
Hugh Bogle
John Myers

Tuckaleechy Cove

Eli Caler
Widow Burns
Rev. Frederick Ernest
Cunningham Dunn
Mr. Levi Dunn
Henry Myers
M. or Mr. Hart
Peter Sneider
Alexander Gamble Esq

Mailing List

Knoxville P.O.
Dr. John Westerfield
Thomas Smith
Rev. Gideon S. White
Wm. Sawyers Esq.
Josiah Sawyers
Rev. John S. Coram
Rev. John Roberts
Joseph Meek Esq.
Mr. Giles S. Bledsoe
Col. James Anderson
Dea. John Smith
Rev. Rufus M. Stephens
Thomas Rogers Esq.
Dr. Wm. Rogers
Dr. James Rogers
John Hillsman Esq.
James C. Moses
Rev. Homer Sears
Rev. R. B. McMullen
Joseph Estabrook M.A.
James H. Cowan Esq.
Horace Maynard Esq.
Rev. Mr. Snoddy
George Hardin
Mrs. Garvin

Church Grove P.O.
John Mynatt Esq.
Rev. Gordon Mynatt

Louisville P.O.

Thomas Boyd
Archibald Walker
John Wills
Will Wills
Elisa Wills
Caroline Wills
David Wills Jr.

Mecklenberg P.O.
John Campbell Esq.
Capt. James Campbell
John M. A. Ramsey
Mary Ann Ramsey
Willaby B. Ramsey
Francis A. Ramsey
Margaret E. Ramsey

Tuckahoe P.O.
Archibald Cullen
Jessee Davis Esq.

Gap Creek P.O.
Samuel Bowman
John Bowman
Esq. Johnson

Clinton
Anderson County
John Jornagin Esq.
W. W. Walker

Boyd's Creek P.O.

Esq. Wesley Huffaker
Rev. James Huffaker
Wm. Thomas

Sevierville
David McCroskey
Eliza McCroskey
Oscar McCroskey
Mrs. Hannah Porter
Miss Maria Porter
Miss Elizabeth Porter
Miss Belinda Porter
Miss Virginia Porter
Miss Ellen Porter
Mr. James C. Porter
Gilbert Porter
George Porter
Jackson Porter
Lieu. Spencer C. Gist
Mrs. Angelina F. Gist
St. Paul Gist
Mimsa Gist
Pinckney H. Toomey Esq.
Dr. Jonathan M. Hammer
John Mullendore Esq.*
Mary Amanda Mullendore*
Abraham Lafayette
   [Mullendore]*
Wm. Wallace [Mullendore]*
Elijah Lunidas {Mullendore]*
Robert Bruce [Mullendore]*
Susan Catharine

*[Mullendore]**
Nancy Matilda *[Mullendore]**
Jane Elizabeth Hitchcock
   Mullendore**: Born
   April 16th 1846
Terresa Ann Lenning
Col. John S. Compton
Rev. Eli Roberts

Walden's Creek P.O.
Rev. James Cummings

Ellijoy P.O.
Blount County
Hugh Bogle
Andrew Bogle
James Black

Maryville
Blount County
John Henry Sen.
James Henry (Care of John
   Sen.)
Jane Henry
Rachel Henry
Wm. Jasper Henry
Samuel Henry
Margaret Elizabeth Henry
Rev. Isaac Anderson D. D.
Rev. Fielding Pope
Rev. John S. Craig
Col. James M. Toole

Knoxville

1846
Margaret Cowan 14
Mary Cowan 13
Lucinda F---te Cowan
Nancy Estabrook Cowan
Susan Perriman Cowan
James Dickinson Cowan
Percy Dickinson Cowan
Joseph Hillsman
[Unclear if the following
names should be included
under Knoxville]
Geo. White Esq.
Joseph King Esq.
Rev. Mr. McInnis
Dea. Elijah Johnson
Rev. Wm. Graves

Part IV

The Original Journal

Mid-1800s illustration. Courtesy of the American Tract Society.

The following pages of *Part IV: The Original Journal* are photocopies of Mr. Hitchcock's journal pages in the exact order they exist in the original.

Original Journal: Inside Front Cover

Knoxville July 3rd 1845
Bought a check of H. White Cashier of the Bank in Knoxville
which runs thus "Bank of Cape Fear
     No. 385   Branch at Ashville April 2nd 1845
Cashier of the Bank of America No 3.
Pay to the order of M. M. Goines   Seventy four Dollars
$74 =   J.F.E. Hardy
                              Cashier

    The above Check wrote on the back
         M. M. Goines
           H. White Cash   Mr White signed his name in
my presence. I paid him $60 in bills & $14 in silver, for discount
I paid him 2 cts ct on pap – 1/2 ct on specie in all $1.40
                              Amos Hitchcock

In Trunk Feb. 1st 1846 Paper $80 Specie $50
added Feb $25
                                     15

1846   1846
March 7th In Trunk Gold.   Silver   Bills   March 7th
                     $52.50 $7.50 $0.00   Total amount now
       21 added $10   deposited with
April 5   Do   James H. Cartan
April 10   Do   10   95.00   in Specie $109.80
       20. Do   Due for money recd for
       22   Do   5   4 Copies of Nelson
May 1st in Trunk   Gold   Silver   Bills $1.76
                    $52.50 $52.50 $35.00   May 21. Now deposited
         added   25.00   with Cowan & Dickin
         Do   & Meade $108.11

Original Journal: Page 2

Dr. The American Tract Society in Stock

1844		$	c
July 1st	To Sales since commencing agency up to date By myself	492	00
	By Tho. H. Aikman	87	95
	" Wm. H. Smith	61	95
	Grants since Commenc't of agency		
	By self	26	65
	" Tho H. Aikman	14	46
	" Wm H. Smith	5	61
1845	To Sales by self & associates to Aug 1st	688	62
	" Grants " " " "	122	79
		17	00
Aug 1st	Publications on hand to balance	829	01
		537	55
		1366	56

Cr. The American Tract Society in Cash ac

1845			
	To Cash remitted as pr dates	150	00
	" " " " "	60	00
	" " " " "	40	00
	" " " " "	44	00
	" " " " "	74	00
Aug 1st	To Cash retained on acct of services expenses &c. of self & associates	387	95
		39	16
Aug 1st	To Cash on hand to balance	795	11

My accts are thus closed with the Society up another place to commence with Aug 1st acct with Amos Hitchcock   Cr.

Publication acct $ cts

1844   By bills of publications
Dec. 16.   Box No 2. as by bill enclosed   99   11
Dec 20.   "   " 1 "   Do   91   14
"   "   "   " 3 "   "   58   25
Dec. 24.   "   " 4 "   "   63   88
            Package of German publications   4   78
                                                           ―――――――
                                                           317   16
1845
April 2.   By 2 boxes of publications as pr bill   163   53
"   23.   By 2 Boxes of   Do   193   45
May 12   By 1- Box of   Do as pr bill enc   54   27
"   16   " 2 Boxes of   Do   "   "   240   16
June 3.   By 1- Box of   Publications as pr bl   109   42
"   17   By 1 Box of   Do   60   75
                                                           ―――――――
                                                          1138   74
July 24.   By 2 boxes Charged, not yet received   227   82
                                                           ―――――――
                                                          1366   56

acct with Amos Hitchcock   Cr. $ cts
Count   1845

         By Cash Recd by self & agents for pub. sold   641   90
         By Do   " " for Messenger   1   00
         By Cash Do   as donations   9   42
         By Cash Do   as outfit   20   00
         By Cash Recd by self & assts. since above   122   79
                                                           ―――――――
                                                           795   11

To date & all my new accts may be found at
1845   Amos Hitchcock Colpt A.T. Soc'y

Tennessee Travels 1844-1845, Journal of Amos Hitchcock

Amos Hitchcocks personal acct.

Date	Description	$	cts
1844 Oct 30	To Cash paid for Silver pencil		92
Oct 31	for blacking Boots		12½
Nov 2	1 Clothes Brush		50
" 11	1 Memorandum Book		09
" 11	1 Temperance Report		10
Nov 12	Postage on letter sent		20
" 13	Postage on 60 papers sent to Brimfield		30
" 12	Refreshments		09
" 13	Donation to A.T. Society N.Y.	5	00
" 20	for 1 paper		06
Dec 12	for postage on letter from Brimfield & papers &c		37½
Dec 19	for postage on letter from N.Y.		25
" 14 & 17	ferriage		12½
Dec 21	for one Horse 5 years old of J.M. Toule	30	00
" "	for Saddle $12. Stirrups & blanket $1.75 bridle & Martingale	15	50
" 28	for Shoeing horse		50
1845			
Jan 2	for 1 pr of Saddle bags	5	50
Jan 4	for 1 bottle of ink		12½
" 6	for 1 pr of leggings or wrappers		37½
Jan 20	postage on letter 25. Feb 3d postage on 2 letters 35		60
"	postage on papers 8		5
Feb 24	Shoeing Horse		50
March 2	Monthly Concert		20
" 20	Postage on letter		25
" 27	for 2 books presented		25
" 26	Shoeing Horse		25
Apr 4	postage on papers up to date		18¾
" 6	Contribution to 3d Creek for Mr Sears Hire		20
Apr 14	Postage on letter from Griffin		18¾
" "	for 1 box of wafers		05
" 16	for Shoeing Horse		18¾
" 18	Postage 25 – working clothes 50. 1 lb of salts 25	1	00
" 23	4 sheets of paper		05
May 4	Monthly Concert		40
" 5	1 silk handkerchief or cravat	1	00
" 12	1 lb of sulphur		25
" 15	6 sheets of paper		10
" 6 & 16	for Shoeing Horse	1	00
" 25	donation for Sil. Beaver Dam		37½
Feb 18	for Saddle Cover		75
		69	60

1845 Amos Hitchcock's personal acct.

Date	Description	$	cts
June 2	Postage on letter from Winfield		25
" 12	for Clothy Trimmings & (Hat $2)	9	56
" 20	Paid for making Coat & pantaloons	3	00
" 18	for Shoeing Horse		25
" 30	for Shoeing Horse		60
July 1st	Postage on letter & papers up to date		39
" 4	1 quire of paper		30
" 18	1 book presented to Mr & Mrs Murray		19
Aug 8	Postage on letter from Winfield		10
" "	In part for Shoeing Horse		62½
Aug 16	for repairing shoes		25
" 17	Contribution at Concord Camp meeting		25
Aug 21	Donation for S.S. Lib. at Westerfields		75
" 24	Contribution at Camp meeting		12½
		16	58
		69	60
Sept 1st	Total up to this date	86	18
Sept 7	Contribution at Camp meeting		20
12	Postage on letter from R.H. Moore		10
14	Contribution 25 – Sept. 24. Contribution 12½		37½
26	for Shoeing Horse		62½
28	Contribution		10
		1	40
Oct. 1st	1 quire of Paper		25
Oct 14	Postage on letters & papers pr qr.		27½
29	1 Phial Oil of Spike		12½
	Postage on letter		10
30	For Shoeing Horse	1	00
31	Postage on Letter		10
		1	85
Nov. 8th	Donation to the A.T. Society	20	00
10	for Pencil points		5
" 22	for Vest pattern & trimmings	1	50
" "	for Silk H'dk'f		75
Dec 1	Postage on Letter from Miss		10
		22	40
Dec 16	To Cleaning Watch 50 – to qt of chesnuts 6¼		56¼
" 20	for one pr of Mitts		2 50
	Total	114	89

Tennessee Travels 1844-1845, Journal of Amos Hitchcock

Dr The American Tract Society Stock or

Date			
1844	To Sales	$	
	" Grants		
Nov 30	For Sale of 4 packages of Tracts & Childrens Tract		7 5
Dec 17	For Cash received for publications	2 3	6 24
Nov 30	For Cash received for Messenger	1	00
Dec 21	For Cash received for publications	2	97
Dec 23	For Cash received for publications	2 3	8 80
Dec 24	For Cash received for publications		6 85
Dec 25	For Cash received for publications		2 68
Dec 26	For Cash received for publications	1 1	52
Dec 27	For Cash received for publications		3 45
Dec 28	For Cash received for publications		8 80
Dec 30	For Cash received for publications		6 71
Dec 31	For Cash received for publications	1 3	96
1845			
Jany 1	For Cash received for publications		12 26
Jan 2	At Marysville for publications		9 75
Jan 3	At Knoxville for publications		12 82
			140 98
	(No of volumes sold at Marysville about 85 vols Amounting to $9.37)		

Original Journal: Page 6

in acct with *Amos Hitchcock* Cr
Publication Acct.

Date		$	
1844	By Bill of Publications		
Dec. 16.	Box No. 2. As by bill enclosed	99	11
Dec. 20	Box No. 1. As by bill enclosed	91	14
Dec. 20	Box No. 3.	58	25
Dec. 24	Box No. 4. As by bill enclosed	63	89
	Package of German publications	4	77
		317	16
1845			
April 2nd	By 2 Boxes of publications as per bill	163	53
April 28	By 2 Boxes of publications as per bill	193	45
May 12	By 1 Box of publications as per bill enclosed	54	27
May 16	By 2 Boxes pub. as per bills each	132	36
June 3	By 1 Box of publications as per bill	189	42
June 12	By 1 Box of publications as per bill	60	45
		1138	74

Transferred & Settled Sept 1st

1845. A. Hitchcock's acct of Sales, Grants visits &c

Date		No. vol. gives grants	No vol. sold at their cts	family pp visited	No of vol Prayer Sold	Cost need for sales $	cts
Jan 7th	Volumes Granted	12		10	140	27	8	37
Jany 4th		2			4	11	2	36
Jany 8	Adam's Alarm	3½	1	8	19	394	17	4	68
Jany 9	2. Baxter's Call	14	2	12½	13	216	11	2	73
Jany 10	1 Alarm &	4	1	6	2	48	7	2	27
Jan. 11		15			16	196	8	1	33
Jan 13	1 B. Call & Almanack	12	3	18	8	144	2		25
Jan 14	1 B. Call	15			12	88	1	3	88
Jan 15	1 A. Alarm. 3 Alman	18	4	25	12	148	6	1	20
Jan 17							10	9	27
Jan 18	1 Almanack	15	1	6	12	204	11	2	0
Jan 20							7		95
Jan 27		13	4	25	13	74	21	5	51
Jan 28		4			4	24	4		56
Jan 29	Settled Sept 17th	2			2	8	1		
Jan 30		28			26	854	34	7	95
Jan 31		25				256	19	2	15

1845 Sept. 17th Rec'd 2 boxes of Publications. Which upon comparing with the invoices I found certain 6 books charged 18¢ which are but 12½. Dying Thoughts, B. Sip. H—, on meekness, 2 of each. Making 37½ cts less than the bill. The above pub are included in the acct. of pub on hand Aug 1st.

Sept 30. Rec'd 1 box of pub. found 10 cts. more than is charged.

1846

March 3d. By Error in bill of Publications Credited to Society in Annual Report of Date $1.50

Sept 11. Society Dr. to Error in bill of Publication Rep. of date 1.51
There was ten books less than charged at 20 cent & 2½ cent charged on 60 Books over price $1.50. (Total $3.) I found 1 Book not charged 15 & 24 cts recont more than charges (Diff 49.) 2.49
$7.51

1845

In My report of Sept. 1st. Is the following

Cash on hand as per last Report Viz Aug 1st	39	16
Rec'd for work & stock sold since	101	43
Total	140	59
Cash paid or remitted to O.R.M. for order	100	00
" " Expenses	12	42
Cash on hand	28	17
	140	59

In My Yr Rept. for Oct 1st. To Stock a/ct $620.19 on hand & Cash a/ct $2.71. Bill of Ser & Exp $112.07 Ret'd to Labour $112.07 Return $45.0 due for the Stum? for S & Smith a/ct in Labour &

Instead of $620.19 in Stock a/ct It should have been $407.07.

Dr The American Tract Society in acct Stock or

1845		$	cts
Sept 1st	To sales of publications since Aug. 1st — self & associates	101	43
"	To grants of Do Do	16	87
Oct. 1st	To Sales of publications since Sept. 1st	75	19¾
"	To Grants of Do Do	19	62
Nov 1st	To Sales of Publications since Oct. 1st	120	10
	To Grants of Do Do	20	68
		353	90

with Amos Hitchcock Cr.

Publication acct.

1845
Aug 1st By publications on hand — 537 35
Oct 1st By publications Rec'd Sept 30th as pr Bill Enclosed — 82 64
                                                                620 19

Sept. 12. By publications Rec'd of
           James Park. 25 books & 6184 pp tracts.   6 75
                                                       626 94
                                                       359 90
Balance as pr Reports ————————————   293 04
Balance as pr Inventory — — — — — —   246 22
Loss — — — — — — — — — — — — — —   26 82
Less as pr Report

Personal acct.

Dr.

Date	Description	$	cts
1846 Jany 1st	Total as per bill of Items up to date. Brot. over	$114	89
Jany 2nd	Postage on 2 Letters from Mass		28
9	For 1 Bible a present to ___		88
15	For Cleaning Watch		5
28	For 1 Copy of Messenger to Esq. John Campbell		17
Feb. 4	For Shoeing Horse for Henry Huffaker Esq.		10
" 9	" 1 Letter from Home		10
" 14	For Repairing Bridle & for medicine &c.		75
21	" Buttons		6¼
23	For Postage on Letter from M. Hitchcock		10

To Cash paid via —

March 2nd	For 1 Inkstand 25 — 1 Comb 25 —		50
		117	25
13th	To Making Vest		25
14	To Shoeing Horse		87½
" 50	1 Pencil		06¼
16	To 1 Saddle blanket of Mrs. J. Campbell	1	50
28	To Postage on Letter from L. Hitchcock		10
April 4th	To Postage 15 — 23d Shoeing Horse 50		65
24	To Cash given to an Indian		5
25	To 1 Bottle Expectorant $1 — 3 blank Books 25	1	25
May 2nd	To Ped. St. Paul & Mimsa		20
3+10	Contribution to S.S. 32½ Do. at Shiloh 25		57½
11+15	Postage & dressing Watch		15
16+18	for Buttons & Sidney		62½
19	Collars Pins & postage		35
21	To Cloth trimmings &c for Pantaloons	4	69
24&25	Shoeing Horse 50 & for 1 Pair of Shoes for Self 87½	1	37½
June 10	Postage 13 — 11th Cloth for Pocket & Making Pants 54		67
19	To Shoeing Horse		60
30	To Cash paid for 1 pr of Stirrups	1	00
" 16	to Do " 1 Pocket of Steel Mrs. Girt		25
July 8	To Cash paid for Book presented to Mrs. John Campbell		12½
13	Messenger for Mrs. Girt		6⅔
10	For 1 Pair of Pantaloons of Mr. Demmes	1	08
		133	83

Original Journal: Page 12

with self —

			$	cts
1844 Oct 30th	By Cash on hand		125	00
1845 Nov. 1st	By Cash received for Salary One Year		150	00
1846 March 3d	By Cash recd. as retained on acct. of services from Nov. 1st To March 1st 4 months		50	00
" "	By Cash recd. for use of Horse since Commencing my Agency to March 1st 1846.		18	32
			343	32
June 1st	By Cash received as retained for services Since March 1st		37	50
" "	By Cash recd as retained for use of Horse Since March 1st		3	75
			384	57

Original Journal: Page 13

1846 Personal Acc't

		$	cts
Aug 2nd	Contribution at Middle Creek Camp meeting		25
3	To Presiding Elder at Do		25
4	For Messenger in part (Horatio Butler)		09
"	to Postage		10
"	Cloth Trimmings &c. & making	1	10
5	For Shoeing Horse (Samuel Hemmer)		31½
6	Postage on letter		10
14	to Shoeing Horse		10
15	One Book in part		13
"	To Patrick Kindred in pining books		25
"	Dr Birdwell one bottle Extract Sersaparilla	1	00
24	For shoeing Horse (Mr Williams)		75
Sept 3d	for linnen for bosoms Collars &c.		75
" 7	Postage on Letter		10
" 12	Postage on two Letters		20
" 17	Bill at Hotel Maryville Self & Henry		75
	Miss Margaret Henry (Sister)		5
" 18	Repairing Watch at Maryville	1	00
" 24	For 3 Maps	2	00
"	For 4 Books presented		85
"	For Messenger Henderson & Toomey		33½
Sept 30	For Shoeing Horse John Myers Tuckaleechy		62½
Oct 4	Contribution at Camp meeting		25
6	Repairing Pencil & 5 yds of Cloth &c		87½
"	To Mr Soule for Repairs &c		16¼
19	To 1 Book presented Mr Dickens		50
21	Two Books presented		40
27	3 Books presented	1	00
	Postage & Pencil leads		07
	1 Packet of Tracts		25
		14	70
		133	83
		148	53
Nov 4th	To Cash paid American Tract Society to constitute myself a Life Director in full ($20 Paid previously)	30	00
Nov 6th	Passage home from Maryville to Springfield $63. (Including above)	33	00
	Total expense	211	53

1846 Personal Acct.

		$	cts
Sept 1st. By Cash received as retained on account of services for 3 month from June 1st		37	50
By Cash Recd. for use of Horse 3 month		3	75
Oct 28. By Cash Retained On Acct of Services		25	00
Do Use of Horse since Sept 1st		2	50
Oct 28 By Cash Recd of Col Jn. M. Toole for Horse Saddle Saddle Bags &c.		50	00
Nov 4. Allowed by the Society for My Expenses home in Part.		30	00
		148	75
Brought Over from June 1st		384	57
		533	32
		211	53
On hand as per Account		321	79
On hand as per inventory		316	37½
		5	41½

Original Journal: Page 15

Dr.   The American Tract Society in Cash

1845		$	cts
Aug 8	To Cash remitted pr. Order from Cain & Dickinson	100	00
Sept 1st	To Cash paid for expenses of Self & associates since Aug. 1st	12	42
Oct 1st	To Cash paid for expenses of Self & associates since Sept 1st	26	64
Nov. 1st	To Cash paid expenses of Self & assocts. since Oct 1st	43	17

Acct with Amos Hitchcock Cr.

acct.
1845		$	ct
Aug 1st	By Cash on hand	39	16
Sept 1st	By Cash rec'd for publications for self & ass'ts sold since Aug 1st	101	43
Oct 1st	By Cash rec'd for publications for self & ass'ts sold since Sept 1st	75	79¼
Nov 1st	By Cash Received for publications pr self & ass ts	120	10

1846   Papers Sent

Nov. 9th Boston Recorder to Wesley Huffaker Esq Boyds Creek E. Tenn
          American Messenger for Nov. To Miss Caroline Wells Loveville E. Tenn.
          Youths Companion to Dea. John Smith Knoxville E. Tenn.
          Youths Companion to John Muillenelare Esq. Sevierville E. Tenn.
          Youths Companion to Samuel Henry Care of John Henry Sen. Maryville
          Youths Companion to St. Paul Gist Sevierville E. Tenn.
          Day Spring to Mr David McCroskey Sevierville E. Tenn.
" 24th   2 Youths Companion to Mr J. E. Porter Sevierville E. Tenn
          2 Youths Companion to Rev. Gideon S. White Academia Knox Co E. Ten
" 30th 1 Youths Companion to Andrew Bogle Ellijoy P.O. Blount Co.
Dec. 10. 1 Christian Almanack to Mrs. Angelina F. Gist Sevierville E. Ten.
" 14 1 Do   To Mr. Wm. Thomas Boyds Creek Sevier Co E. Ten
" 14 1 Messenger to Col. Jm. M. Toole Maryville E. Ten
"   " 1   Do   To Mr Wm. H. Smith   Do — E. Ten
"   " 1   Do   To Mr James Black Ellijoy P.O. Blount Co E. Ten
"   " 1   Do   To Rev. Gorden Mynatt Church Grove P.O. Knox Co.
"   " 1   Do   To Mr David Wells Greenville Green Co E. Ten.
" 17 1 Messenger to Rev. John S. Craig Maryville E. Ten
" 24 1 Recorder to John Hillsman Knoxville E. Ten
" 24 1 Springfield Gazette to Eliza Wells Sevierville Knox Co E. Ten
" 24 1 American Messenger to Rev Robert Hamburgh Co. Architectural Works
" 30 1 Day Spring to Rev. H. Sears Knoxville E. Ten.
Jan. 2 1 Johnery Messenger to Mr Thomas Boyd Sevierville Knox Co E. Ten
"   " 1   Do   Do   to Thomas Rogers Esq Knoxville E. Ten
"   7 1 Almanack to Dr Birdwell Sevierville E. Ten
"   " 1   Do   to Dr J. M. Hammer   Do   Do
"   " 1 Paid Do   to David McCroskey   Do   Do
"   " 1   Do   to Rev. Eli Robert   Do   Do
"   " 1 Messenger to Joshua Jarnigin Esq. Clinton E. Ten
"   " 1 (Jan 13) Do   to John Henry Sen. Maryville Do
" 28 1 Jm. Day spring to Rev. Johnson Adams Weirs Cove E. Ten
Feb. 1st 1 Messenger to Wm. E. Trewitt Elijoy P.O. Blount Co
         1   Do   to John Henry Sen. Maryville

                    Papers Rec'd
  1847
Jany 12 Register — Baptist & Episcopalian from Porter Gist & Co.
"   12   Christian Mirror Portland. Letter on Colpatage.
         One Circular & Baptist Minutes of Association Knoxville

1846   Letters ~~Sent~~ Written

Nov. 10 & 11. One to Mr James C. Porter Sevierville E. Tennessee
" 14 One to Mr John Henry Sen. Maryville E. Tenn.
Nov. 19th One to Mr John Mullendon Esq. Sevierville E. Tenn.
Nov. 21st One to Mr John Mynatt Esq. Church Grove Knox Co. E. Tenn.
Nov. 26. One to James Moses Esq. Knoxville E. Tenn.
Nov. —— Two to American Tract Society New York N.Y.
Nov. 30 One to Samuel Bowman Gap Creek P.O. Knox Co. E. Tenn.
Dec. 2 One to Rev. Seth Bliss Secy A. Tract Society 28 Cornhill Boston Mass.
Dec. 5 One to Martin Moore Proprietor of Boston Recorder Boston Mass.
Dec. 15 One to Mr David Wells Greenville E. Tenn.
" 16th One to Rev. John S. Craig Maryville E. Tenn.
" 17 One to Rev. Seth Bliss Sec A.T.S. Boston (Remittance & Request)
" 30 One to Mr Thomas Smith Academia Knox Co. E. Tenn.
Jan. 2nd One to Mr Thomas Boyd Louisville Knox Co. E. Tenn.
" 7th One to Rev. Seth Bliss 28 Cornhill Boston Remittance $15.
" 12 One to Mr John Hillsman Esq. Knoxville E. Tenn.
" 15 One to Rev. Seth Bliss 28 Cornhill Boston (Remittance $10.)
" 19th One to Mr Joseph Meek Esq. Academia Knox Co. E. Tenn.
" 20th One to Col. James M Toole Maryville E. Tenn.
" 26 One to Boston Recorder (Martin Moore Proprietor)
" 28 One to Mr Wesley Huffaker Esq. Boyds Creek Sevier Co. E. Tenn.
" 28. One to Rev. N. Sears Knoxville E. Tenn.

Letters Recd

Dec. 10 1 from Rev Seth Bliss Sec A.T.S. Boston
" 11 1 " Do ——
" 24 1 From Rev. Seth Bliss Sec A.T.S. Boston
" " 1 From Rev. O. Eastman & Circular Newport
1847
Jan. 8 1 From John Henry Sen. Blount City E. Tenn
" 13 1 From Rev. Seth Bliss Boston
" 23 1 From Rev. Seth Bliss Boston
" 25 1 From Rev. Norman Sears Knoxville E. Pa. Dated Jan 30th
" " 1 From James C. Porter Sevier City E. Tenn

Tennessee Travels 1844-1845, Journal of Amos Hitchcock

Dr John Westerfield — Thomas Smith — Rev. Gideon S. White
Wm. Sawyers Esq. — Josiah Sawyers — Rev. John S. Coram — Rev. John Roberts
Joseph Meek Esq. — Mrs. Bledsoe — Col. James Anderson
Dea. John Smith — Rev. Rufus M. Stephens — Thomas Rogers Esq.
Dr. Wm Rogers — Dr. James Rogers — John Hillsman Esq.
James C. Moses — Rev. Homer Sears — Rev. N. B. McMullen
Joseph Estabrook M.A. — James H. Cowan Esq. — Horace Maynard Esq.
Rev. M. Snoddy — George Hurlin — Mrs. Genin. (All Knoxville P.O.)
John Mynatt Esq. Rev. Gordon Mynatt. (Church Grove P.O.)
Thomas Boyd. Archibald Walker. John Wills. Will. Wills.
Eliza Wills — Caroline Wills — David Wills Jr. (Louisville P.O.)
John Campbell Esq. — Capt. James Campbell — John M. A. Ramsey,
Mary Ann Ramsey, Wellaby B. Ramsey — Francis A. Ramsey. Margaret E. Ramsey
(Mecklenburg P.O.)
Archibald Cullen — Jesse Davis Esq. Tuckahoe P.O. E. Tenn.
Samuel Bowman. John Bowman. Esq. Johnson (Gap Creek P.O.)
John Jornagin Esq. W. W. Walker. Clinton Anderson Co. Tenn.
Esq. Wesley Huffaker. Rev. James Huffaker. Wm. Thomas Boyds Creek
David McCroskey Eliza McCroskey. Osler McCroskey. Mrs Harriet Porter
Miss Maria Porter. Miss Elizabeth Porter. Miss Belinda Porter — Miss Virginia Porter
Miss Ellen Porter. Mr. James C. Porter — Gilbert Porter. George Porter. Jackson Porter
Lieu. Spencer C. Gist. Mrs Angelina F. Gist. St Paul Gist. Minerva Gist.
Pinkney Toomer Esq. Dr. Jonathan M. Hammer — John Mullendore Esq.
Mary Amanda Mullendore — Abraham Lafayette — Wm Wallace
Elijah Leniston — Robert Bruce — Susan Catharine — Nancy Matilda
Jane Elizabeth Hitchcock Mullendore Born April 16th 1846
Teresa Ann Lenning. (Col) John S. Compton Rev. Eli Roberts. (Sevierville)
Rev James Cummings Waldens Creek P.O. of Hugh Bogle —
Andrew Bogle. James Black. Ellijoy P.O. E. Tenn (Blount Co)
John Henry Sen. James Henry Son of John sen., Jane Henry, Rachel Henry
Wm Jasper Henry — Samuel Henry. Margaret Elizabeth Henry
Rev Isaac Anderson D.D. Rev. Fielding Pope — Rev. John S. Craig —
Col. James M. Toole. Maryville Blount Co. E. Tennessee.
1846. Margaret Cowan 14. Mary Cowan 13. Lucinda Foute Cowan,
Nancy Estabrook Cowan, Susan Penniman Cowan, James Dickinson Cowan
Pereu Dickinson Cowan. Joseph Hillsman. Knoxville Tenn.
Geo. White Esq.; Joseph King Esq.; Rev. M. Manning
Dea Elijah Johnson; Rev. Wm. Eaves.

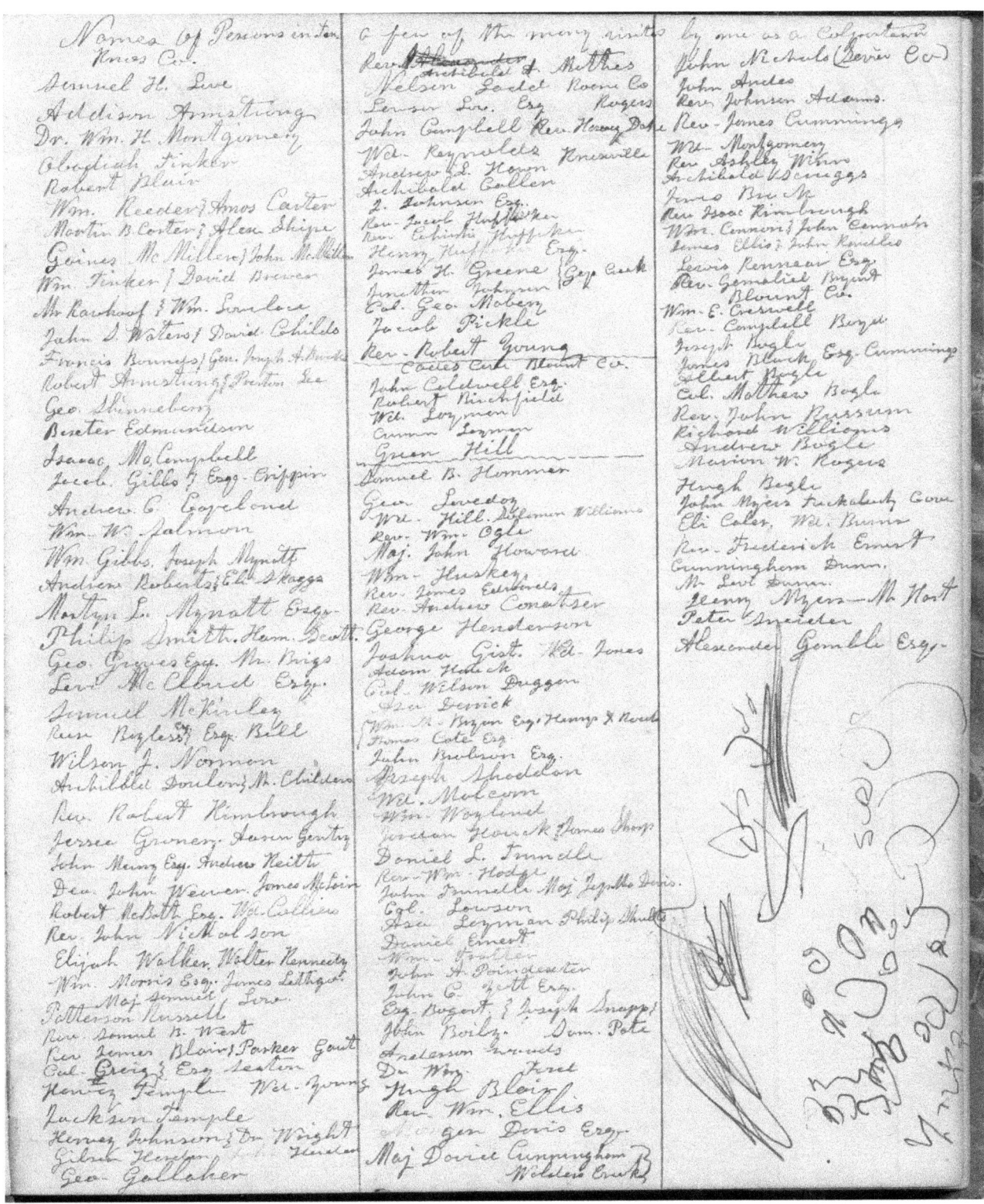

Dr The American Tract Society

		$	cts
Oct	To Cash remitted		
"	Cash paid Expenses viz		
1844			
Nov 8	To Cash paid Mrs Maver for Board	9	00
" 1?	To Cash paid for ponies &c	4	06
Nov 13	To Cash paid Thomas Lyon Master of Brig Clint for passage to Savannah	20	00
		33	06
Nov 19	To Cash paid for transporting Trunk		25
Nov 20	To Cash paid for transporting Boxes to Depot		25
Nov 21	To Cash paid for passage to Depot		50
	for passage to Macon	8	00
	for breakfast & Dinner	1	00
	for passage from Depot to Hotel		50
Nov 22	To Cash paid for Crackers & Raisins		25
	for Board at Hotel Macon	2	25
Nov 23	for freight on box from S. to M.	3	05
	for passage in Omnibus to Depot		50
	for passage from Macon to Griffin	3	00
		52	91

Original Journal: Page 22

in acct with Amos Hitchcock   Cr

Date		$	cts
	By Cash rec'd as profit		
	By Cash received for sales		
	" " " " Managers		
1844	" " donation from Mr. ___		
Nov 8	By Cash received to pay for board	9	00
13	By Cash received to defray expenses in reaching New York	4	06
	By Cash Rec'd as outfit — Settled Nov 9 /44	20	00
		33	06

1846

June	Money to Loan			July 4th in Trust			
	Gold	Silver	Bills		Gold	Silver	Bills
5	$52.50	$32.50	$	deposit	$2.50	$22.50	$10
13	$8.00	$40.00		9th	$25	$10	$32.00
20	$5.00	$8.00		Aug 15	$5.50	$2.50	
				27	5.00	5.00	
				Aug 31		15.00	
				Sept 6		16.00	
				Oct 2	10.00	8.00	
				" 6	7.00		

Dr The American Tract Society

Nov 28	To Cash paid for passage from Griffin to Marietta	5	00
Nov 28	To cash paid for board at Griffin 5½ d	3	50
Nov 29	To cash paid for freight on Boxes from Macon to Griffin	2	22
Nov 29	To cash paid for Breakfast & Dinner		58
Dec. 4	for Sup. lodging & Breakfast		93½
" 5	—		40
Dec. 9	to Mr Legg for transporting Self & Boxes	12	00
	to Mr Cochran for hauling to Maryville	5	00
	to Mr Harris for Sup. lodg. & breakfast		25
	for dinner		10
Dec. 10	for ferriage, meals & lodging		94
	for passage from Athens to Maryville	9	75
Dec. 11	for supper & lodging		40
Dec. 12	for passage from M. to Knoxville		75
Dec. 21	for one Horse 5 yrs old	90	
	for one Saddle $12 Stirrups & blanket 1.75	13	75
	for one Bridle & Martingale	1	50
Dec 28	for Shoeing Horse		50

Original Journal: Page 24

in acct. with Amos Hitchcock

Tennessee Travels 1844-1845, Journal of Amos Hitchcock

Dr The American Tract Society in acct

1845

Jany 2	To Cash paid for hauling tracts from Maryville to Knoxville Dec. 20	1	50
Jany 2	To Cash paid for saddle bags	5	50
Jan 18	for ferriage		12½
Jan 20	for postage on letter to Athens		10
Jan 25	for premium on $160 — to Cowan & Dickinson	2	40
Feb 3d	for postage on letter from Society		25
Feb 6	for keeping horse several nights to Dr W		57
Feb 12	for ferriage 10 Feb 24 Shoeing horse 50		60
March 3	Postage on letter from Society		25
March 20	premium on $40		60
March 20	Shoeing horse		25
April 2d	postage on letter from Society		25
April 2d	freight on 2 boxes of books 312 lbs 5 cts	15	60
April 10	postage on letter from Society		25
April 16	for Shoeing horse		18¾
April 24	for freight on 2 boxes of books from N.Y.	19	25
April 25	for postage on letter from Society		25

Original Journal: Page 26

with Amos Hitchcock

1845		$	cts
Jan. 16	Rec'd of Miss Temple Treasurer of the Female Tract Society Knoxville for Tracts bought of A.T. Society N.Y.	10	00
Jany 16	Committed to Mr Cowan the above sum together with money Rec'd for pub. to the amount of $150. to be remitted by him.	150	00
Feb. 13	The Society acknowledge the recpt of the above		

Tennessee Travels 1844-1845, Journal of Amos Hitchcock

Dr.   American Tract Society in acc't

1844			
Nov 13	To Cash paid for passage from N.Y. to Savannah	20	00
Dec.	To Cash paid for pas passage, freight Meals, lodging &c. from S. to Knoxville	62	06
1845			
March 3	Cash paid for Horse keeping & Shoeing, ferriage, postage premium &c. Since Arriving	4	94
March 1st	Dr for 4 months Service from Nov 1st. To March 1st	50	
Jany 16	To Cash remitted pr Cowan & Dickinson	160	00
Dec 21	To Cash paid for Horse $30 Saddle $12	42	
	Bridle, blanket, Martingale & Saddle bags $10.75	10	75
March 4	To Cash remitted by draft from John T. King	60	00
March 4.	To Cash proved Counterfeit $1.10		
March 20.	To Cash Remitted by draft from John T. King	40	00
April 1st	To Cash paid for premium & to Cash paid for Shoeing Horse		85
April 2d.	Postage on letter from society		25
April 10	for freight on 2 boxes of Books 312 lbs	15	60
April 10	for Postage on letter from society		25
April 16	for shoeing horse		18
April 24	for freight on 2 boxes of Books	19	25
April 25	postage on letter from society		25
April 29	To Cash remitted by drafts from John T. King	44	00

with Amos Hitchcock   Cr.

1844				
Nov 13	By Cash Received as outfit		20	00
1845				
March 1st	By Cash recd for Sales up to date		262	81
	By Cash recd for Messenger		1	00
	By Cash received of Tract Society Knoxville		10	00
March 20	By Cash received of Tract Society Knoxville		9	42
April 1st	By Cash received for publications from March 1st		7	41
May 1st	By Cash recd for publications from April 1st to May 1st		80	15
May 31st	By Cash recd for publications			

Dr. American Tract Society in
1845

		$	ct
May 6th	To Cash paid for Shoeing Horse		50
15"	Postage on letter from Kingston		10
16	For Shoeing Horse		50
24	Postage on letter from A.T.S. N.Y.		25
31st	To Cash paid Bratton & Tule for Freight 5 boxes of Books from N.Y. to Maryville 1924 lbs	41	58
	To Cash paid for transporting 4 Boxes from M. to K.	1	42
30	Postage on letter from T. H. Aikmen Roane Co		6¼
30 & 31	for ferriage		11
	for Services from March 1st to June 1st	37	50
June	Discount on Gold proportion to $5.		25
June 7	Freight on Books from K. to Esq. Hillsman		50
June 11	Postage on Letter from T. H. A. Roane Co		6¼
June 13	Postage on Letter from A.T.S. New York		25
June 18	For Shoeing Horse		25
June 19	Postage on Letter from T. H. A. Roane Co		6¼
June 25	Postage on Letter from A.T.S. New York		25
June 30	for Shoeing Horse by Levi McCloud		80
July 1	Postage on paper for Qr. ending this date		20
July 1	Postage on letter from Roane T. H. Aikmen Rept		10
		2	52½
July 3d	To Cash remitted by Check in letter dated July 3d addressed to "The Secretaries of the American Tract Society No. 150 Nassau Street New York"	74	00
July 3	To cash paid for discount on the above	1	41
July 28	To cash paid for postage on letter from Roane Co		5
Aug 1st	To Cash paid for postage on letter from N.Y. & also 1 from Roane		15
			61
Aug 8th	To Cash paid Cowan & Dickinson for an order on a firm in N.Y.	100	00
"	To Cash paid for premium on the above at 2 prct.	2	00
Aug 8	postage on 2 letters 15 Freight on books 56		71
" 22	Postage on letter 5. 26th ferriage 5. 29th postage 5.		15
		2	86

Original Journal: Page 30

Acct. with Amos Hitchcock Cr.

1845

Date	Description	$	cts
May 31st	By Cash Recd. for publications from May 1st to May 31st	88	13
July 1st	By Cash recd. for pub. from June 1st to July 1st	53	94
July 1st	By cash Received of Wm. H. Smith Colpt.	35	00
July 10	By Cash Recd. of Tho. H. Aikman Colpt.	88	00
Aug 1st	By Cash Received for publications from July 1st to Aug 1st	41	03
Sept 1st	By Cash Received for publications from Aug 1st to Sept 1st	43	78
Oct 1st	By Cash Recd for pub. since Sept. 1st	95	17
Nov 1st	By cash Recd Do since Oct 1st	42	97
Oct 25	By cash Recd of Tho. H. Aikman asst Colpt	38	03
Oct 31	By cash Recd of Wm. H. Smith Do	61	42

1845.

Items of Expenses. Self for Society

		$	cts
Sept. 1st	Postage 12½ Moving Books 40.		52½
3.	Postage 10. Sept 5th Postage 5.		15
12 & 18	Postage 2 — 5. Sept 30 Postage 5		12
20.	Freight on 2 Boxes Books 467 lbs. 4½ p lb	21.	00
		21	79½
Oct. 14	Postage on Letter from Society		10
"	Do — on Papers Pamphlets &c. pr gr.		40
29	Do on Letter from Society		10
30.	To Cash paid for freight on 1 Box of Books 200 @ 4½	9	00
31.	To Cash " for do on 2 Box of Books 708 lbs 4	28	32
		37	92

Original Journal: Page 32

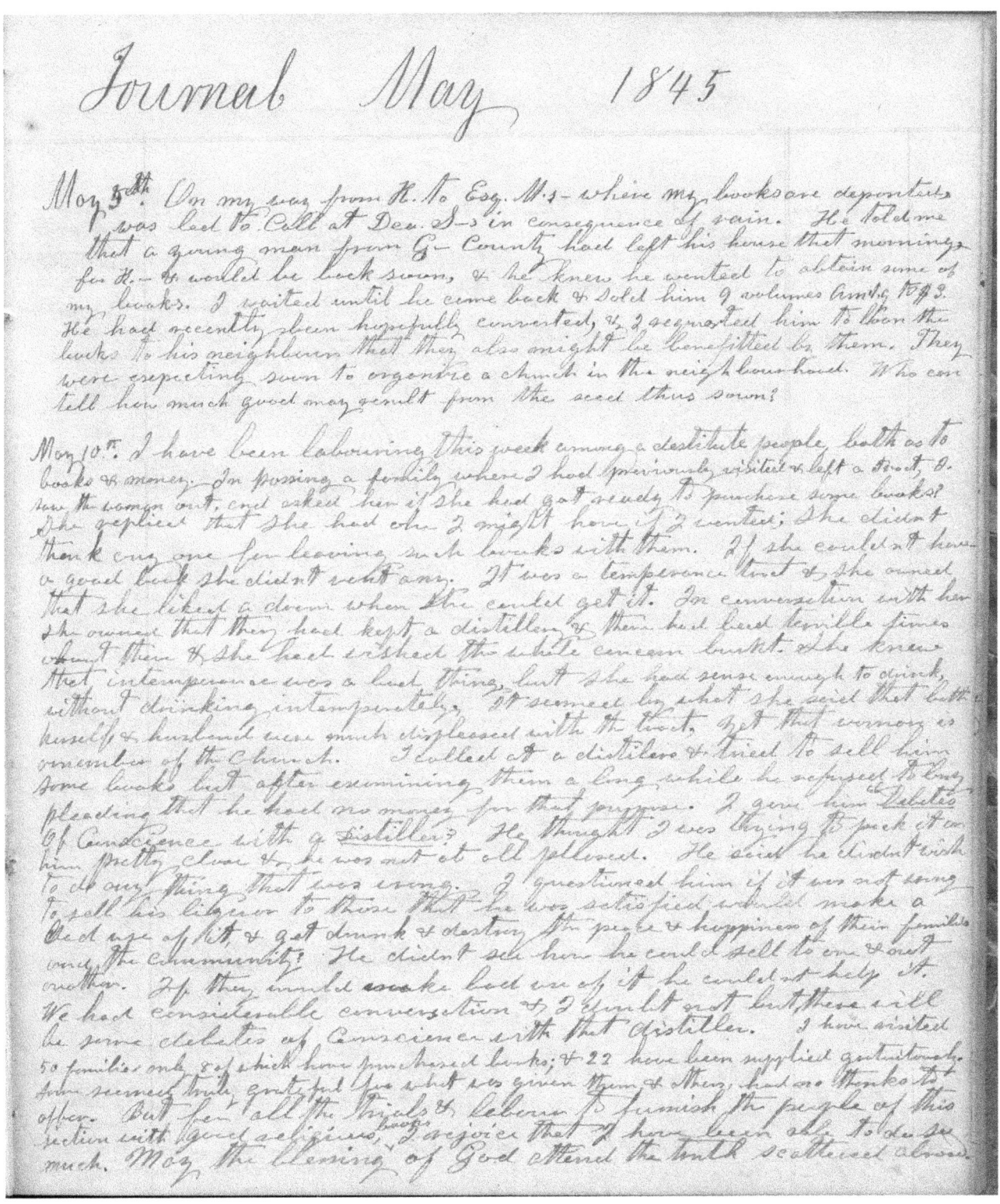

Journal May 1845

May 5th. On my way from H. to Esq. M.s— where my books are deposited, was led to call at Dea. S—'s in consequence of rain. He told me that a young man from G— County had left his house that morning for H.— & would be back soon, & he knew he wanted to obtain some of my books. I waited until he came back & sold him 9 volumes Amt'g to $3. He had recently been hopefully converted, & I exhorted him to loan the books to his neighbours that they also might be benefitted by them. They were expecting soon to organize a church in the neighbourhood. Who can tell how much good may result from the seed thus sown?

May 10th. I have been labouring this week among a destitute people, both as to books & money. In passing a family where I had previously visited & left a tract, I saw the woman out, and asked her if she had got ready to purchase some books? She replied that she had rather I might have if I wanted; she didn't thank any one for leaving such books with them. If she could n't have a good book she didn't want any. It was a temperance tract & she owned that she liked a dram when she could get it. In conversation with her she owned that they had kept a distillery & there had been terrible times among them & she had wished the whole concern burnt. She knew that intemperance was a bad thing, but she had sense enough to drink without drinking intemperately. It seemed by what she said that both herself & husband were much displeased with the tract. Yet that woman is a member of the Church. I called at a distiller's & tried to sell him some books but after examining them a long while he refused to buy, pleading that he had no money for that purpose. I gave him Debates of Conscience with a Distiller? He thought I was trying to pick it in him pretty close & he was not at all pleased. He said he didn't wish to do any thing that was wrong. I questioned him if it was not wrong to sell his liquor to those that he was satisfied would make a bad use of it, & get drunk & destroy the peace & happiness of their families & the community? He didn't see how he could sell to one & not another. If they would make bad use of it he couldn't help it. We had considerable conversation & I doubt not but there will be some debates of Conscience with that distiller. I have visited 50 families, only 5 of which have purchased books; & 22 have been supplied gratuitously. Some seemed truly grateful for what was given them & others had no thanks to offer. But for all the trials & labour to furnish the people of this section with good religious books, I rejoice that I have been able to do so much. May the blessing of God attend the truth scattered abroad

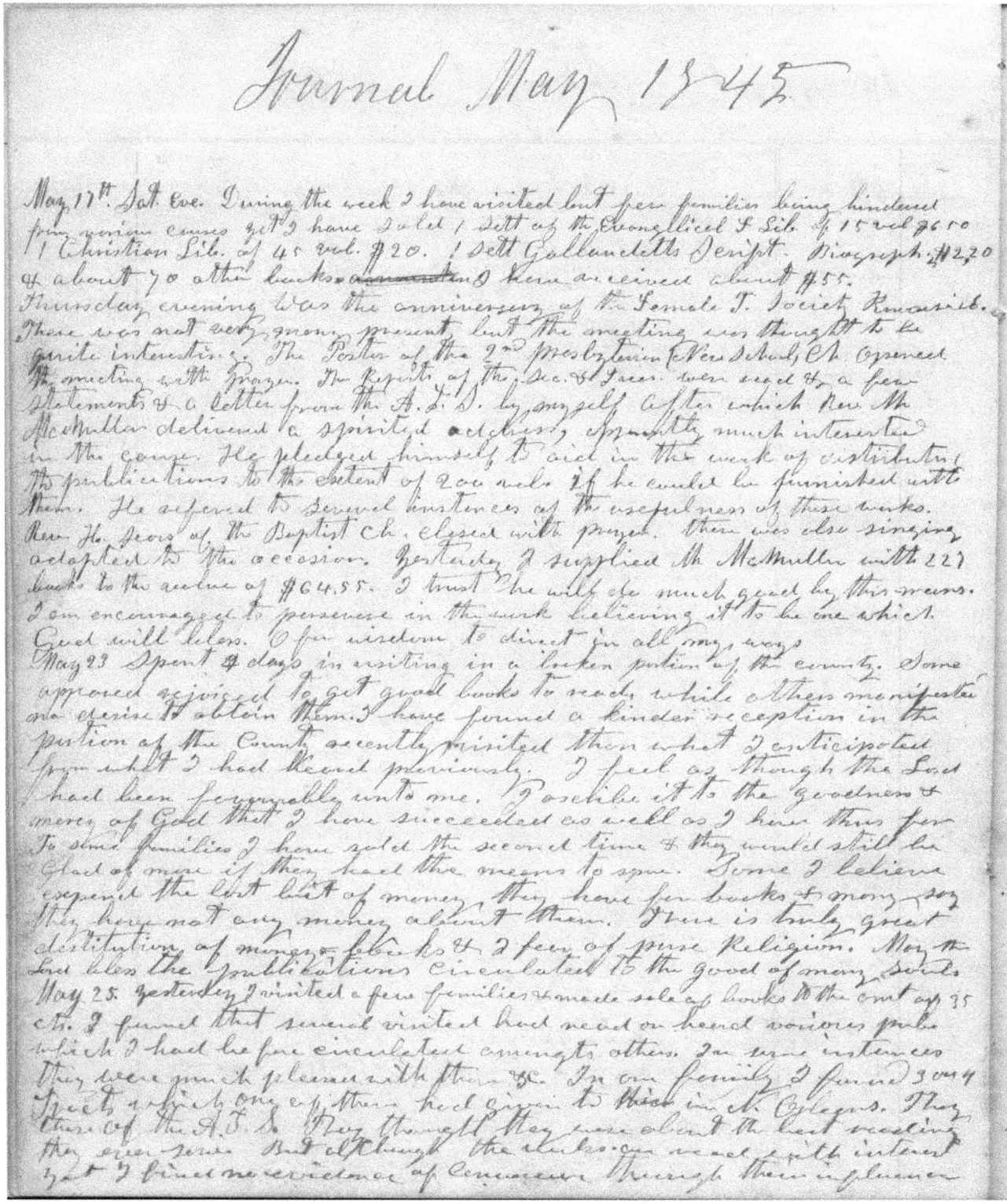

Original Journal: Page 34

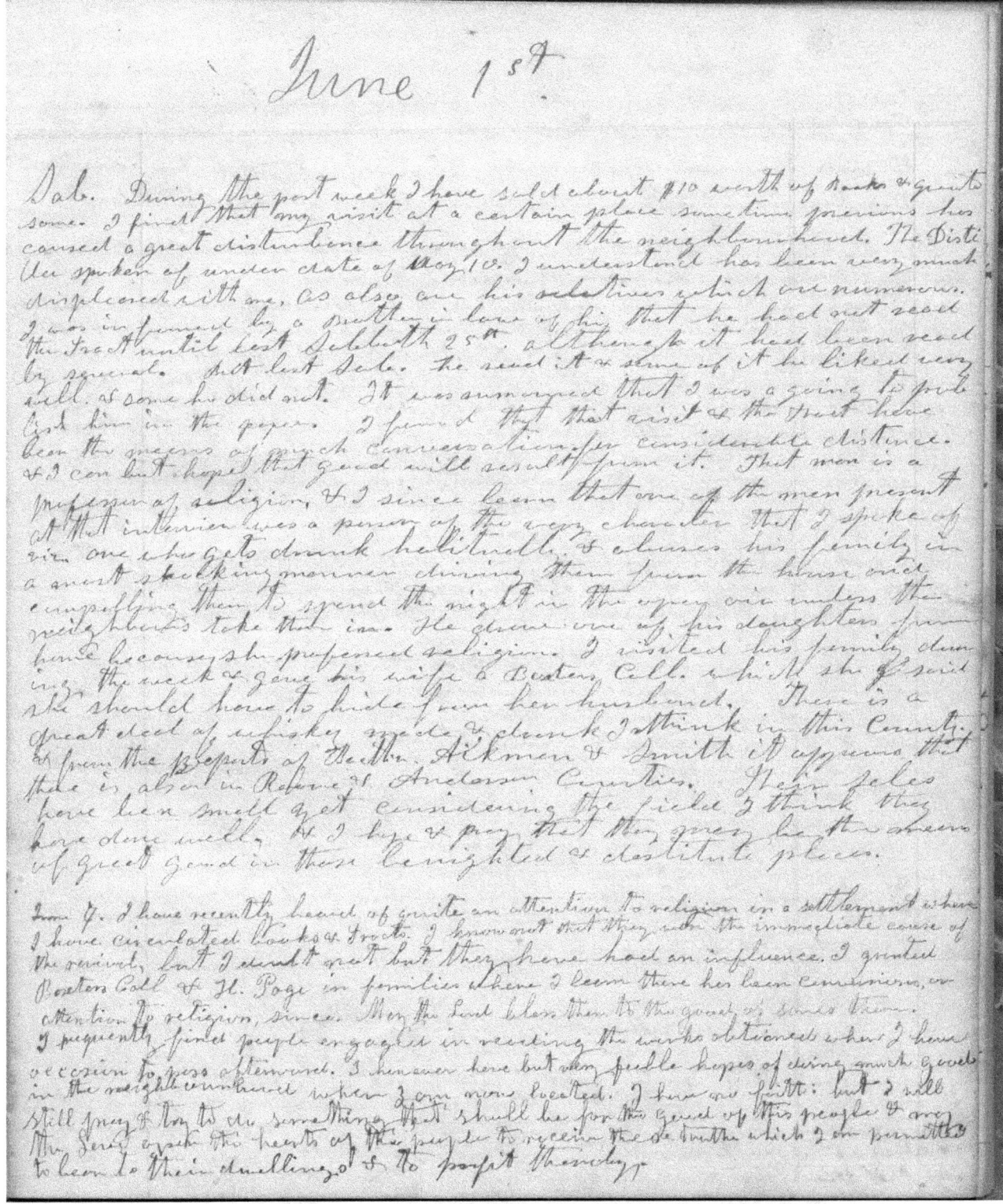

June 14th

Sat. eve. My visits during the week have been but very few, owing in part to the weather & partly to receiving a call from my associate in Roan Co. to send him more books, as he was nearly out of a suitable assortment. I rejoice that he is able to circulate such good books in that Co. I sent him a box yesterday by stage to the value of $72.59. His health has been bad but was much better when he wrote. I met a gentleman in Knoxville who hailed me but I did not recognise him. He spoke of getting the History of the Great Reformation from me & said he had read it with a great deal of interest, & he had two children which he wanted to have a sett each & he wanted to get two more setts. I met another gentleman Esq. B— who had purchased the Spirit of Popery & 8 other books to the value of $1.75. He said he had read some in the Spirit of Popery & thought it worth much as he gave for all. I frequently hear of the people speaking of the books as being about the best books they ever read. I sometimes sell a book where at first there is no encouragement at all, but after reading some from it they are induced to buy. But I have as yet heard of no conversions resulting from the reading of these works, but I labor in hope that some of the good seed sown will bring forth fruit to eternal life by the blessing of God.

June 29. Sab. During my visits the past week I found one man who would not receive any of the pubs. He seemed opposed to any thing of the kind & did not often go to meeting because those who pretended to preach would not preach the gospel. I understood from good authority that he afterward swore awfully about the books & tracts. An intelligent Christian Slave who was a near neighbor to him tried to have him read a tract which I gave him, but he would not, & he asked him if he would hear it read, at the same time turning to a woman present asking her to read it which she did. The Tract was the Anxious Prayer. He listened with attention & made some remarks at the close indicating that his feelings were touched. Thus truth has been presented to his mind, which may be the means of good. I sold the servant C. S. Reste. At one house at which I called, a neighbour was present who was quite a wealthy gentleman it was supposed or had been but his appearance shewed that he was a friend of strong drink. After awhile I proposed the subject in which I am engaged & asked if he would not like to examine & purchase some of the books? He promptly answered no, he had seen books aplenty of that kind. I asked him if he was familiar with the history of the Reformation? He seemed to wish for no conversation with me. After awhile I mentioned the name of Calvin & asked him if he ever was acquainted with Dr. Daniel Nelson of E. Ten.

He seemed to have some knowledge of him. I told him I had a book written by him on the cause & cure of Infidelity, at the same time getting the book. He borrowed some spectacles & read awhile when he asked the price. I told him the price which he immediately paid. Some of his acquaintances thought it was the very book he ought to have. A few days ago I called at a house where the man was closely considerable distance in the field but as I had had some encouragement that a young man, a relative, who was at work with him would purchase some books I ventured to visit the field which I did. But such swearing & vile profane language & cursing about the books & tracts &c &c. I have not met with in our travels since engaging in the work. I endeavoured to deal plainly with him & gave him a tract & sold his nephew a dollar worth of Books. I am obliged to scatter gospel books often among bad persons & I cherish the hope that the efforts of the Society for E. Young will not be in vain. A week yesterday I visited a neighbourhood about 7 miles from this & sold them at Tile. for their Sab. School which had been in operation but 2 or 3 Sab. They purchased $10 worth & I think there was some interest in the work.

July 5th Sab. The pastor of the church where they purchased the Lib. spoken of above attended meeting in this neighbourhood (3d Creek) to day and in speaking of the enterprise, said he had never known so much said about books in so short a time before. The youths and the adults seemed much pleased with the works. Said one Mother (Eng. M.) they are some of the most spiritual works I ever saw. Said a Sister I would not grudge the amount paid for all, for one book she had read. A general interest was manifest in the reading of the works.

Dec Johnson who had purchased the History of Redemption, told me he was much pleased with the work. Mr P. who had bought Nevins Poor Pious & 1 other work told me he had read them with much interest. They were powerful works, & he wanted to get some more but had not the means. I constantly receive testimony of the approval of the books.

July 13th Sab. Morn. During the past week I have visited & supplied about 60 families with religious readings and generally conversing with them according to my ability, on the all important subject of religion & frequently reading from the works I had to the Christian & the impenitent. I visited a neighbourhood properly called the Great bend, but from some cause had acquired the name of Sodom, from what was told me before entering the place, I had no anticipation of selling any books. but I succeeded in selling about $2.60 worth & in some instances where vice, ignorance & poverty reigned. I endeavoured to be faithful & do them good; & I was kindly received & treated with usual respect. My sales during the week have been nearing of $12. I am sometime told by the people that there is no use in visiting such & such families they are so wicked; but I tell them, they are the ones I want to visit if by any means I may do them good, & in several such

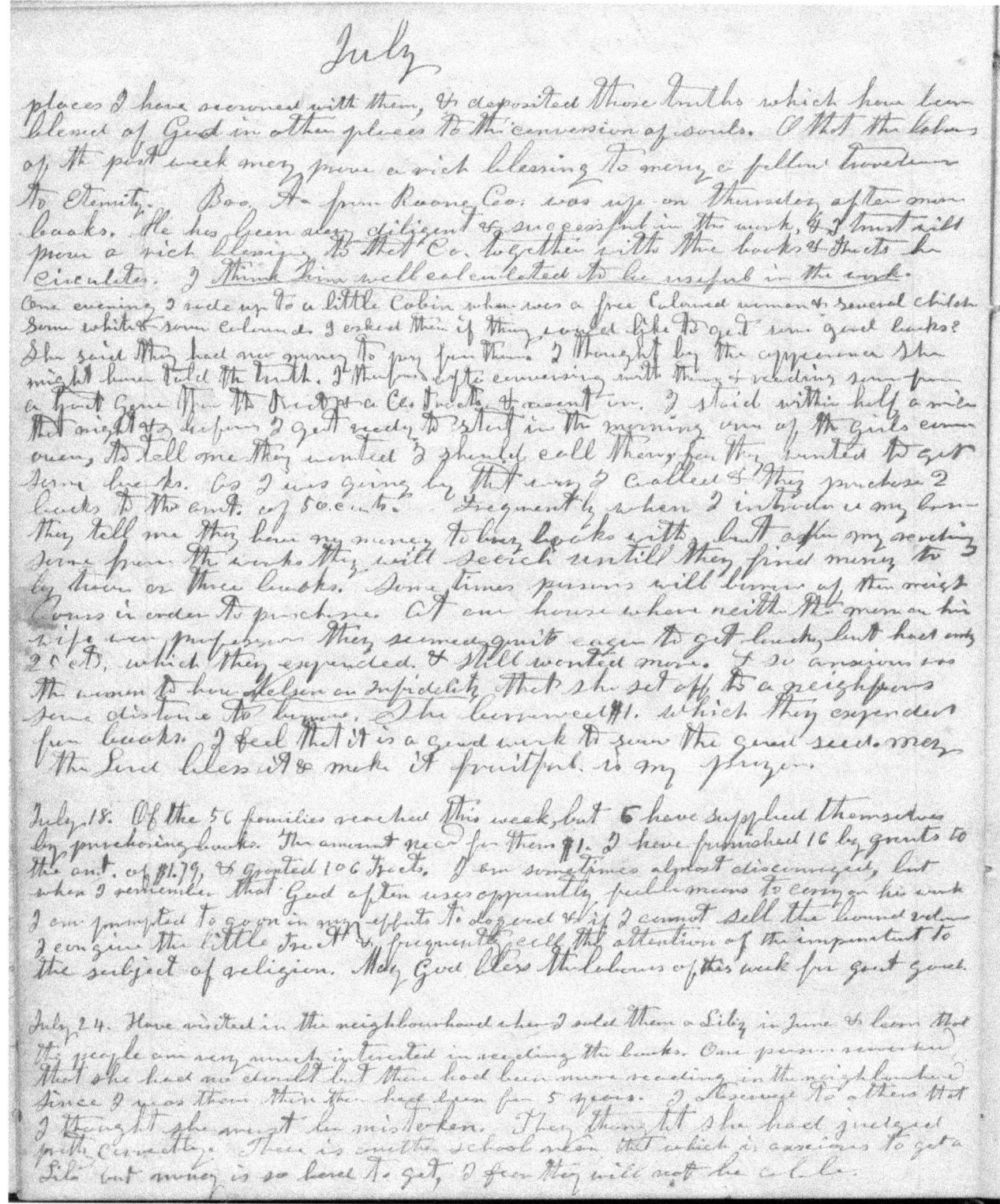

July

places I have sojourned with them, & deposited those truths which have been blessed of God in other places to the conversion of souls. O that the labours of the past week may prove a rich blessing to many a fellow traveller to Eternity. Bro. H. from Roane Co. was up on Thursday afternoon last. He has been very diligent & successful in the work, & I trust will prove a rich blessing to that Co. together with the books & tracts he circulates. I think him well calculated to be useful in the work. One evening I rode up to a little Cabin where was a free Coloured woman & several children, some white & some coloured. I asked them if they would like to get some good books? She said they had no money to pay for them. I thought by the appearance she might have told the truth. However after conversing with them & reading some from a tract & some from the Rec[?] a Co. tract, I went in. I staid within half a mile that night & before I got ready to start in the morning one of the girls came over, to tell me they wanted I should call, there, for they wanted to get some books. As I was going by that way I called & they purchased books to the amt. of 50 cents. Frequently when I introduce my business they tell me they have no money to buy books with, but after my reading some from the works they will search untill they find money to [get?] by two or three books. Sometimes persons will borrow of their neighbours in order to purchase. At one house where neither the man or his wife were professors they seemed quite eager to get books, but had only 20 cts. which they expended, & still wanted more. I so anxious was the woman to have Nelson on Infidelity that she set off to a neighbours some distance to borrow. She borrowed $1. which they expended for books. I feel that it is a good work to sow the good seed. may the Lord bless it & make it fruitful is my prayer.

July 18. Of the 56 families reached this week, but 6 have supplied themselves by purchasing books. The amount nec. for them $1. I have furnished 16 by grants to the amt. of $1.79, & granted 106 tracts. I am sometimes almost discouraged, but when I remember that God often uses apparently feeble means to carry on his work I am prompted to go on in my efforts to do good & if I cannot sell the bound volumes I can give the little tracts & frequently call the attention of the impenitent to the subject of religion. May God bless the labours of this week for great good.

July 24. Have visited in the neighbourhood where I sold them a Bible in June & learn that the people are very much interested in reading the books. One person remarked that she had no doubt but there had been more reading in the neighbourhood since I was there than there had been for 5 years. I answered to others that I thought she must be mistaken. They thought she had judged pretty correctly. There is another school near that which is anxious to get a Bible but money is so hard to get, I fear they will not be able

August

22nd. From various causes I have visited but few families since my last date. I have scattered some religious works however, which may God bless. I have attended some religious meetings. At two of them I presented some statements relative to the operations of the society, its object & aim, the plan & extent of its operations & some of the results. I found that it was a means of awakening considerable interest & of leading many to desire the most precious books I had. I was encouraged & led to hope that good would be the result. I have the cooperation of the pastors generally. My small books are now about all gone & I need a new supply. My societies I think are faithful & devoted to the work & I rejoice that they engaged in the work. Several instances of an interesting nature are reported, which I will omit inserting here, as I have reported them already. There have been several revivals in this vicinity. And I doubt not but the books & tracts have had an influence. Wherever I hear from them they are much liked. O may the Lord —

Sept 11th. I have just received a new supply of Publications which I hope yet as I will ever circulate. But I feel unwilling to abandon the field without trying to do more for the cause of Christ & the good of my fellow men in this region. There is great wickedness in this region. Murder, Robberies, Theft &c. is very common. It is considered unsafe to travel without being armed & I have been advised by Ministers & others to go armed, so that I might defend myself in case of necessity. Yet I am reluctant to take that course & for the present think I shall not. But I intend to have with me the sword of the spirit, & I desire to have a good shield, & that by the blessing of God will I trust protect me. I feel that the Lord has been good to me & I desire to love him more & serve him better. There is considerable rumour of war & I feel that it is very likely there will be, for we are a sinful nation & deserve chastisements. But O God deal with with us then ever best. Hear the prayer of thy people & extend the Kingdom of the Redeemer rapidly & may the kingdom of Satan be overthrown. Bless all societies that exist for to aid in this glorious work. Bless the American Tract Society, its Officers & agents in their labours & bless the publications wherever circulated. O that many may be brought to the Saviour in this region by these means & may the hearts of the people here & elsewhere be opened to come up to the support of this noble & glorious enterprise. The Lord has blessed it at other times & in other places. May he bless here also is the desire of my heart. O for a spirit of prayer

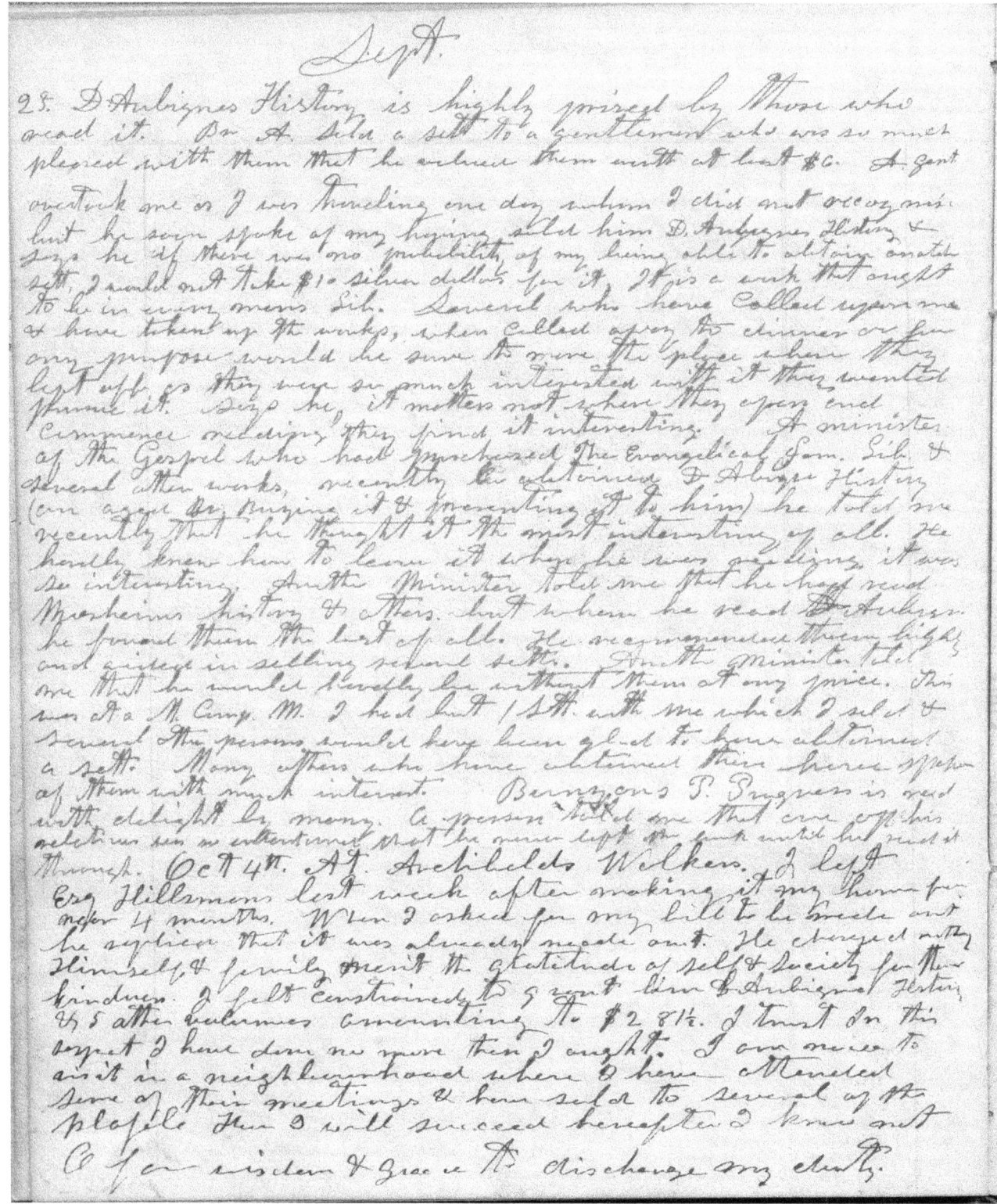

Sept.

28. D'Aubignes History is highly prized by those who read it. Br. A. sold a sett to a gentleman who was so much pleased with them that he valued them worth at least $6. A gent overtook me as I was traveling one day whom I did not recognise, but he soon spoke of my having sold him D'Aubignes History & says he if there was one probability of my being able to obtain another sett, I would not take $10 silver dollars for it. It is a work that ought to be in every man's Lib. Several who have called upon me & have taken up the works, when called upon to dinner or for any purpose would be sure to mark the place where they left off, as they were so much interested with it they wanted to resume it. Says he, it matters not where they open and commence reading, they find it interesting. A minister of the Gospel who had purchased the Evangelical Fam. Lib & several other works, recently obtained D'Aubigne's History (an agent by buying it & presenting it to him) he told me recently that he thought it the most interesting of all. He hardly knew how to leave it when he was reading it, it was so interesting. Anoth'r Minister told me that he had read Mosheim's history & others, but when he read D'Aubigne he found them the best of all. He recommended them highly and aided in selling several setts. Anoth'r Minister told me that he would hardly be without them at any price. This was at a M. Camp. M. I had but 1 sett with me which I sold & several other persons would have been glad to have obtained a sett. Many others who have obtained them have spoken of them with much interest. Bunyan's P. Progress is read with delight by many. A person told me that one of his relatives was so entertained that he never left the book until he read it through. Oct 4th. At Archibalds Walkers. I left Esq Hillsmans last week after making it my home for over 4 months. When I asked for my bill to be made out he replied that it was already made out. He charged nothing himself & family merit the gratitude of self & society for their kindness. I felt constrained to grant him D'Aubigne's History & 5 other volumes amounting to $2.81½. I trust in this respect I have done no more than I ought. I am now to visit in a neighborhood where I have attended some of their meetings & have sold to several of the people. How I will succeed hereafter I know not. O for wisdom & grace to discharge my duty.

Oct.

15th Visited Mr. B— sold D'Aubigne's History & Memoir of Mrs. Graham. Hence to Mrs. A_____. Poverty to the extreme. No professor. No books but Bible. Gave Anxious Inquirer— Next No religious books. Gave A. Alarm— Next no books but Bible—gave a book. Next poor family, gave a book— Next a Wicked family. Sold Baxter's Call.

16th Visited several very poor families seemingly as destitute of the decent comforts of life as I almost ever saw. Granted several books. Conversed with nearly all visited on the subject of Religion. Visited one family where a young lady had been sick for several weeks & was much deranged. It was truly grievous to see & hear the poor creature. It is a family of affliction indeed. The mother has recently died, & another of the daughters was sick. Gave the sister who was able to be about Flavel on Keeping the Heart. I trust she is a Christian, but she is greatly tried. O may the Lord bless the poor efforts of his unworthy servant & the publications circulated.

Nov 11th. One year has passed away since I entered upon the service of the Society as a Colporteur. I feel that I have been an unprofitable servant yet by the blessing of God I have been the means of sowing some good seed, but whether any of it has fallen into good ground where it will yield fruit I know not. During the year I have put in circulation by sale about $1070 worth of Publications & about $120. by Grants. With the aid which I have had. We have visited about 3,760 families with many of whom we held religious conversations & almost without exception left something of a Religious character for them to read. Several who were destitute have been supplied with the Bible.

1846
Jan. 25. Sab. Since my last date I have been able to prosecute my work but slowly, yet I have been pressing forward. Many interesting scenes have I witnessed, & many interviews enjoyed, which tend to strengthen my attachment to this country, the people— & the work in which I am engaged. But while this has been the case, I have experienced trials of various kinds which have at times depressed my spirits, & led me to feel that perhaps, duty required me to occupy some other field of labour in my sojourn in this world. Recent letters from my kindred have stirred up my mind on the subject of withdrawing from my present field of labour & returning to the home of my childhood & youth, to engage in my former occupations. But I know not what to do. I did feel that it was a clear case that it was the Lord that I was led to come forth to their region. Is it his will that I should tarry or return? May I be guided aright in this matter is my prayer.

1846 Journal Continued

March 6th. My time has been principally occupied since the month came in with making out my Annual Report & with other duties connected with my station beside visiting. Yesterday I visited a few families & made sales to the amount of $4.40. I endeavoured to be faithful in my conversation with those visited. Several were not religious, but acknowledged its importance & necessity. I hope that the truth presented in conversation & on the printed page will exert an influence for good. I found one family with no Bible or other religious Book. I had no Bible with me but gave them the "Book of Proverbs." Gave the "Backslider" to an old man who had been in the church but was not now. Had one R. Book but Test. & H. Book. Could not read but wife could. Gave Book of Proverbs to a Family who had no Bible or R. Bks. The man had been a member of the church but was not now. Gave "Dying Thoughts" to a poor family. Dest. of R. Bks & no money to buy. The man could not read, but his wife could.

March 8th. Sab. Sales during the week 20 vol. Am'tng to $5.40. Fam. Vis. 20. Con. 18. Dest. of Bible 4. Of R. Bks. 8. May it be found at last that the labours of the week were not in vain.

March 9th. Proceeded to my work. First house, family had no Bible or other good book & no money to buy. Gave Baxter's Dying Thoughts. Had next Sem. Gave Almanack Children Tract &c. The next was a place represented by the neighbours as being next to nowhere. I found it however. The Woman said that herself & husband were both members of the church, but from what I had learned, I was induced to leave Preacher or Intermixed its reading also. At the next house was a woman & her children. Dest. of R. Bks. I asked if she was a professor of Religion? She said her daughter was. I told her that would not answer her turn. She said she had been a professor but was not now. I asked her why? She said she didn't know, unless it was her own unworthiness. I warned her of her danger & exhorted her to examine herself, whether she was in the road to heaven or hell. Gave her Flavel on "Keeping the Heart" with such advice as I was able. At the next cabin lived a couple of women of reputed lewd character. They had several children. They could both read but had no Books. I gave them "Village in the Mountain" & tract & warned them to prepare for Death Judgment & Eternity. At two or three of the next families I made small sales. At one of them I spent the night, & although professors of religion & belonging to a sect very strenuous (Seceders) yet I was asked if I wouldnt have a Dram. It seemed that old & young partook of the poisonous liquid. May their eyes be opened to see their folly & danger.

10. Visited 18 families 9 of whom were destitute of Religious Books & 5 of the Bible. To 6 families I granted a hundred vol. & to others Almanacks & Tracts. Yesterday & today I have visited 30 families found 16 Dest. of R. B. My grants am't to $2.18. My sales to $3.24. Thus I have left light & knowledge behind me & I pray God

1846
March   Continued

to make it the means of promoting righteousness Peace & Joy in the Holy Ghost but my faith is weak. Astonishing wickedness prevails. Sabbath breaking Profane Swearing Intemperance Gambling & lewdness, appear to be very common. Professors of Religion take their dram of Liquor. More than one instance have asked me if I would have one too? One time I took occasion to testify against the use of Whiskey. The parents seemed to think that it was good to use a little. They said they had but one child that was a drunkard. I asked them if that was not enough? They thought that somebody else was to blame in making him a drunkard. I asked them if they had any assurance that some of the others would not become drunkards too? They thought there was no danger at all. For my own part I thought there was danger. Several in the neighbourhood have recently been so loaded with whiskey as to lay out at night. Fighting is common in the neighbourhood especially at public gatherings &c. I would say the such but it seems almost like casting Pearls before

16th Sevier County. Saw a young man in a field & hailed him. He came to the fence & I commenced talking with him & showing my books. He concluded not to purchase. He said he had formerly belonged to the church but had neglected duty & was now a wild young man. I said what I could to persuade him to break off his sins & return to duty. He finally bought Persuasives to E. Piety. The next house was a family of Blacks. None of them could read. They had a Testament & several other books but no Bible. I sold them one & gave them such tracts as I judged suited to them. Some of them were professors but others were not. At the next house found a widow & her children. She would be very glad of the books, but had no money to buy with. The next I sold to amt of $1.50. At the next house I found a woman & children but they could not read. She was a wicked person. I read from some of the works & warned her to flee from the wrath to come.

18th In the three past days I have visited 97 families. 25 of whom were destitute of religious books if we except the Bible & Hymn book & in nearly every instance I had to grant them a book or leave them destitute still. There seemed a very good desire to obtain them, but the means to do so were not at hand. I judge that nearly one half of the heads of families were unable to read. In 3 or 4 cases there was not a reader in the family. I read considerable & endeavoured to be faithful in conversation. I sold to the amt of $3.64 & got $2.89. In several instances the people expressed their hearty thanks for the gift bestowed. The country is very hilly & the people very poor. The friends of the Bible the country supplied them with the scriptures so that I found but 3 destitute, 2 of which had a testament. I supplied 2 of them & the other I think will get one such although not a member of the Fam. can read. I had no Bible with one but sold

1846
March.

them a good book. The head of the fam. was a professor & said he liked to hear reading if he could not read himself. I sold Baxter's Call to a young man who was not religious & said he could not read any of account. I told him I believed he might learn if he would. His wife could read some. I saw his father afterwards who said that his son sat down & studied his book a good while & remarked that he meant to read it through & through. In consequence of reading from Alleine's Alarm an impenitent young woman persuaded her husband to purchase the book. I think the books will be read with interest & I hope they may be with profit.

21st. Yesterday visited 9 families, sold 10 books, had conversation with most. At the first house the man was not a professor, but owned the importance of Religion. I sold him Religion & Eternal Life? & a young woman present bought Baxter's Call. At the next house found a young man who had been very vicious. His whole frame shook & trembled, as I suppose from the effects of his dissipation. He had a wife & children but no religious books. Mr. H— a young man who was visiting with me bought a Bible & gave them, & the woman gave me 10 cents for a good book. I conversed freely & thought I discovered some evidence of feeling & reflection on his part. At another house we found a Widow & several children, young ones. I think none of them were religious. They bought Nelson on Infidelity & it was said by some afterwards that it was a very suitable book for them. For if there was any place where that work was needed, it was there. One of the sons remarked to his mother after he had been reading it some time, that it contained more doctrine than any book she had set her eyes on for a long while. At the last place we found a member of two different families & sold one of them Nelson & the other Pike's Persuasive. They were both non professors. Today attended a meeting at Baxter Creek Ch. B.S. The Pastor Rev. Wm. Billew spoke a few words to that point with reference to my business & recommended the people to purchase. I sold a few & distributed several tracts. I feel as though the way was prepared for a more extensive circulation of the works by my attendance at that meeting. It is a needy region. The people need just such reading as this society furnishes.

March 28. Sat. During the week I have been able to prosecute the work to some extent, but my sales have been few. Of 33 families visited in 2 days 18 were dest. of R. Books except Bible & in almost every instance I found an expression of poverty & the appearance of it. Of the 33 only 4 purchased books. In one of these instances I found five women at one house representatives of six different families. I made known my business. The woman of the house said they did not wish to purchase. I commenced reading from Baxter's Call. When I paused

1846 Continued

March 28. one of them remarked that, that was a good book. I took occasion to make some remarks, & the woman of the house told one of her visitors if she had the money, if she would pay for it, she would pay her again. She said she would have to go home for it which she did. In the mean time I commenced reading from "Religion and Eternal Life" having learned that but one of the six were professors of religion. When the woman came back with the money, they concluded to take it instead of the Colt. I said what I could to persuade them to seek the one thing needfull. The people are mostly very poor, having but little of what is considered in some places of the comforts of Life.

April 4th Sat. During the week have visited 35 families—sold 42 books amtg. to $11.28 & granted to the amt of $2.22. At one house the people wished for one of the books but did not know how to pay for it, at the time. as I was to be back that way soon I let him have Baxter's Call @ 15 cent. When I returned he brought out the money & paid me but wanted to know if I just took the books about to sell? He said several persons had been there since I was along which told him he was a fool for buying the book—that I was Known to give the books—that money was contributed a good while ago for this very purpose, & they thought I was selling what I could & pocketing the money. I told him plainly, the principles of the society & read a letter of Explanation & Recommendation, Given by Minister in Knoxville. He said he had no reason to find fault, as he did not contribute any thing. He wanted a Bible for a friend, and as I had none with me, he wanted I should send him one which I did & he sent the pay for it. I endeavour to tell the truth plainly, & to prove it to be so by my works but I suppose some will not believe. I found one family destitute of Bible or Religious books. I conversed with them & gave them a Bible & other religious reading. They were poor indeed if we might judge from testimony & appearance. not a Chair in the house, but children plenty.

Esq Johnson who purchased some $3— worth of books & Subscribed for the Messenger saw me passing & hailed me. In the course of our conversation he said he had read his papers & the Books he had purchased, with a great deal of pleasure. He admired their character, and viewed them as emminently calculated to do good. His children also were much interested in reading them. He considered the Messenger as one of the most valuable religious papers he ever saw. Others have expressed their delight in the works, & a desire to have more if they had the means to purchase.

April 12. During the past week I have visited but 43 families but my sales have been greater than I have effected some previous weeks, when more family were visited, being to the amt of $15.81. My grants amt to $2.63. At one house I found a Wd. & her children. At one house I found had no R.B. but Bible & Hymn book. She was a professer & one of her daughters was in the church as a seeker. I conversed with them & judged

Original Journal: Page 45

1846 Journal

April 12th. that "The Anxious Inquirer" would be a very suitable book for the daughter, which I gave her. At another found a Ud. without Bible or any reading of consequence. Gave her a Bible & other religious reading for which she seemed very grateful. Another Cabin visited contained a numerous family but no Books. It appeared to be the abode of poverty. I had no Bible but gave them "Scripture Promises" & tracts. I frequently find publications which I distributed several weeks ago, have been ahead of me several miles. At a house, said to be a place of wickedness, after conversing awhile the woman said she had an excellent good book, which she brought forth to show me. I knew the book at first sight & told her that I sold the book to a man at ____ naming the place, for 15 cents & changed a $5 bill to do it. She blushed some but said it was so. The Book was "Baxter's Call." She said she knew she was doing wrong living as she was, but she hoped to do better some day. I told her God's time for her to repent was now, but the devil would persuade her that by & by would do as well. I warned & exhorted her to break off her sins, & turn to God, & left some reading with her to stir up her mind when I was gone. I might speak of other instances but I forbear. I still feel that it is a blessed work, to live & labour for the cause of Christ & the Good of Souls. May the Lord follow with his rich blessing.

April 19th. During the past week my sales have amounted to about $16. and my grants to about $5. besides Bibles. At one house there was a family without Books & if I mistake not without ability to read. I gave them a Bible. One of the young ladies said she intended to learn to read. I think she was a member of the B. Church. At another place I found a man who had been in the Church, but was addicted to intemperance. He was very friendly & proposed to ride with me through his neighbourhood which he did. He was very full of his talk & friendships. I must take dinner with him & come back & spend the night with him. He spoke freely of his dissipation — he knew it was ruining him, and he had determined never to get drunk again. But he had promised so many times before that his friends have but little confidence in him. He is a young man of talent & education & possessed a handsome property. Liquor has quite a different effect upon him from what it has upon many. Instead of prostrating him into the gutter dead drunk it makes a fool & a mad man of him. According to his own testimony, & that of his acquaintances, a very little will make him raving distracted. Reason leaves the throne, while the evil spirit seems to take entire possession. I conversed plainly & earnestly with him if he would avoid drunkenness & its consequences, never to let the first drop pass his lips — that there was no safety on any other plan than entire abstinence. I told him he had occasion to be thankful that he was alive & had not been ushered into eternity in his

1846
April.   Journal

drunken sprees. I told him to look at the injury he had done to the cause of Christ—to his family—his friends & himself, that he had occasion to exercise deep repentance for the past, & seek forgiveness, & to implore divine assistance to withstand temptation and to overcome in future. During the evening he commenced reading the tract "Fool's Pence" but could not well proceed. I took it & finished it. We conversed & read till after 11 O'clock. He felt a confidence that his folks would never have to weep on account of his drinking again. May it be even so.
At another place family had no books save Bible. The woman brought forth all the money she had as she said. 6½ cts. & I gave her a book at 12½ cts. & the reading. One of the neighbors said she thought that she had better have bought some meat with the money as they had none. I hope the book will prove more beneficial to the soul than the meat would have been to the body. Men seem to be more care for the body than for the soul.

April 30. During the last 10 days I have made but little progress in the work of visiting, having visited but 69 families. I found 11 of these destitute of the Bible & of whom I supplied. My sales have amounted to $32.79 and my grants to $5.75 besides Bibles.
At a mill I found a pew men which purchased $1. worth of books among which was Baxter's Call. He let a neighbour have it & he called at my desire, & bought another; this he disposed of also, & when he saw me, he bought the 3d. He seemed to be more interested in giving the works circulation. At another house I could neither sell nor give them any thing. At another place found a family of free blacks. Sold them two books. They seemed desirous of attaining knowledge & of doing what was right.
At another place found a house where the children were quite reluctant about taking tracts. The parents were away from home. They however took two or three small tracts. I since learn that they were afraid that the folks would burn them. I found the parents at a neighbours house. When I made known my business, the men commenced abusing the society—their publications, & their agents, according to his ability of using language, if we except profanity. He was very wise in his own conceit, as well as righteous in his own eyes. All these societies which were abroad in the land, & all the denominations, but the one to which he belonged (for he was a professor & a preacher) he thought were not aiming at the Glory of God, or the good of their fellow men, but at self aggrandisement & exaltation. He said the Bible was not light, or a means of Grace, & that the spread of the Bible was not a means of spreading light. I tried in calmness to tell him the truth, but he seemed to be devoid of reason. I have since been informed that he drinks to excess, & I know not but he was under the influence of strong drink at that time, for I found him on the bed.

1846   Journal
April
30th I since learn that he had determined to insult me as bad as he could, when I should come along. I think I have not met with such ill treatment since I have been engaged in the work as from this same (Rev. Samuel Pate) Preacher. The next day I saw one of his sons at a mill where I was distributing some of the works. He selected a tract which he seemed to want, & I told him if he wished it, he might take it. He did so. I was pleased to be able to bring any of the works to bear upon any of the family. May he see his error & be converted therefrom. Several purchased works from the fact that conscience was on the side of truth, as set forth in the books & brought before their mind by my reading to them. Today visited but 4 families. Supplied them with something valuable. It Clouding over & Commencing raining fast, together with loosing my way prevented my doing as much as I wished, but thanks be to god I was enable to sow some truth, where greatly needed. May it prove a —
May 6th Have as yet visited but 96 families this month, conversed with 27, Loaned 21 Dest. of R.B. except the Bible & 6 Dest. of that 3 of whom I supplied. My sales amount to $9.72 & my grants to $4.05 besides the Bible. One day I found 18 families 6 Dest. of Bible & 17 Dest. of R.B. 15 of whom I supplied with Religious Books. Tracts, Almanacs &c. & the other 3 with a Bible. My Sales amounted to 10 cents, & I should judge that there was not much money left. The people generally seemed favourable but were dest. of means to purchase. I gave sixteen calls to on old men who seemed to be on the verge of eternity & was living without a well founded hope of heaven. I did what I could to persuade him to attend to the concerns of his soul. In nearly every instance I labored to bring some important Bible truth before the mind, & I can but hope that good will result from my labors in that neighbourhood. I sometimes am disheartened & almost feel induced to let the work alone for others to perform, but when I consider, I can but view it as a good work, & that God has blessed me in it, & although I may not be permitted to behold the fruit of my labors, I doubt not but some will bless God in eternity for the visit of the Colporter in this region, & when I remember too that I have an urgent call from man at least if not from God to labor on, I am prompted to go forward & do what I can for the advancement of the Cause of Christ & the good of my fellow men. O that I could do more in this blessed work, for as such I view it & I trust I ever shall.

May 1846   Journal

7th. Visited 18 families — found 5 dest. of the Bible — Supplied 2. Distributed 37 Tracts, & Sold Publications amounting to $2.12½ and Granted to the amount of .56 — Besides Bibles & Tracts. I endeavored in connection with the distribution of the works to add a word or two, as opportunity occurred. At one place I called at the house — the man was in the field, but was sent for. He declined coming as he was busy at work although not far from the house. His wife seemed desirous to obtain a Book but, for reasons best known to herself did not. As I started from the house I went so as to see the man & after some conversation & examination he called to his wife to bring his money, which she did when he purchased the Persuasives to Early Piety. May it prove a rich blessing.

8th. Visited 15 fams. Sold 1 Bill & 33 books & a Pocket of Tracts. Amount of Sales $7.69. Granted 2 books & 39 Tracts. Col. Crompton rode with me this day. We found the people generally able & willing to purchase one or more books. Found but one Fam Dest. of Bible & 3 Dest of R. Books all of which I supplied. The work was looked upon as a good work.

13th. During the last three days have been travelling in the 10 Dis. or as is frequently & timely called Knob District. I have visited about 40 families, with whom I had some conversation on the subject of Religion. It was a very difficult section to visit, but a very needy one. There were those that told me they thought there was no use in visiting a certain neighborhood, as the people couldn't read, & wouldn't try to do as they ought. I told them my business was to visit them & see if I could not do them some good. I was generally kindly received, & the people manifested expressed an interest in subject of education & religion although many of them could not read. Found 11. Fam. Dest. of the Bible. Supplied 4. 26 Fam. reputed thereabout as Dest. of R. B. except Bible. 26 of the 40 visited were supplied with one or more Books & the other with Tracts. My Sales amounted to $7.32 or my Gts to about $4.00 besides 4 Bibles. I called on one man to whom I had previously sold Doddridge's Rise & Progress. He said Doddridge had given him a pretty good rub. He thought it an excellent book. He purchased 12 more to the amt of $3.32. remarking that he thought by the time he read them all through he ought to be a pretty good man. I told him I had no doubt he would be if he practiced according to the instructions which they contained. He was an experienced man, and I think will

Tennessee Travels 1844-1845, Journal of Amos Hitchcock

1846
May
13th read his book. Another man said he didn't wish to look at the works. I asked him if he did not like to read good books? He had the Bible & that was good enough. He said he viewed the work in which I was engaged as a speculation. I asked him in what respect? He answered that he thought those who wrote the books & those who were circulating them were speculating. I asked him if he would like to engage in such a speculation, for the sake of the gain? He would not consent. I then told him plainly the principles of the Society & how the works were furnished, & told him the salary of the Colporteur &c. Well says he if it is a good work go ahead, I'll keep my hands clean from it. Says I you will not oppose it then will you? He said he would not. I told him that in the sincerity of my heart I believed it to be a good work or I should not have been there, for if I was after gain I should have been in some other business, but the object of the Society was to do good, & if my heart deceived me not it was my desire also. & I believed that the enterprise in which I was engaged was eminently calculated to effect that object.

At another place I found a family out in the field, on rather on the side of a Mountain where it was too steep to stand or walk without difficulty. They had no Bible & no H. Book & none of them could read. I conversed with them & gave them a Bible & tracts they promised that they would have it read, and they were calculating to send their children to school. At another place was a family which I was told might not treat me very civilly. I found the man at home & entered into conversation with him on the subject of religion & found that he was ready to admit his guilt & danger & the importance of religion. I gave him the tract on Keeping the Heart. He got his spekes immediately & commenced reading. Soon he remarked that he fealted it already. I asked him what objection he had to it? He said it was to great to look for him. I told him I knew it was addressed to Christians, but if he was not one I wanted him to be come one & then it would just suit him. He thought it would be a fine thing if he was one. Another young man was with me a part of one day to aid me in getting about as it was very difficult, there being nothing but

1846
May.
13th

Journal

paths & many times not even that, without letting down fences. In the course of conversation he said that he had formerly been trying to live as he ought, but he had mixed with bad company & it seemed now that he was worse than ever. I talked plainly & faithfully with him & he seemed to feel the importance of abandoning his sinful habits. As the Lord enabled me, I endeavored to speak & read for his case & the good of the people, & my hope & prayer is that good may result from my visit there.

21. Went to Knoxville to attend a meeting of the Juvenile Tract Society. Sold some few books in K. Had a good meeting. Exercises of the meeting were Prayer, Singing, Reading of the Report — Report & Statements by self, respecting my labors — Addresses by Rev. Messrs. Sears — McMullen & Myers — Singing & prayer. It was thought by some that the meeting would do good.

23. Spent last night with a gentleman who was thought by some to be tinctured with infidelity. He purchased Nelson's work of me last winter, & afterwards told me he was much pleased with it. He recommended it to others also. He afterwards purchased other books — & this Morning himself & wife purchased 4 more. They had several books borrowed from their neighbors which I had sold. One was Doddridge's Rise & Progress which the wife said she thought had considerable impression on his mind. I read with & prayed for them & hope the Lord will have mercy upon their souls.

26th During the last 4 days have visited 70 families, conversed with 62 — found 21 destitute of the Bible — Sup. 7 — Granted 36 Books & 180 Tracts and Almanacks. Value of Grants 7.16. My Sales were 100 vol. amting to $93.11½. At one place the man was quite advanced in life, but was not a professor. One of his daughters selected Baxter's Call for him to buy, remarking that he needed something to lead him to do differently. He bought the Book. II At another place found the fam. dest. of Bible, & of Money to buy. I offered to give them one. The woman said she hated to take it without paying for it. She said they were able to pay for it but had not the money then. I told her she might leave the pay if she chose with one of the Merchants of Sevierville. She said that she would do so. They lived several miles from town, but I soon found the money for the Bible there. I believe that most of the dest. might pay for them if they had a disposition & could be waited upon awhile.

+ Mr Sears spoke in his address of one young man when giving in his experience previous to baptism stating that it was Doddridge's Rise & Progress which I had circulated that was the means of leading him to the Savior.

1846 Journal

May

30 (Continued) At another place the man instantly charged me with being engaged in a speculating business. I told him that he was entirely mistaken, & if he was at all acquainted with the value of books, he could not pronounce it a speculation. He acknowledged his ignorance respecting them & said he could not read. I told him the principles & object of the society, & read to him from some of the works. He finally bought Bouton's Call. He had a large family. At another place I met in my way representatives from 3 or 4 different families. I conversed with them freely, & noticed that one of them was considerably affected. I furnished them with Books, Tracts &c. & hope that the interview may be blessed. Much of the route was very bad travelling & caused me much fatigue. The people were very poor & destitute of Books & money. But they are now supplied with something that is calculated to do them good. May the Lord bless it unto them. My labours for the month have exceeded my expectations. My receipts for sales exceed those of any month since commencing my agency if we except the first when I laboured in Knoxville. They amount to $89.38 & my Grants to about $19. Beside Bibles I visited about 200 families 46 of whom reputed themselves Dest. of the Bible, only 18 of which I supplied. I have not the convenience for supplying the County in full, yet I rejoice that I am able to bear some humble part in the great & glorious work of Circulating the Bible, & Bible truth as presented in the works of the American Tract Society. O that it may prove a rich blessing to many souls.

June

6th During the past week my visits have been but few owing to various causes being lost 36. I found 8 Dest. of the Bible 4 of whom I supplied. My sales amount to $19.25 & my grants to $3.18. Some of the time my health has been so feeble that I have been constrained to solicit a resting place in the day time, yet from day to day I have been engaged in the prosecution of the work, though in much weakness of faith as well as body. I have been a portion of the time in Wear's Cove some part of which was very difficult to get at the people. There was generally a very good disposition manifest towards the enterprise. Esq. Mullendore & Maj. Cunningham were with me, & my success thus far in that section may be attributed in some degree to their influence. We called upon one man who had no Bible but after a long & trying effort we succeeded in selling him $2.50 worth of Books, a thing at which we had heard of it seemed astonished, but when the subject was fully explained they were not so much surprised. The man was a clear lover of silver & having a $10 bill which he feared was not good, he wished to exchange it for specie for which I made arrangements to do so although I did not do it wholly at the time. At another place I found a family retired far from society in the mountains. The woman had been a cripple for years, her joints being displaced by the power of disease, neither she or any of the family could perform. I converse freely with them & sell them a Pocket Bible, although they had but means to pay in full.

1846
June.   Journal

13th. During the past week have completed one district & commenced another. Found the people generally poor, but there were exceptions. Some of those who had the means to purchase, lacked the disposition. One instance where the man seemed somewhat desirous for some of the books, his wife was so much opposed that he did not purchase. She seemed to be a hard shell in reality. Another man I saw away from home & conversed with him & read to him from Doddridge's 'Rise & Progress' which he seemed pleased with. He was not a professor & could not read, but said he would love to take that book if he was at home. I was going by his house in the course of my route, but when I got there he had been talking with the women about it & they did not want any of the books. It seems as though some of the people did not wish for any aid in religious instruction except it be from some of their own nation. They reject the different benevolent enterprises of the day & have no christian fellowship with those who engage in them. I also sold one man who said he could not read $2. worth of Books, some of his children could read some. He carried on a Distillery, & from the indications I would think that he took freely of the Liquid Poison. Another to whom I had sold $4. worth before, afterwards bought The Fountain Of Life & Method Of Grace. In my last tour I had to travel several miles to reach the first house, & to ford the Pigeon River I think some 6 or 8 times; in some places the ford being very bad on account of large stones & rock. Yet I succeeded in reaching the neighbourhood in safety & in selling more books than I expected. If money had been as plenty as honey, I think the people would have supplied themselves with a good assortment of Books, but as it was many that wished for the books were unable to purchase a single book even at 10 cents. I found 3 families out of 17 destitute of the Bible & of means to purchase, which I supplied. One man on whom I called wanted some of the books but had no money by him. He had money due him & thought probably he could procure from his next neighbour until he could get his money. He accordingly went on with me. But his neighbour was in pretty much the same situation. He had no money on hand, but a neighbour of his (living about 3 miles out in the mountains) was owing him & he thought he could get some of it. It was a place very difficult to get at there being no road excepting a kind of trail over logs, rocks, & mountains &c a place which I had been advised by several to omit visiting, as it was so bad and so far beyond the settlement being about two miles. I resolved however to go, if this man would go with me, which he consented to do. As it was a rainy evening & getting too late to undertake such a trip I concluded to spend the night where I was. In the morning, we started, & although difficult & dangerous in some places we arrived in safety. The man is is a kind of herdsman employed in keeping cattle in the mountains. He was apparently a man of great natural abilities & disposition & abilities, but was not a professor of Religion. He stated that he had seen some of my books in an adjoining county, & would have been glad to have got some of them then. He said his means were now

1846   Journal

June 13th] but small, yet he would buy $2. worth which he did, & also let my Guide have a dollar which he expended for books.

There was another family about half a mile farther on, which we were compelled to visit on foot if at all as the way was impossible for a horse. We found a little Cabin with the ground for a floor. There were two families living here the feth & son with their wives. There was none but the young women in. She said they had no Bible or other Religious books. She was a professor of Religion & could read some, & would be very glad of a Bible, but had nothing to pay for it. I gave her one & some tracts, with such advice as I was able. I had been informed that the old men was a very wicked opposer to religion & that he would not allow the Bible in the house nor religious singing, with how much truth this information was clothed I knew not. The women appeared grateful for the gift & said she would keep it & read it. May the blessing of God attend the truth circulated in these families. On returning we called upon another family the man I had seen some days before in another district where he was at work. He urged us to stop to dinner which we did & during our stay they seemed anxious that I should read from the books which I did. He said that the folks where he was at work were very much pleased with the books & he wanted to get some of the same kind. The women said they had collected a little money to pay their taxes with, but the Good Lord had sent the Good man with his books first & she was glad of it. They said if they had $5.00 they would be glad to spend it for good books. I have been cheered to witness the manifest desire of some to obtain the tracts, yet I would not wish to convey the idea that the desire is general & strong as I could wish. For many seem to care for none of these things.

June 20. During the week my visits have been few & my sales small. Nothing of special interest brought to view. To one family living far out in the mountains I sold $5. worth of books. The parents could read but little & the children none. I think there was 14 children at home & 3 absent. They solicited & obtained the promise, that if no providential hindrance prevented me, that I would visit them again, & help them read the books. I said what I could to encourage them to obtain a teacher for their children, & by some means or other be sure to give them education sufficient to enable them to read. I found some of the tracts which I had given to a minister near S— 20 miles distant in the mountains. One old man which got one of them, said that he gave it to a son of his which had been neglecting duty & it seemed to do him a great deal of good. I found 10 families destitute of the Bible & supplied 4. I found 21 Dest. of Religious books cured Vz N & H B.

My sales amount to $11.43 & my grants to $3.41 Some of the people had no wish for the books, but generally they seemed a desire to obtain them. Some seed has been sown. May it yield

1846 Journal

June 30. Since the 20th I have visited 79 families, turned 21 D. of Bibles, supplied 13. Made sales of publications to the amt. of $20.53. & granted to the amount $7.04. A good degree of interest manifested by many. Not uncommon for persons who have purchased previously, to buy again. Some however have no use for such things. I called at one place where the man did not wish to purchase. I asked him if he ever read tracts? he said no. I asked him if he would like to have some of them? he said no, he didn't want any. I told him that there was as good preaching in some of them as he would likely ever hear. I took the one containing the writings of Hester Page Makers to Early Piety & read much of it to him. He said that was very good, but he had seen some that he did not believe was true & he had decided to have nothing to do with any of them. I told him that although he might never have witnessed anything like what was stated in there he had seen, yet it might be none the less true. He said there was so many different kinds of books about he didn't know what were good, only the Bible & Hymn Book. I told him there were not denominational, the Society which published them being of different branches of the Christian Church. I read from different works to none of which he could find any fault, but as he had determined not to read such things he would not receive any. §§ Another place where I called the man had a distillery & appeared to be quite too much addicted to the use of whiskey. I showed him the books & told him their object & their price. He got hold of Beecher on Intemperance & after looking at it awhile he remarked that the Doctors ought to read that (Dr. H— was with me) & asked me if it was not a medicine book. I told him that it might be; & that doctors were much pleased with it. He after some hesitation bought it; which very much pleased the gentleman who was with me, as he was anxious to have him have it, but did not wish to let him know it.

I called upon an old man who was a cripple. Had no religious books but Bible & Hymn book. Neither he nor his wife I think were professors. I conversed with them on the importance of Religion & gave him Beecher's Call. § Another place the folks were away from. The man was teaching school. He had no Bible. I supplied him with with a copy charging him to make good use of it. He as I afterward learned was a great drunkard, although his appearance was that of a sober temperate man. May the Lord bless the labors of this month.

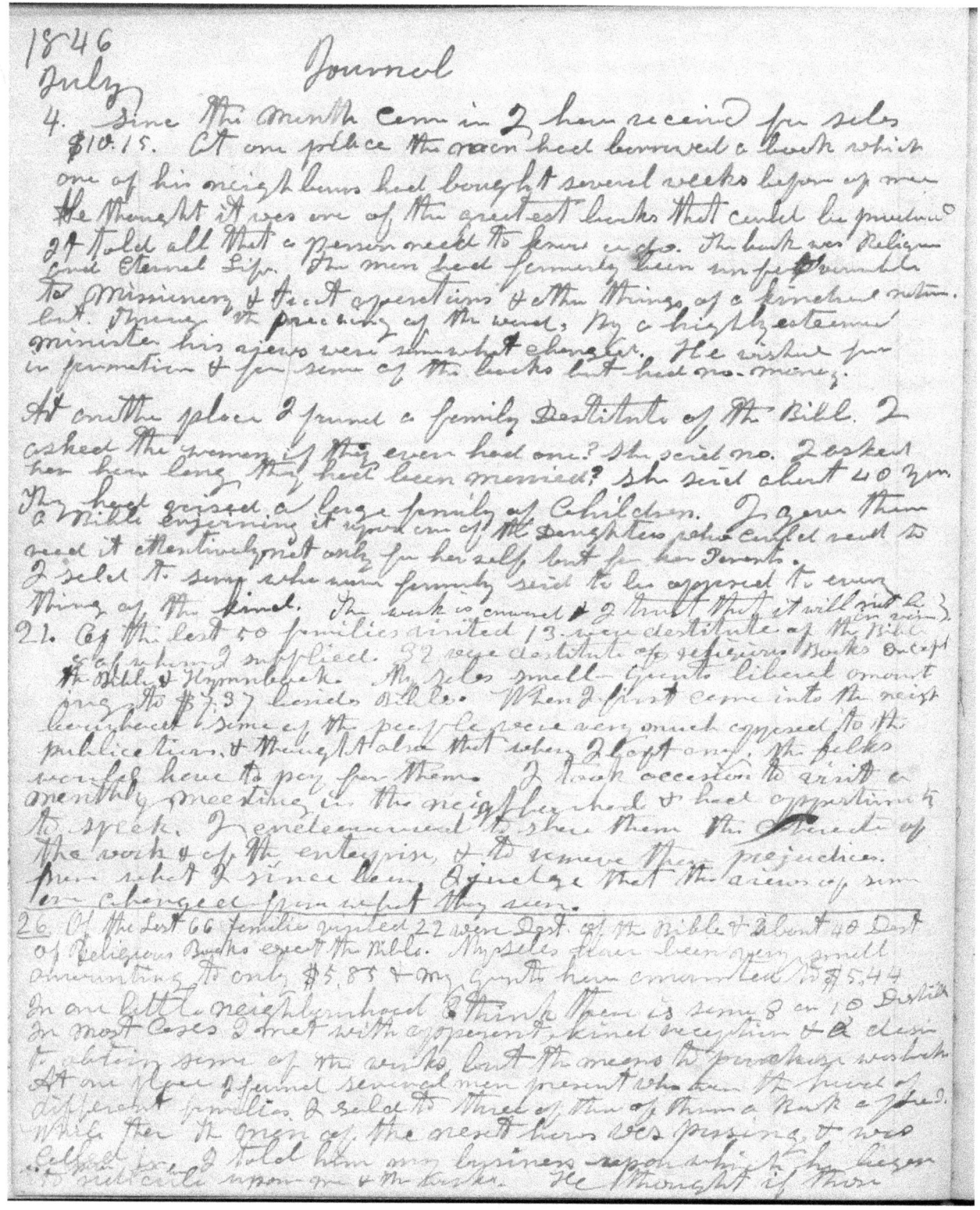

1846   Journal

July 26
while we are going about living on the people & getting every fourpence there was in the country would take the mattock or the tools & go to work it might be as well. I told him the object of this enterprise was not to swindle the people out of their fourpences, but it was to teach them with religious truth that was calculated to do them good. After considerable conversation he invited me to call at his house at dinner. I did so. And I learned then & from other means what I think was the cause of his being so full of his laugh & jests in the morning. He is a distiller & a dram drinker & before dinner the bottle must be passed around for children & all who would to partake of. I tried in vain to sell him some of the books, but gave his daughter several tracts. I left several of Beecher's Sermons in the neighbourhood which I hope will do some good, but my faith is weak. At another place I found the men drunk. I asked the daughter if they had religious books besides the Bible? she said they had not. I asked her if they would be glad to purchase, she said she would be glad to have some but her father was not in a situation to purchase & she was thinking although they had money to purchase if they would. Yet I was constrained to give the girl the D[iscipline] & Daughter & such advice & counsel as I could. In here had conversation with several eager sinners & endeavoured to deal plainly & faithfully with them. I have often felt that it was truly good to go from place to place & converse on the all important subject to they who there is but little if any reason to believe think much of it. I read & furnish them with reading suitable for them & leave them expecting to see them no more until the judgment of the great day. O may it be found then that my labours have not been in vain.

About the middle of this month was the coldest weather ever known at this time of the year it was near dry some. It was colder than I was accustomed to wither in the north of them. Then has been some very warm sultry days. First ripe peaches that I had was July 20th. Since which I have had several times. Rye & apples are abundant. My health is improving. I think I am now at Mr. Samuel B. Flemmons a methodist both I find himself & family very agreeable.

Aug 1846

Journal

1st. Have just Completed Sevier County having been engaged about 4½ months. It is a very rough broken mountainous Section of Country. The people are settled among the knobs & hills without much regard to roads or conveniences. The paths to many of their dwellings lies through fields which renders it necessary to let down bars & fences. In other instances it is unsafe to ride a horse and it becomes necessary to walk. There are I would judge about 1000 families in the county. I have visited 952. Of this number 220 were destitute of the Bible & about half destitute of Religious Books except the Bible. A large portion of the people cannot read. Common schools are very scarce & I would judge inferior to what they should be. I have supplied 207 destitute families with the Bible & granted about 350 volumes mostly to the destitute of religious books beside more than 1900 tracts on various subjects. The value of Sales is about $300. value of grants about $57. The people generally seemed to view it as a good work, although there were some exceptions. I have endeavoured to sow the good seed as extensively as I could consistently. I am happily disappointed in being able to put in the hands of the people of this county so much with reading. May it be the means of rich blessing.

Aug. 23. **Blount County**

Commenced labouring in this Co. on the 17th. Have visited 78 families, found 9 destitute of the Bible & 24 of other religious books. I had Company most of the time which made my labours more pleasant. Found a general desire to obtain the books, but little means to purchase. Sales amounted to $26.96 — Grants $5.47. Endeavoured to speak a few words in most of the families on the subject religion. The Conscience seems to be on the side of vital godliness, but alas, the life of too many is manifestly on the side of the world the flesh & the devil. May the Spirit of the Lord be poured out & the truth as set forth in the books of this Society be a savour of Life unto Life.

Sept 1st. Visited 19 fam. Sold pub. to the amt. of $1.20. People poor — Money scarce. Visited 3 fam. free blacks. Two of them purchased. At one of the places a little boy of 10 years could read well. Gave him the ten commandments to commit to memory. At another place a free black woman bought a book for her son. Was well received in general & left something good with all. Mr. John Henry with whom I am staying rode with me

1846
Sept.

Journal

5th. Sat. Eve. Have visited during the week 76 families. Sales have been small, amounting to only $8.15 & my gets to $4.17 found 9 fam. without the Bible. A portion of the week has been spent among a poor destitute people and in visiting 22 fam. my sales amounted to only 57 cents. Many things render it discouraging yet when I remember the object of the enterprise, and its adaptation to prove useful I am prompted to hold on. I am permitted to bestow a precious gift to many families who receive such as the A.T. Society send forth. May the God of blessing bestow his favor upon the the generous of this society that they may prove a rich & lasting blessing to the people ——

Sept. 15. During the two past days have been visiting in millers Cove. & visited 37 families granted 17 books & 37 Trots sold 12 books. amounting to $20b. People generally very poor and destitute. I conversed with some of them on the subject of religion & the salvation of the soul. I fear but still hope. May the Lord add his blessing to my feeble efforts & for men faith & a deeper work of grace in my own soul. At one place the men who was very old & decripid after hearing me read awhile from Beecher Call thought it was the best kind of preaching he brought the book. At another house the people said that they had heard me & the Books spoken of in another

Dr.	The American Tract Society Boston Stock	$	cts
1846			
~~Dec. 12th To Publications Sold~~			
Dec. 17th To Cash Remitted to Rev. Seth Bliss		10	00
1847			
Jany 7th To Cash Remitted to Rev. Seth Bliss		15	00
" — 13th To Cash Remitted to Rev. Seth Bliss		10	00
" — 15th To 94 F.C. Almanacks returned		2	35
Feb. 11th To Cash Remitted to Rev. Seth Bliss		10	00
March 3d To Cash Remitted to Rev. Seth Bliss 2s Campbell		5	00
		52	35
(Balance on hand Cash $1.2c, in all $81.24)			
March 26th To Cash Remitted to Rev. Seth Bliss Boston		15	00
May 4th To twenty-nine Vol. drawn by Miss Sarah Hitchcock to which she was entitled in consideration of Life Membership		10	00
May 27 To Cash Remitted to Rev. S. H. Bliss		5	00
Sept. 16 To Publications on hand		31	13
" " To Discount on Life		2	00
" " To Cash on hand		45	00
		160	48

in Acct. with Amos Hitchcock   Cr.

Acct.
1846 $ cts

Dec. 11. By 1 Case of Publications as pr Bill   91   42

".. ..   By Error in Bill - - - - - - - - - - - - - - -   25

".. ..   By 399 Tracts = 3160 pp. value – $2.10¾ also)
         76 Copies of Messenger, All Grants)

Dec. 25th By 1 Box of Publications as per Bill   42   41
         (By 452 Tracts — 2582 pp. value $1.32 also)
         (82 Copies of American Messenger & 24 Tracts Respting Gospostage)
         (All grants to be distributed

1847

Feby 1st By two Emily Maria 10 - - -   20
                                                       134   28

April 24 By 1 Package of Publications   13   90
.. .. (By 292 pp. of Tracts gratis 2.0)

May 3d By 1 Package of Books   11   86
.. .. (By 1232 pp. of tracts 82 cents gratis)

~~May 1st~~ June 14 By 1 Tract Vol. No. 1st   42
                                                         160   48

Reported to Society families visited 234. vols sold 487.
Amounting to $125. Tracts distributed Gratis 7266.
value $4.45 Also 150 Numbers of Am. Mess.
About 15 days labour.

Dr. The American Tract Society Boston

		Cash	
1846		$	cts
Dec- 11th	To Cash paid for freight on 1 Box. of Pub-ns. from Boston to Warren Depot		44
" 17th	To Cash Remitted in Letter to "Rev. Seth Bliss Sec. A.T.S. No 28 Cornhill Boston Mass."	10	00
" 25th	To Cash paid for freight on 1 Box from Boston to Warren		25
1847			
Jany. 7th	To Cash Remitted to Rev. Seth Bliss Sec A.T.S. No. 28 Cornhill Boston (in Letter of Date)	15	00
" 15th	To Cash Remitted to Rev. Seth Bliss Boston	10	00
Feby 11th	To Cash Remitted to Rev. Seth Bliss Boston	10	00
March 3d	To Cash Remitted to Rev. Seth Bliss Boston	5	00
		50	69
March 26	To Cash Remitted to Rev Seth Bliss Boston	15	00
April 24th	To Cash paid for freight on Package		25
May 3	To Cash paid for freight on Package		25
May 27	To Cash Remitted to Rev Seth Bliss	5	00
		71	19
Sept 17th	To Cash on hand (On account)	43	81
May 4th	To Hitchcock due (or bought $10. with not included above)	15	00
		10	00
		125	00

in Acct with Ames Hitchcock   Cr.

Acct
1846 $ cts

Dec. 12   By Cash Rec'd for Sales up to Date   7   72½
" – 19   By Cash Rec'd for Sales Since Dec. 12th   6   83
" – 26   By Cash Rec'd for Sales Since Dec. 19th   6   35½
1847
Jany 2nd By Cash Rec'd for Sales Since Dec. 26th   2   63
" – 9th By Cash Rec'd for Sales Since Jany 2nd   4   98
" – 14   By Cash Rec'd for Sales Since Jany. 9th   8   36½
" – 23   By Cash Rec'd for Sales Since Jany. 14th   2   07
" – 30th By Cash Rec'd for Sales Since Jany. 23rd   1   50¼
Feb. 11   By Cash Rec'd for Sales Since Jan. 30th   5   09
" – 16   By Cash Rec'd for Sales Since Feby 11th   3   40
" – 27   By Cash Rec'd for Sales Since Feb 16 & Women 13 B. 3 00
                                                      51   95
March 2d Families visited up to date 50 · Vol. sold 196.
          Packets of tracts sold 5 Children tract 4 (Repeated)
March 10th (Since above) Fam. Vis. 17 – Vol. Sold 44 – P. Tracts 5 – C. Tr. 1. Cash Recd   11 46
"   20   Since 10th   Do .. 5 – Do .. 13 – P. Tracts 0 – .. 1   4 17½
April 24   Since above Fam. Vis. 6 – Vol. sold 14 .. .. .. 1 – Cash Recd   3 46½
May   4th Total up to date   Do. 267   amounting to   74 05
      "   Deducted tract vols ___ 17   7 84
           which leaves true amount   256 vol + ____ ___ ___ $ 66 21
      5th Since the above for Vis. 1 – Vol. sold 15   Cash Recd   3 50
Jun. 1st   for 1 Fam. & vol. No 1st   44
           per vol. Dan. Moulton   25
Augt 14   Since the above .. .. .. 16 Chil– tr– 62   3 73
" 20&21   Fam. 23. Vis 74. vol 28 –   5   6 29
Sept 3d   Fam 55 .. 14 .. 69 ·   16 27
"   8th   Fam. 32 .. 42½ .. 36   7 38½
Sept 16   45   32   10 01
           Not Paid   35
           Drawn by Sarah Hitchcock 29 vol $1.a   119 88
                                    1 Do. $1. 12¢   124 00

Original Journal: Page 64

Original Journal: Page 65

1846. Brimfield. Personal Account
Dr.

Date	Description	$	cts
Nov. 6	To 1 Pr of Boots $2. & 1 Pr. of slippers 50 cent	2	50
" 11	To 1 Silk neck Handkerchief 5/0		83
" "	To 5 Yds red flannel 30¢ per Yd.	1	50
" "	To 1 Vest $1.50 & 1 Hat $2.75	4	25
" "	To Almer Hitchcock for taxes paid for me	3 8	20
" 17	To 10 sheets of Letter Paper & 1 Box of Wafers		16
" 18	To C.R. Brown for Mrs Symns for Medicine		25
" 22	To John E. Callihan in behalf of Wm. Eton		25
Dec. 1st	For 12 sheets of Paper		10
Dec. 5	For postage on letter to Boston Recorder		5
" "	For 1 pr. of Wollen Gloves lined		33
" 10	Postage on 2 Almanacks Sent		5
" 12	Donation to American Education Society		25
	Postage on Circular		2
Dec. 15	To Cash paid D.F. McGilvray for Over Coat Dress Coat & Pants & Over Coat	34	00
" 16	To Cash Paid for two Books (Presented)		28¼
" 19	To Cash Paid Just Hitchcock for 1 Bottle Ex. Sarspla		75
" 18	To Cash Paid for 1 Bottl. Hungarian Balsam	1	00
" 25	To Cash Paid for 1 Umbrella (J.F. Hitchcock)	1	33
Jan. 3	To Monthly Concert		25
" 4	To pay for 12 sheets letter paper		10
Jan. 8	Postage on Letter & 4 Almanack 20 cts / pr Combs 1 ct.		21
" 12	Postage on four Papers Recd		6¼
" 22nd	For 5 Books Bought of Wm. E. Hitchcock	2	00
" 24	For 4 Copies of Am. Messenger & Postage	1	00
" 28	For Postage on two Letters from Tenn.		20
" "	For Postage on two Letters Sent		15
Feby 6	To Postage on Letter from J. Mullendore 10 & for ½ quire of Paper 10		20
" 11 & 16	To Postage on Papers from Knoxville Postage		04
"	To 1 Bottle Wistar Balsam	1	00
"	To 1 pr of Rubbers $1 — to 1 Concordance 33	1	33
"	To 1 Book presented to Black Boy with 12½ cts Cash (Mrs Webster)		22½
March 10th	For postage on letter Papers & (up to date)		08
" 7th	To Cash Contributed at Monthly Concert		25
"	To Do. for 1 Book presented to Mrs Whitney by		10
	To Edward		01
" 13th	Donation to Am. Tr. Society	2	00
"	For 2 Books presented to Mr & Mrs Partridge (Postage on Papers)	1	00
" 15	For 1 Bottle of Wistar's Balsam of Wild Cherry	1	00
"	For 1 pr of spectacles		37½
		98	71

1846	Brimfield. Personal Account.	Cr.	
		$	cts
Nov 6.	By Cash on hand as pr Inventory Errors excepted	316	37½
Nov. 12.	By Cash rec'd as interest on S. & N. S. Hubbard Note	36	00
" 22	~~By Cash Rec'd of L. H. B. for 2 Books~~		
Dec. 7.	~~By Cash Rec'd of Dea. Bishop for 1 package of Tea~~		
1847			
Jany. 7th	By Cash Rec'd of Abner Hitchcock (on Note)	15	00
" "	By Cash Rec'd of Abner Hitchcock Balance on Settlement		25
Jany 28	By Cash Rec'd of S. Homer in part of Note	400	00
April 10th	By Cash Rec'd of S. & N. S. Hubbard as interest	54	00

1847		Dr	
March 17th	Postage on Letter from Joseph Meek Esq. Rawn Co.		10
" "	For ½ quire of Letter paper		10
" 26	Postage on Letter from Greenville & on 1 paper sent		12
April 1st	For 2 bottles of Wistar's Balsam of W. Cherry	2	00
" "	For Perforated Paper & two Sermons 4		12
" 3	Loaned Wm. E. Hitchcock $2. for a week or two		
		1	00
" 8	For 2 papers from Jen.		03
" "	To make direction up to $40.		
" 12	For postage on Letter from Jen		10
" 13	Postage on 4 Messengers sent		12
" 15	Postage on Paper		2
" 16	Postage on Letter sent to Springfield		5
" 17	1 Bottle Burns Sarsaparilla & Tomato Bitters	1	00
" "	To 2 Oranges		06¼
" 19	For Another Watson		6¼
" "	Postage on Letter from D. McCroskey Bowie Co. Jan.		10
" 24	Book presented to My Mother		10
" 24			50
" "			60

1847. Papers Sent

Feby 1st 1 Messenger to Dea John Smith Knoxville
" "   1 Do (Feb. No) to John Henry Sen. Maryville
" "   1 Do to Wm E. Crenwell Ellijoy Blount Co
" "   1 Boston Recorder to Mr Hugh Blair Sevierville
" 5th 3 Youths Companions to James C. Porter Sevierville (Up to Jan 28)
" 5th 1 Companion, Dayspring &c &c No. 1 to Mrs Drayton & Girl Sevierville
" 9th Feb. No. Am. Mess. to Dr. J. M. Ramsey Mecklenburg E. Ten
" "   2 Youths Companions to John M. A. Ramsey Mecklenburg E. Ten
" 12th 1 Boston Recorder to James C. Moses Esq. Knoxville
March 4th 1 B. Recorder & 1 Christian Citizen to James C. Porter Sevierville
" 10th   Am. Mess. to John Myers Tuckaleechee Cove Blount Co E. Ten
" "   Am. Mess. to Joshua Girt Sevierville E. Ten
" "   Am. Mess. to Caroline Wells Sevierville Knox Co. E. Ten
" "   Am. Mess. to Wm. Bryan Esq. Henrys Cross Roads Knox Co
" "   1 Dayspring to Alexander Gemble Esq. Maryville E. Ten
" 17 3 Youths Companions to Mrs. Hannah Porter Sevierville E. Ten
" 26 1 Boston Recorder to Joseph Meek Esq. Academia Knox Co E. Ten
April 12th Am. Messenger to Dea John Smith Knoxville E. Ten
         Am. Messenger to Dea. Elijah Johnson Knoxville E. Ten
         Am. Messenger to Rev Ashley Wynn Sevierville E. Ten
         Am. Messenger to Mr Hugh Blair Sevierville E. Ten
May 7th Am. Messenger to Calvin Mynatt Church Grove E. Ten
         Am. Messenger to Thomas Smith Academia E. Ten
         Am. Messenger to Jordan Houck Boyers C. Neck E. Ten
         Am. Messenger to James C. Porter Sevierville E. Ten
         Am. Messenger to Dr. J. M. Ramsey Sevierville E. Ten
         Am. No. Mess. to David Wells Campbells Station
         Am. Mess. to John Henry Maryville
June 14 Am. Mess. to Dea John Smith Knoxville } E. Ten
         Am. Mess. to John Jernigan Esq. Clinton
         Am. Mess to John Hillsman Esq. Knoxville
July 22 Am. Mess to Gen. Keutin Knoxville
         Am. Mess to Rev. John S. Cunn Academia
         Am. Mess to Samuel Hammer Sevierville
         Am. No Mess to Andrew Bogle Ellijoy Blount Co
Aug 9th Am. Mess to John Henry Sen. Maryville E. Ten
         Am. Mess to Rev John Smith Knoxville
         Am. Mess to Joseph Meek Esq. Academia

1847. Letters written

Feby 2nd 1 To Joseph Estabrook Pres E. Ten. University Knoxville E. Ten.
"   3d 1 To David McCuskey Sevierville E. Tennessee
"   8th 1 To Pinckney H. Toomey Esq. Sevierville E. Ten.
" 11   1 To Rev. Seth Bliss Boston Mass.
" 17   1 To Rev. James Cumming Waldens Creek P.O. Sevier Co. E. Ten.
" 18   1 To Dea. John Smith Knoxville E. Tenn.

March 4th 1 To Rev. Seth Bliss Boston (Receipt & Remittance)
"   "   1 To Mr. John Henry, sen. Maryville E. Tenn. (Porter Sevierville)
"   "   1 To Little Pigeon Sabbath School & James, Monroe & Elizabeth
" 10   1 To John Mullendore Esq. Sevierville E. Ten.
" 17   1 To Rev. Mr. Sanford Holland Mass.
" 26   1 To Rev. Seth Bliss Sec. Am. Tr. Society 28 Cornhill Boston Mass.
           Containing $15. on acc't of $20. to constitute Miss Sarah Hitchcock a mem for life
" 27   1 To Mr. Archibald Walker Loveville P.O. Knox Co. E. Ten.
"   "   1 To Mr. Hugh Bogle Ellijay P.O. Blount Co. E. Ten

April 8 1 To Rev. Seth Bliss Sec. Am. Tr. Soc'y 28 Cornhill Boston Mass.
           Enclosing $40 ea donations from Ninifield
"   8   1 To Mr. Wm. Thomas Boyds Creek Sevier County E. Ten
"   9   1 To Mr. Joseph Meek Esq. Accademia P.O. Knox Co. E. Ten
" 16   1 To Mr. Wm. Stowe Esq. Springfield Mass.
"   "   1 To Rev. Seth Bliss Boston Request for Books
" 19   1 To Mr. David Wills Campbells Station Knox Co. E. Ten.
" 22   1 To Col James M. Toole Maryville E. Tenn.
" 23   1 To Col Thomas Rogers Esq. Knoxville E. Ten.

             Letters Received & Papers

Feby 6th 1 From John Mullendore Esq. Sevier Co. E. Tenn.
"   16 1 From Rev. Seth Bliss Boston
March 9th 1 From Rev. Seth Bliss Boston (Rec'pt)
"   "   1 From Col James M. Toole Maryville E. Tenn. (Written at New York)
"   17 1 From Joseph Meek Esq. Knox Co. E. Tenn
"   "   1 From Wesley Huffaker Esq. Sevier Co. E. Ten
"   26 1 From David Wills Tusculum College Green Co. E. Ten.

April 3d 1 From Rev. Seth Bliss Boston
"   8   2 Papers from Tenn.
"   11   1 From Dea. John Smith Knox County E. Ten
"   13   1 From Tract Society Boston Mass.
"   15   1 Paper from P.E. Moses Knoxville E. Ten.
"   19   1 Letter from Tract Society Boston
"   "   1 Letter from David McCuskey Sevier Co. E. Ten
"   "   1 Baptist Report from D. McCuskey
"   "   1 Report from Knoxville

		1846
Dr. The American Tract Society		Stock
Sept 11th To Error in bill of Publications	1	51
Oct 1st. Publications Granted since Sept 1st.	12	46
Oct 28 Publications Granted since Oct 1st.	13	51
Oct 28. Publications sold since Sept 1st.	78	97
Oct 28 Publications invoiced & left at Brobsons		
& dealers from Boston well packed	296	50
	403	35
Loss Of which I can give no account	2	71

1847 Letters written & Papers sent

April 26. 1 Letter to James C. Moses Knoxville E. Ten
" " 1 Do Rev Seth Bliss Boston Remittance $6. & Order for Books
" 29. 1 Tract to Rev S. C. Gist Sevierville E. Ten
May " 2 Monthly Concert
" 4 1 Letter to Mr Aaron Bliss Warren Mass.
" 8 1 Do to see Mr F. Ruck 150 Nassau St NY
" 13 Boston Recorder to David McCroskey Sevierville E. Ten
" — " Springfield Gazette to Mrs. Dickinson Knoxville E. Ten
" 20 Boston Recorder to Rev R. B. McMullen Knoxville E. Ten
" 26 1 Letter to Rev Joseph N. S. Shipton Jonesborough E. Ten
" 27 1 Ditto to Rev Seth Bliss with letter rewritten
June 4 1 Letter to Dr. Cowan Porter & Maria Sevierville E. Ten
" — " Book mark Enclosed to Elizabeth & Maria
" 14 1 do Do. Am Tr. Soc New York Enc $1. for Mess.
" " Youth Companion to John Mullendore Esq.
" " Do. J. C. Porter } Sevierville
June 26 1 Letter to Thomas Smith Cherokee Academy io Ten
June 30 1 do to Rev S. S. George Haden Knoxville

1846
Acct. in Acct. with Amos Hitchcock Cr
$ cts

Sept. 1st Publications on hand as per
      Quarterly Report of date   73   79
Sept. 11th By Publications Recd. as per Bill. 333   27
                                                   407   06
                                                   403   35
                                                           3   71

1847   Letters & Papers &c. Received

May 3d   1 Letter from Seth Bliss 23 Cornhill Boston
May 6   1 Letter from Thomas Smith Knox Co.
" 13   1 Knoxville Register of Apr. 28 from the Office
" 16   1 Do Do May 5 Do
"   1 Letter from pr. Jones Huffaker Jonesborough Tenn
" 26   1 Letter from Dr. J. M. Harmer Sevierville $1. for 6 Messengers
         Register of May 12 from Office
Jun 1st   1 Letter from J. C. Maria Porter Sevierville
         1 from Rev. S. H. Bliss Boston
         1 from Rev. C. Cartman New York (Circular)
" 10   1 Letter from Presby. Bd. of Education Knoxville
         Do from Col J. D. Compton Sevierville
" 24   1 From Wm. Thurman Sevier Co. Co.

1846

Dr. The American Tract Society $ Cts

Sept.
7 & 11   Postage on Circular & Letter   07
11th   Cash paid Brabson & Toole for freight on
          four Boxes of Publications   20   20
Oct 2   Postage on 2 Letter   10
" 5   Do   on Letter & Paper   15
" 20   Fuirage   11
                                                                  20   63

Oct 28   Services since Sept 1st   25   00
          Use of Horse   2   50
                                                                  48   13

Dr 1847 Personal Acct

April 26 To make donations up to $6. for Dr. S.   23
    "   Do 4 Books presented & 1 Sheet of Paper used   07
     29   Postage on Tract sent Rev. J. C. Gist   03
May 2   Monthly Concert   25
     3   2 Oranges   4
     6   To 1 Sett of D. Aubignes History of Reformation   1   50
     7   To Postage on 5 Messengers sent to Sab. Schols   15
     13   To Postage on paper sent & Recd.   07
     16   To Postage on Letter & Paper from Gen.   11
     26   Postage on Paper   7
June 1   Postage on Letter from J. C. B. Snr.   10
     5   Do on Papers Recd   3
     10   Postage on 2 Letters from Paris & Paper sent   23
     11   For 1 Box of Blacking   10
     14   Postage on 8 papers sent to E ten   24
     18   For 1 Quart of Strawberries & gum   5
     24   Postage on Letter & paper   13
     "   1/2 Quire of Letter pape   10
     "   2 Pencil & pen   8

1846 in Acct with Amos Hitchcock Cr.

Acct. $ Cts

Sept 1st By Cash on hand as per
          Report of date. (Quarterly Rept)   42 79
Oct 1st   By Cash Rec'd for sales since Sept 1st.   41 90
Oct 2d   By Cash Rec'd for sales since Oct 1st.   37 07
                                                    121 76
                                                     48 13
Oct 2d   By Cash on hand Due Society ---   73 63

Nov 4th. Settled all accounts with the Society

1847   Personal Acct. $ Cts
April 26 ~~To make duplicates of &c. &c. up to $6~~
          ~~on sheet of paper~~
May 27   ~~To 4 Childrens books presented~~
May 7.   By Cash Rec'd for 1 Bottle Westers Balsam   1 00

1846
Letters Written

Sept. 1st	1	To Rev. R. S. Cook New York (qr. Report)
8th	1	To Lucy H. Bliss Warren Mass.
26	1	To Ruth Ca. Bliss Warren
Oct 2	1	To Rev. R. S. Cook New York (M. Rept.)
6	1	To Rev Shepherd Wells Columbia Tenn
"	1	To Abner Hitchcock Brimfield
27	1	To Sarah Hitchcock Brimfield
28	1	To Rev R S Cook New York
"	1	To Rev Shepherd Wells Sen g. gft Columbia Tn
"	1	To James H. Cowan Esq. Knoxville
"	1	New Energy Paper Anderson

1847   Personal Acc.t $ cts

July 4th	Monthly Concert		20
8	Postage on Letter New York		5
18	Contributn to For. Evangelical Socity		25
31st	Since above Postage on Letters Papers &c		50
August 9th	Postage on Papers sent		12
Aug 18th	Fares per R.y.	13	42
"	Postage on Letter & two papers		13
20	Paper & Cah.l. Tus.		5
25	1 Wallet 12½ 1 Hair Brush 4 — 1 Cahilds Inst		16½
27	1 Umbrella 1.33. 2¾ yds common 57 - 2.29. Silk & Twist		
"	1 yd Drilling & Buttons 10. 6 yds Cotton 75. 1 Pack Cards		
15	1½ yds Linnen 1.12. Thread 5. Gloves 67	6	63
"	1 Silk Pocket Hdkf. 75. 1 Penknife 54		
	2 pr Suspender 30. ½ Quire Letter Paper	1	65
Sept 8	Donation to Am. Bible Socy		50
"	Postage 3. Books Given 6		09
7	1 Scripture Manual & pockets		87½
8	Postage 10. Books presented 11½ Qr. Postage 1		22
16	Postage 2. Books bought 18. Cloth 21		42
18	50. Cutting Pants		25

Original Journal: Page 74

1846
Letters Received

Sept. 7	1 From Lucy H. Bliss Warren Dat 2.426.		10
"	1 Circular from A.T. Society		2
"	1 From Rev Shepherd Wells Jonesborough (dat Sept 30)		5
12	1 From Sarah Hitchcock Pinfield (date Aug 27)		10
"	1 From Ruth C. Bliss Warren		10
Oct 2	2 From Rev Shepherd Wells		10
" 5	1 From Rev O. Eastman & Z. Ackley		10

1847   Personal Acct   Cr

Sept 13th	By Five hundred dollars on Note of N. S. & L. Hubbard		500	00
" 18	By Cash Recd Of N. S. Hubbard		116	68
" "	By Cash Recd per Mr Yed. Linner			37½

Dr

Sept 20th	To Postage to Porter 2.05		2	05
21st	To 1 Library co mel. 2.50 — 2 rakes 6 – 1 Blank Book 75		3	31
" "	To Subscription for Am Sun Sch. Jour. to be sent to Ten.		1	00
" "	To Youth Companion to be sent to Jr. C. Post	1	1	00
" "	To Passage fare to Mr Dept Porter 50 Bunker Hill & 11½			62½
" "	To 1 Bible 94. Repayment 8.6		1	00
" "	To Ten from Note A. Warren		2	05
" "	To Admittance to Lect on Physiology			25
" 22	To 3 Daguerreotype Likenesses		3	75
" "	To 3 Blank Books			46
" "	To Postage on Letter			10
" 25	To fare from Palmer to Lenox & back $4.55 Newspaper 3		4	58
" 20	Deposited Six hundred dollars in the savings Bank Springfield			20
" 28	Fare from Calent ville to Springfield			20
" "	Postage on Letter sent to Phil			5

Original Journal: Page 75

1846
Dr. The American Tract Society Stock

		$	cts
April 1st	Publications Granted from Mar. 1st to April 1st	13	34
April 30th	Publications Granted from April 1st to April 30th	13	12
June 1st	Publications Granted from May 1st to June 1st	19	06
	Error in Bill of Pub. Rec'd. May 16th		25
		45	77
May 21	Remittance to O. R. Kingsbury N.Y. per Order	150	00
June 1st	Loss of Publications since Mar. 1st as per inventory to date	4	21
	Services & Expenses since March 1st	1.99	58
		1.24	32
	Balance Due me as per Report of Date	78	76
July 1st	Publications Granted Since June 1st	17	59
Aug 1st	Publications Granted Since July 1st	26	58
	Cash on hand as per Report of Date ×	36	24
Sept 1st	Publications Granted Since Aug 1st	9	48
	Sales Since June 1st	163	58
	subtract ×	253	47
		36	24
		.217	2B
	On hand as per Inventory	73	75
	Less. Of which I can give no account	2	25
		253	27

1846.
in Acct with Amos Hitchcock Cr.
account.

		$	cts
March 3d. By Publications on hand as pr Ann.l Report.		404	10
May 16. By Publications Recd. as pr Bill		134	71
		538	81
June 1st. Balance on hand as per quarterly Report of Date		293	27

Sept 1st. Publications on hand as per Report 73 79
Transferred

1847 Dr Renewd Acct.
Oct. 3d Postage on papers
"   4. To Cash Paid Abner Hitchcock for Book of &c.   102 25

Cr
1847. Oct.   By Cash Recd for 12 Books
         By Cash Recd from Simeon Homer   119 55
         By Cash Recd from Abner Hitchcock for Note. 293 03
         By Cash Recd from Do   for work —   50

Tennessee Travels 1844-1845, Journal of Amos Hitchcock

1846

Dr. The American Tract Society   Cash

		$	Ct
March 3d	To Balance due me as pr Annual Report	66	87
5th	To discount on uncurrent money		09
5	To Ferriage		10
11	To Cash paid for Meals lodging, Horse Keeping &c.		27
21	To " " for Freight on Books pr Mr. Thomas	1	00
28	To " " " Ferriage to Esq Henry Huffaker		50
April 1st	To " " " Postage on Letter from N.Y.		10
4th	" Total as pr monthly report of Date	68	93
4th	" Postage pr qr .45 — 13th Postage on Letter 10		55
4th	" Ferriage 5, — 24 Ferriage 5		10
April 30th	Total up to date including Balance as pr Report		65
		69	58
May 14	Postage on Letter		5
21	Remittance pr Order from C. Wallace Knoxville	150	00
	Premium on Above (2 pr Cent)	3	00
"	To Cash Paid Craven & Dickinson for freight on Case of Pub from N.Y. Wt. 261 lbs. 4 ct pr lb.	10	44
June 1st	To Cash paid Self as Retained on Acct of Services & use of Horse	41	25
		274	32
June 10 & 11th	Postage on Circulars & Papers		09
July 3d & 7th	Postage on Letters for Society		22
" 9th	Ferriage 5. Postage on Report, Papers &c 12½		17½
Aug 5	Postage on Papers		5
28	Do on Letters		15
29	To Hugh Bogle for making Deposit at his house 2 weeks		45
June 1st	Balance Due me as pr Quarterly Report of Date	78	76
Sept 1st	To Cash paid Self for services & use of Horse since June 1st	41	25
		129	14

1846

in acct with Amos Hitchcock Cr.
acct.

		$	cts.
April 1st.	By Cash Rec'd for Sales Since March 1st.	41	29
April 30th	By Cash rec'd for Sales Since April 1st.	64	89
June 1st.	By Cash Rec'd for Sales Since May 1st.	89	38
		195	56
July 1st.	By Cash Rec'd for Sales Since June 1st.	72	48
Aug 1st.	By Cash Rec'd for Sales Since July 1st.	40	68
"	By Cash Rec'd for 14 Copies of Messenger to Commence with July 1846	2	33
Sept. 1st	By Cash rec'd for Sales since Aug. 1st.	50	42
		165	91
	Services & Expenses subtracted	123	14
	Balance on hand as per Report	42	77

| Sept 1st. | Balance on hand as above Transfered | 42 | 77 |

Dr. A. Hitchcock Acct with

1845

		$	cts
April 26	To 1 box of publications	87	76
	Also to 4 German books	1	22
May 30	for publication	5	20
July 1st	To 1 box of publications	71	23
Sept 10	1 vol. German & 500 pp. tracts		64
Sept 19	1 box. publications	68	14
Sept 30	To selected publications	7	14
Oct 27	to 4 vol.	1	44
Oct 31	by 1 vol.	242	26
			40
		242	40

Wm. H. Smith Associate Colporteur Co.

1845

		$	ct
July 1st	My Cash Rec'd —	35	00
Sept 10.	By His Receipt for thirty seven & 50/100 Dollars retained for 3 months service ending July 31st 1845 —	37	50
Oct 31.	By Rec't for 3 months service ending Oct 31st 1845 $37.50/100	37	50
	By Publications Returned	28	00
	By Do. Granted	31	70
	By Cash returned for expense	6	70
	By Cash Received	61	82
	By Discount on Sales	4	58
	By amount	242	70

1846

| April 30 | Cash on hand as per Report of date | 86 | 60 |

Dr. A. Hitchcock in acct with Thomas H. Aikman
1845

April 25	T. H. Aikman Dr for 1 box of Books	89	62
May 23	for picked up tracts 25	2	00
June 12	for 1 Box of Publications sent by Stage	72	59
July 10	for 1 Box of Books & tracts to be sent by Stage	82	74
Aug 4	for 1 Pocket _____ ____ Sent by ___		25
Sept 1	for 1 box of ____ put to be sent by stage & River	26	05
Sept 13	for Books & Tracts	7	25
Oct 2	for 1 Family Library sent by stage	6	50
Sept 29	for Books & Tracts	4	26
		291	86

<u>Associate Colporteurs for 6 months</u>   Cr.

July 10. Rec'd of Sh. H. Aikman	88	00
Sept. 12 Rec'd of Sh. H. Aikman	62	00
Sept 12. By Receipt of Sh. H. Aikman for three months Service ending July 25th	37	50
Oct 24. Publications Returned	10	50
Oct 24. By Cash as per Rec't. for three months Service ending Oct. 25	37	50
Oct 24. By Rec't for Expenses to Bal. Acct	8	
By Grant of Publications (Total)	45	87
Discount on books Sold	2	42
Expenses for 6 months		
By Sales of Publications	234	07
By Grants of Do	45	87
By Discounts on Sales of Pub.	2	42
By Publications Returned	10	50
	291	86
Cash Rec'd of Sh. H. Aikman	126	00
allowed for services for 6 months	75	00
allow'd for Discount on Sales	2	42
allow'd for Grants	45	87
allow'd for Expenses		
Pub'ns Returned		
	291	86

1845

July 5 Rev. Wm. Rogers Dr. for 31 books
to be forwarded him by Joseph Hillsman
he wishing them to distribute as a volunteer.   7   12½

Aug 28. Settled the above receiving $6.75 & 1 book 37½   7   12½

Aug 28. Left with Rev Wm. Rogers for sale 8 books paid   2   00

A. H. $42 75   132.85   42.85   42,75
W. B.   31 15   42 75
2 S B   31 15   21 4 25
7 nson   12 00   29 5 50
         13 10   85 7 0
         ―――――   17140
         132 85   132,89)18318.35(13,78
          50   132 89
         42,85   50 33
     13285 42 85 31 15   50
           31 15   5 85 5
          21 4 25
                                   104)787
                                     925 5
         12 85   1175 25
)13 8 4)775)10.04   1062 80
        132 85   0.04
        ―――――
        000.62)55

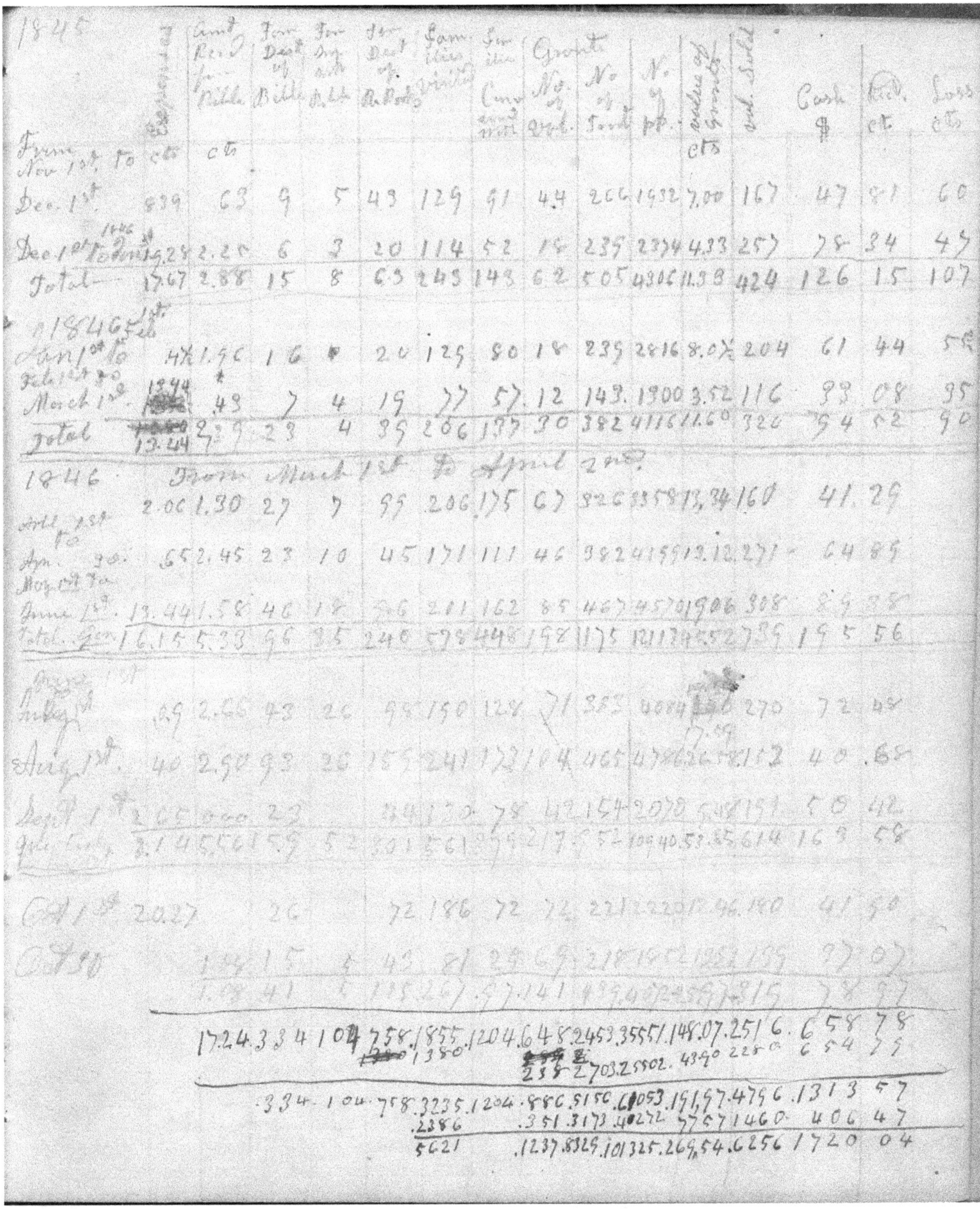

1845	Expenses	Amt Rec'd for Bible	For Dest of Bible	For Sy. sch. Bible	For Dest of R. Books	Families visited	For the Conv and ...	Grants No. of Vol.	No of Tracts	No of pp.	value of Grants	Vol. Sold	Cash $	Rec. ct.	Loss cts
From Nov 1st. to	cts	cts									cts				
Dec. 1st.	839	63	9	5	43	129	91	44	266	1932	7.00	167	47	81	60
Dec 1st 1846 to Jany	9.28	2.25	6	3	20	114	52	18	239	2374	4.33	257	78	34	47
Total	17.67	2.88	15	8	63	243	143	62	505	4306	11.33	424	126	15	107
1846 Jan 1st to Feb 1st	4.8	1.96	16		20	129	80	18	239	2816	8.07	204	61	44	55
Feb 1st to March 1st	1.44	.43	7	4	19	77	57	12	143	1900	3.52	116	33	08	95
Total	13.44	2.39	23	4	39	206	137	30	382	4116	11.60	326	94	52	90
1846 From March 1st to April 2nd.	2.06	1.30	27	7	95	206	175	67	826	3358	13.34	160	41	29	
April 1st to Ap. 30.	.65	2.45	23	10	45	171	111	46	382	4155	13.12	271	64	85	
May 1st to June 1st.	13.44	1.58	46	18	96	211	162	85	467	4570	19.06	308	89	38	
Total. Gen	16.15	5.33	96	35	240	578	448	198	1175	12117	45.52	739	195	56	
June 1st to July 1st	.69	2.66	43	26	98	150	128	71	383	4084	17.59	270	72	48	
Aug 1st.	.40	2.50	93	26	159	241	172	104	465	4786	26.58	152	40	.68	
Sept 1st	2.05	0.00	23		34	130	78	42	154	2070	5.48	191	50	42	
Gen. Total	3.14	5.56	159	52	301	561	399	217	552	10940	53.85	614	169	58	
Oct 1st	20.27		26		72	186	72	72	221	2220	15.46	180	41	50	
Oct 30		1.84	15	5	43	81	29	69	218	1852	19.81	135	97	07	
		1.08	41	5	115	267	57	141	439	4072	35.27	315	78	97	

17.24.3 3 4 1 04 758.1855.1204.648.2453.3555.148.07.2516.658 78
1380 ... 6 54 77
238 2703.25502. 4340 2280
.334. 104. 758.3235.1204.886.5156.61053.191,57.4796.1313 57
.2386 .351.3173.40272 77571460. 406 47
5621 .1237.8325.101325.269,54.6256 1720 04

Original Journal: Page 85

Report of Feb. 5, 1845

		#	
Cash on hand as per last report		139	86
Received for vol. & Tracts sold since		59	83
		199	19
Cash Remitted		150	
Expenses		2	62
Cash on hand		40	37
		199	19

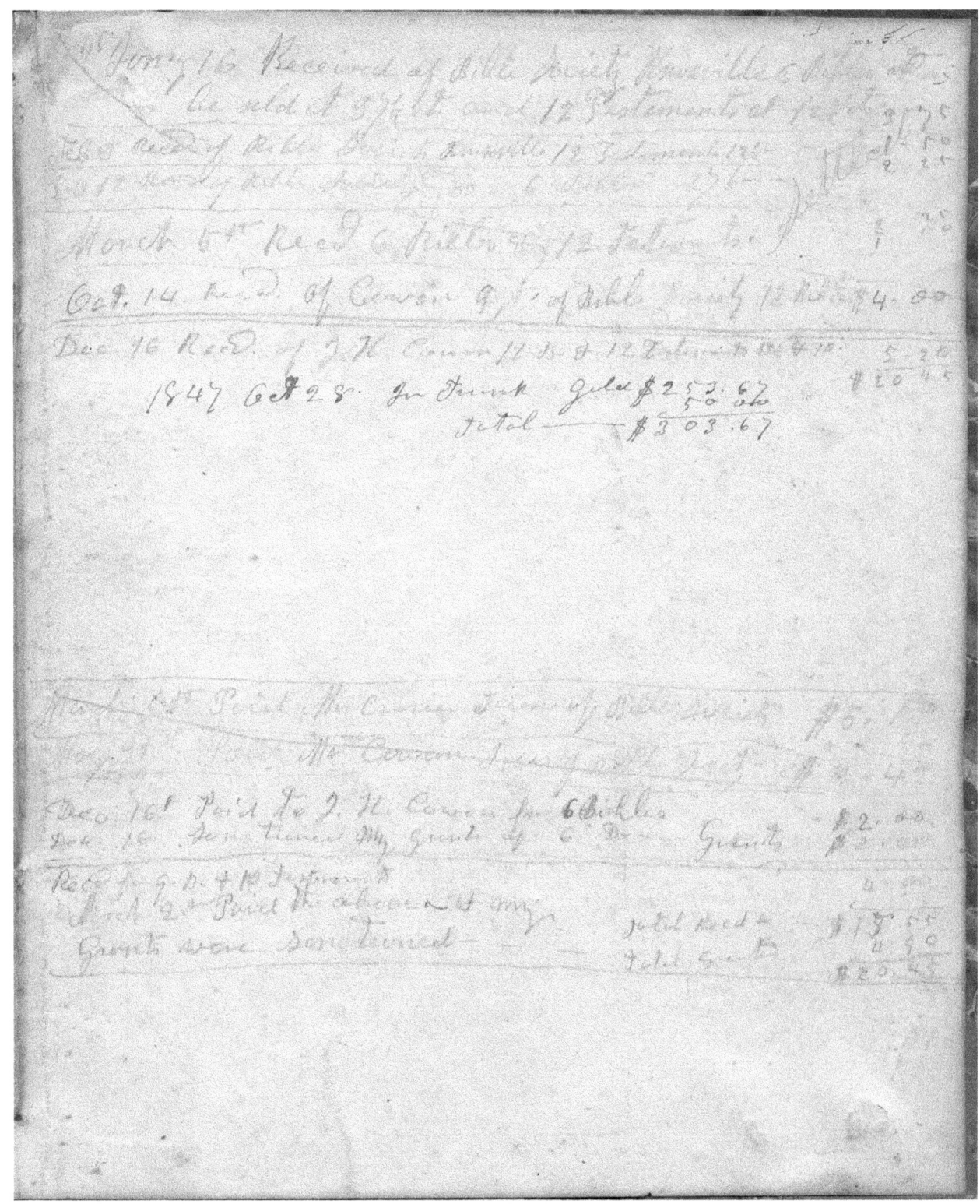

Original Journal: Inside Back Cover

Part V

The Hitchcock Family

Part V
The Hitchcock Family

Amos's Lineage

The Hitchcocks have been in America since Colonial days. Amos's great, great, great, great grandfather, Luke Hitchcock, settled in New Haven, Connecticut in 1644. [1]

Luke's son, John, moved to Springfield, Massachusetts. [1]

John's son, Nathaniel, who died in the 1760s, had at least seven children, including Joseph born in 1719. [1]

Joseph married three times and had at least fifteen children. He and his second wife, Patience Stebbins, were the parents of Nathaniel born in 1746. [2]

Nathaniel lived through both the American Revolution and the War of 1812. He married Ruth of Brimfield, Massachusetts. Nathaniel and Ruth had Ira in March 1777. [3]

Ira married Persis Newell.[10] Some sources give her name as "Percy." [4] Church records show that Persis became a member of the Congregational Church in Brimfield, Massachusetts in 1832, as did a great number of other Hitchcocks. [5]

Nathaniel and Persis had at least seven children. The last documented is our Amos, the author of this journal, born March 16, 1818 in Brimfield, Hampden County, Massachusetts. [4]

Amos was 26 years old when he became a colporteur and embarked on his journey to East Tennessee. He traveled to New York where he picked up supplies at the American Tract Society headquarters. Then he sailed on the Brig *Clint* to Savannah Georgia, and made his way overland. He made his first journal entry on October 30, 1844.

In East Tennessee, he distributed literature for the American Tract Society, meeting hundreds of local residents. Among the people whose names he records in his journal is the Porter family of East Tennessee, which included Elizabeth Porter, his future wife.

On November 6, 1846, Amos bought passage back to Brimfield, ending his colporteur travels, though he continued to correspond and send literature to East Tennessee. In April 1848, he and Elizabeth Porter married and began life together in Brimfield. They had at least five children: Ellen F., Lucy N., Alvin P., Alice C., and Thomas.[6]

Ellen was born in Brimfield, September 25, 1850.[7] The Hitchcocks moved to and settled in Alabama where their daughter, Lucy was born around 1853. All the rest of their children were also born in Alabama: Alvin around 1857, Alice around 1861, and Thomas around 1865.[6]

In 1860, the Hitchcocks lived and farmed near Fayetteville in Talladega County, Alabama. By this time, Amos appears to have made a comfortable living, owning considerable real estate, cash, and personal property.[8]

They still resided in Talladega County in or near the town of Childersburg in 1870. Their next-door neighbors were Elizabeth's sister, Maria, her husband and a 15-year-old daughter. Maria's house also included her mother, Hannah Porter, and her sister, Belinda Porter.[6]

Amos's daughter, Ellen, married Joseph W. Burke in 1874. Sadly, she died July 14, 1875, before her first wedding anniversary at the age of 24.[7]

Amos died April 27, 1876 at the age of 58. Apparently he remained faithful to the Christian beliefs he sets down in his journal, for after his death in Talladega County, Alabama, the Fayetteville Methodist Church paid tribute to him.[9]

Four years after his death, his wife, Elizabeth is still living in Fayetteville, Alabama. Three of her children, Lucy, Alvin, and Thomas live with her. Elizabeth Porter Hitchcock died June 7, 1887 at the age of 62.[12]

Other Hitchcocks in Amos's Journal

Abner Hitchcock   Abner was Amos's brother.[4] He sometimes took care of business for and had business dealings with Amos. Abner's 1847 marriage to Lucinda Barber is recorded in the *Vital Records of Brimfield*.

Sarah or Sally Hitchcock   Amos wrote letters to and receives letters from Miss Sarah Hitchcock. He bought a bottle of extract from her. He paid for her lifetime membership to the American Tract Society. Amos did have a sister named Sally.[4] Since Sally was a common nickname for Sarah, Sarah and Sally are probably the same person.

William Hitchcock   Church records state that a William Hitchcock was admitted to the Congregational Church in Brimfield, Massachusetts in November 1831. Two Williams can be documented, one distant relative and the other Amos's first cousin.[15] In his journal, Amos records a purchase of five books from William as well as a $2.00 loan he made to William. This is probably his first cousin, son of Artemas Hitchcock, Amos's father's brother.

The Bliss Family

The Hitchcocks and the Blisses were associated by marriage[4] as well as American Tract Society business. Amos kept in contact with several Blisses during his journal writing, 1844-1847. During his years as a colporteur, many letters, receipts, and monies went back and forth between Amos and Reverend Seth Bliss, as Seth was the Secretary of the American Tract Society in Boston.

Amos's sister Lucy married Samuel Hopkins Bliss, February 23, 1831.[4] His Aunt Ruth Hitchcock married Isaac Bliss in Brimfield in 1783.[2]

Amos wrote letters to Lucy H. Bliss, Ruth C. Bliss, and Aaron Bliss 1844-1847; all lived in Warren, Massachusetts. Aaron had been a member of the Congregational Church in Brimfield, Massachusetts in November 1831, the same church to which Amos's mother belonged.[5]

Tennessee Travels 1844-1845, Journal of Amos Hitchcock

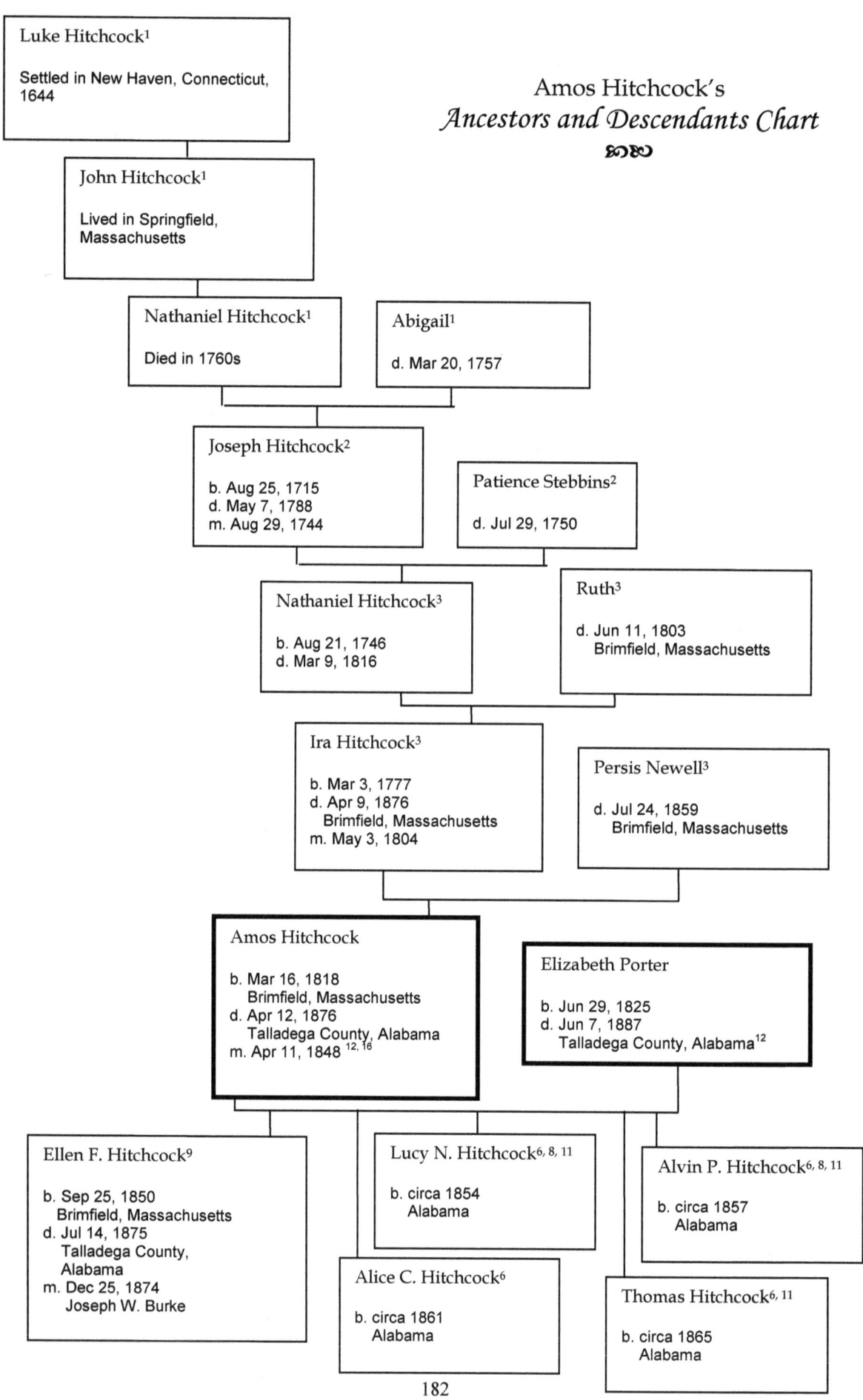

Part V: The Hitchcock Family

Endnotes

1. *Historical Celebration of the Town of Brimfield, Hampden County, Massachusetts* Published by Vote of the Town. Springfield, Massachusetts, 1879. Printer: Clark W. Bryan Company. p. 409.
2. *Historical Celebration of the Town of Brimfield, Hampden County, Massachusetts* Published by Vote of the Town, 1879. p. 410
3. *Historical Celebration of the Town of Brimfield, Hampden County, Massachusetts* Published by Vote of the Town, 1879. p 412
4. *Historical Celebration of the Town of Brimfield, Hampden County, Massachusetts* Published by Vote of the Town, 1879. p. 413
5. Morse, Jason. *Annals of the Church in Brimfield*. Springfield, Massachusetts 1856. p.67
6. United States Federal Census 1870. Childersburg P.O., Talladega County, Alabama; p. 61, Families and Dwellings 36 and 37, Lines 15-26; July 18, 1870.
7. Smith, Jonathan Kennon Thompson, transcriber. *Death Notices from the Christian Advocate, Nashville, Tennessee 1874-1876.* Transcription copyright: Jonathan K. T. Smith, 2000. p. 57. Found: www.TNGenWeb.org.
8. United States Federal Census 1860. Fayetteville P.O., Talladega County, Alabama; p. 48, Dwelling 342, Family 354, Lines 19-23; June 18, 1860.
9. Smith, Jonathan Kennon Thompson, transcriber. *Death Notices from the Christian Advocate, Nashville, Tennessee 1874-1876.* Transcription copyright: Jonathan K. T. Smith, 2000. p. 74. Found: www.TNGenWeb.org.
10. *Vital Records of Brimfield Massachusetts to the Year 1850*. The New England Historic Genealogical Society 1931. p. 293.
11. United States Federal Census 1880. Fayetteville, Talladega County, Alabama; p. 30; Dwelling and Family 202; Lines 30-33; June 25, 1880.
12. Smith, Jonathan Kennon Thompson, transcriber. *Genealogical Abstracts from Recorded Deaths, the Nashville Christian Advocate, 1887-1899*. 2002. Found: www.TNGenWeb.org. October 22, 1887 Edition.
13. *Historical Celebration of the Town of Brimfield, Hampden County, Massachusetts* Published by Vote of the Town, 1879. p. 415
14. *Vital Records of Brimfield Massachusetts to the Year 1850*. The New England Historic Genealogical Society 1931. p. 202.
15. *Historical Celebration of the Town of Brimfield, Hampden County, Massachusetts* Published by Vote of the Town, 1879. p. 414
16. *Vital Records of Brimfield Massachusetts to the Year 1850*. The New England Historic Genealogical Society 1931. p. 201.

Appendixes and References

Appendix 1: Publications

Amos Hitchcock distributed and listed in his journal several publications. Some were periodicals that would be mailed to his acquaintances. Others were books, pamphlets, and tracts that he would carry and sell door-to-door. Since Amos usually mentions the publications by title rather than author, this list is alphabetical by title.

The American Tract Society's Twentieth Annual Report *published in 1845, lists an astounding number of publications. The Society published over 480 different titles of tracts in English and hundreds of tracts in German, French, Spanish, Portuguese, Italian, Welsh, Danish, Swedish and Dutch. The 1845 Report lists 105 children's tracts printed in English and 85 unique titles presented as broadsheets, handbills, and cards. Books by various authors were grouped together in collections called "libraries." Collections included the 15-volumed* Evangelical Family Library, *the 45-volumed* Christian Library, *and the 40-volumed* Youth's Christian Library. *Dozens of books were also sold separately including volumes in foreign languages.*

Alphabetical By Title

Alarm to Unconverted Sinners in a Serious Treatise on Conversion, An
By Joseph Alleine
Book published by the American Tract Society. It was published as Volume 9 of the *Evangelical Family Library*. First published in 1672 it has gone through centuries of reprints.

American Messenger
Newspaper published by the American Tract Society of national news, missionary news, religious commentary, and many international cultural articles. According to David Nord, Indiana University professor and colporteur expert, the *American Messenger* was founded in 1843, making Amos Hitchcock's acquaintances some of the earliest subscribers to what became a popular monthly publication. On April 4, 1846, Amos writes, "…Esquire Johnson said the *Messenger* was one of the most valuable religious papers he ever saw." By 1848, the circulation had reached 100,000.

American Sunday School Journal
Publication distributed by Amos Hitchcock.

Anxious Inquirer After Salvation, The

By Rev. John Angell James

Published by the American Tract Society. Author was a widely respected, evangelical, English Congregational minister.

B. Life

Amos Hitchcock's shorthand for the book *The Life of the Reverend David Brainerd.*
See entry: *Life of the Reverend David Brainerd, The.*

B. S. Rest

Amos Hitchcock's shorthand for the book *The Saint's Everlasting Rest.*
See entry: *Saint's Everlasting Rest, The.*

Backslider: Or an Enquiry into the Nature, Symptoms, and Effects, The

By Andrew Fuller

Pamphlet published by the American Tract Society.

Author was an English, Baptist preacher.

Children's Tract
2 ½" x 3 ½"

Boston Recorder

A newspaper that included missionary reports, shipping reports, and social news including marriages and deaths. Mr. Hitchcock corresponded with its proprietor, Martin Moore. On February 4th of one of the years when Amos kept his journal, the *Boston Recorder* carried an article called "(The) Necessity of Colporteurs," which he mailed to several acquaintances.

Call to the Unconverted to Turn and Live, A

By Reverend Richard Baxter

Book published by the American Tract Society.

Cause and Cure of Infidelity: Including a Notice of the Author's Unbelief and the Means of His Rescue, The

By Rev. David Nelson

Book published by the American Tract Society.

Appendix 1: Publications

Children's Tracts

The American Tract Society published many tracts for children. Amos doesn't name them specifically in his journal, however, one tract published during Amos Hitchcock's tenure was entitled *Pretty Stories for Good Children*. See illustrations: pages 24 and 188.

Christian Advocate

A publication of the Methodist and Methodist Episcopal Church. The Methodist church divided (and still divides) the country into regions called "conferences." Each conference published a magazine providing church and church membership news including obituaries, births, and marriages. In the mid-1800s the *Daily Christian Advocate* was published in Nashville; the *Christian Advocate* was published in New Orleans. In the 1870s the *Daily Christian Advocate* was published in Louisville. The *Southern Christian Advocate* served the South Carolina, Georgia, and Florida conferences. Through the years, other places of publications of this official Methodist publication have been Baltimore, Atlanta, Chattanooga, Memphis, Asheville, Birmingham, and Oklahoma City.

Christian Almanac

See entry: *Family Christian Almanac, The.*

Christian Library, A Weekly Republication of the Most Popular Religious Works

By various authors

These volumes were published by Thomas George in New York. *The Twentieth Annual Report of the American Tract Society*, printed at the Society's House, Opposite the City-Hall, No. 150 Nassau-Street, New York by Daniel Fanshaw, 1845, page 209, describes the *Christian Library* as "…neatly and uniformly bound and lettered, in firm sheep, adapted to permanent use… The set embraces 19,530 pages…" Amos Hitchcock writes that he sold a set of 45 volumes for $20.

Christian Mirror

Amos received this publication on August 12, 1847. Affiliated with the Congregational Church, this newspaper was published in Portland, Maine between 1822 and 1899.

Dairyman's Daughter, An Authentic Narrative

By Rev. Legh Richmond

Published by the American Tract Society, New York. Christian morality tale geared towards children.

Dayspring

An illustrated, Christian, monthly newspaper published by the American Board of Commissioners for Foreign Missions.

Debates of Conscience with a Distiller, a Wholesale Dealer, and a Retailer

By Herman Humphrey

This work was probably a pamphlet or tract. It is included in a later compilation called *Publications of the American Tract Society*.

Discourse on Meekness and Quietness of Spirit, A

By Matthew Henry

Book published by the American Tract Society.

Dying Thoughts of the Reverend Richard Baxter

By Richard Baxter

Book published by the American Tract Society. Perhaps published in more than one volume.

Evangelical Family Library, The

Set of fifteen volumes published by the American Tract Society. Titles included in this set: *Volume 1: The Rise and Progress of Religion in the Soul* by **Doddridge**; *Volume 2: Practical View of the Prevailing Religious System* by **Wilberforce**; *Volume 3: A Treatise on Religious Affections* by **Edwards**; *Volume 4: The Pilgrim's Progress* by **Bunyan**; *Volume 5: The Saint's Everlasting Rest* by **Baxter**; *Volume 6: A Call to the Unconverted to Turn and Live* by **Baxter**; *Volume 7: Life of the Reverend David Brainerd* by **Edwards**; *Volume 8: A Memoir of Reverend Henry Martyn* by **Sargent**; *Volume 9: An Alarm to Unconverted Sinners* by **Alleine**; *Volume 10: Persuasives to Early Piety*; *Volume 11: A Guide for Young Disciples of the Holy Savior*; *Volume 13: Practical Thoughts, Thoughts on Popery*; *Volume 14: Infidelity* and other works by various authors; *Volume 15: Memoir of James Brainerd Taylor*.

Amos sold the set of 15 volumes for $6.50. He also sold the volumes separately.

Family Christian Almanac, The

Published by the American Tract Society

Almanac published for the American Tract Society. Truly a utilitarian publication. Versions were published for several geographical regions showing tides, moon phases, sunrises and sunsets for each particular region. They were also chock full of inspirational poems, thoughts, aphorisms, and suggestions for Christian living such as "A little wrong done to another is a great wrong done to ourselves." From *The Family Christian Almanac*, 1845.

Fool's Pence, The
Published by the American Tract Society. This smaller work is included in a volume with several other short works. Perhaps it was also sold separately as a pamphlet or tract.

Fountain of Life, Or a Display of Christ in His Essential and Mediatorial Glory
By John Flavel
Book published by the American Tract Society.

H. on Meekness
Amos Hitchcock's shorthand for *A Discourse on Meekness and Quietness of Spirit*
See entry: *Discourse on Meekness and Quietness of Spirit, A.*

Harlan Page
See entry: *Memoir of Harlan Page or the Power of Prayer and Personal Effort for the Souls.*

Highway to Your Immortality: A Comparative Religious Study of Eternal Life
By H. G. Liem
Book.

History of the Reformation of the Sixteenth Century
By J. H. (Jean Henri) Merle D'Aubigne
Published by the American Tract Society. A comprehensive history of the Protestant Reformation in five volumes. Author, D'Aubigne, was a Swiss theologian. He first published this five-volume work in French. The first volume was completed in 1835 and the last in 1853. Obviously, translation into English began before all of the volumes were finished. Amos Hitchcock was already selling the first volume or volumes in the United States during his sojourn in East Tennessee from 1844-1847. Several of his customers commented on the excellence of the work.
By D'Aubigne's time, the political and intellectual significance of the Reformation was recognized, but the religious significance had been virtually forgotten or ignored. He wrote this work, he said, because "I want this history to be truly Christian and to give a proper impulse to the religious spirit."

D'Aubigne also wrote an eight-volume work, *The History of the Reformation in Europe in the Time of Calvin*, published between 1863-1878.

It was said that D'Aubigne's works were the most widely read and circulated books on church history. No doubt Colporteur Amos Hitchcock and others like him contributed to this wide circulation.

Intemperance

Amos Hitchcock's shorthand for *Six Sermons on the Nature, Occasions, Signs, Evils and Remedy of Intemperance*.

See entry: *Six Sermons on the Nature, Occasions, Signs, Evils and Remedy of Intemperance*.

Keeping the Heart

By John Flavel

See entry: *Saint Indeed or the Great Work of a Christian Opened and Pressed, A*.

Life of the Reverend David Brainerd, The

By Edwards

Volume 7 of *The Evangelical Family Library*.

See entry: *Evangelical Family Library*.

Memoirs of Harlan Page or the Power of Prayer and Personal Effort for the Souls of Individuals

By William A. Hallock

Book published by the American Tract Society.

Memoirs of Mrs. Graham

Amos Hitchcock's shorthand for the book *The Power of Faith Exemplified in the Life and Writings of the Late Mrs. Isabella Graham*.

See entry: *Power of Faith Exemplified in the Life and Writings of the Late Mrs. Isabella Graham, The*.

Messenger, The

Amos Hitchcock's shorthand for the *American Messenger*.

See Entry: *American Messenger, The*.

Method of Grace in the Holy Spirit's Applying to the Souls of Men the Eternal Redemption Contrived by the Father and Accomplished by the Son

By John Flavel

Book published by the American Tract Society. Sequel to Flavel's *The Fountain of Life*.

Persuasives to Early Piety, Interspersed with Suitable Prayers

By J. G. (John Gregory) Pike

Book published by the American Tract Society.

Pilgrim's Progress

By John Bunyan

This allegorical Christian classic was Volume 4 of *The Evangelical Family Library*.

Power of Faith Exemplified in the Life and Writings of the Late Mrs. Isabella Graham, The

By Isabella Graham

Book published by the American Tract Society.

Religion and Eternal Life or Irreligion and Perpetual Ruin, the Only Alternative to Mankind

By John Gregory Pike

Book published by the American Tract Society.

Rise and Progress of Religion in the Soul, The

By Philip Doddridge

A book published by The American Tract Society. It was also sold as Volume I in the *Evangelical Family Library* Set. "Illustrated in a Course of Serious and Practical Addresses Suited to Persons of Every Character and Circumstance, with A Devout Meditation or Prayer Subjoined to Each Chapter."

Saint Indeed or the Great Work of a Christian Opened and Pressed, A

By John Flavel

Such a classic Christian book that it has gone through many reprints. The American Tract Society published it under the name *Treatise on Keeping the Heart* and, in 1830, as *Keeping the Heart; the Saint Indeed*. Other editions: 1826 by Joseph Martin; 1971 and 1972 by Sovereign Grace Publishers; 1998 by Christian Focus Publications, Ltd and Soli Deo Gloria.

Flavel was born in England around 1628 and died in 1691. An ordained Presbyterian minister during the reign of King James, he was persecuted for his evangelical beliefs and his non-conformity to the Church of England.

Saint's Everlasting Rest, The
By Reverend Richard Baxter
Volume 5 of *The Evangelical Family Library*.

Scripture Biography for the Young with Critical Illustrations and Practical Remarks
By Reverend T. H. Gallaudet.
A 7-volumed set published by the American Tract Society. Biblical biographies. The *Scripture Biography* was included as the first seven volumes of a 40-volumed collection entitled the *Youth's Christian Library*. Current American Tract Society archivist, Kristin Mitrisin, explained that the *Scripture Biography* collection was begun and compiled by Gallaudet. After he died, Gallaudet's material was organized and edited by Thomas Hooker. Amos Hitchcock sold a set for $2.20. See Illustration: page 8.

Scripture Promises or the Christian's Inheritance
By Samuel Clark D.D.
Book published by the American Tract Society.

Sermons
Amos Hitchcock's shorthand for *Six Sermons on the Nature, Occasions, Signs, Evils and Remedy of Intemperance*.
See entry: Six Sermons on the Nature, Occasions, Signs, Evils and Remedy of Intemperance.

Sinner's Prayer, The
A tract, probably published by the American Tract Society.

Six Sermons on the Nature, Occasions, Signs, Evils and Remedy of Intemperance
By Lyman Beecher
Book published by the American Tract Society, New York. The author, a Presbyterian and Congregationalist minister, helped found the Bible Society in

Lyman Beecher, c. 1850. Courtesy of The Harriet Beecher Stowe Center.

1816 and was the first president of Lane Theological Seminary. He was also the father of Harriet Beecher Stowe, the author of *Uncle Tom's Cabin.*

Spirit of Popery: An Exposure of Its Origin, Character, and Results in Letters from a Father to His Children, The
By not stated
Book published by the American Tract Society in New York. Another edition was published by the Religious Tract Society in London.

Springfield Gazette
Published in Springfield, Massachusetts, Amos Hitchcock mailed these to some of his acquaintances.

Treatise on Keeping the Heart
See entry: *A Saint Indeed or the Great Work of a Christian Opened and Pressed.*

Village in the Mountains, The
By Anonymous
Book published by the American Tract Society. Included in one volume with two other works. Perhaps also published separately as a tract.

Youth's Christian Library
See entry: *Scripture Biography for the Young with Critical Illustrations and Practical Remarks.*

Youth's Companion
An illustrated periodical newspaper for young people featuring wholesome stories and poems and Christian moral tales. "A family paper, devoted to piety, morality, brotherly love – no sectarianism, no controversy." In the 1840s it was published by Nathaniel Willis, who also published the *Boston Recorder,* at 11 Cornhill, Boston, Massachusetts, right down the street from the American Tract Society, which was located at 28 Cornhill.

Youth's Dayspring
An illustrated, Christian, monthly magazine for young people, published by the American Board of Commissioners for Foreign Missions.

Appendix 2: Resources

Excellent resources for researchers.

1. The American Tract Society
   1624 North First Street, Garland, Texas 75046-2008
   www.atstracts.org

2. W. E. B. Du Bois Library
   University of Massachusetts
   154 Hicks Way
   Amherst, Massachusetts 01003-9275
   www. library.umass.edu

3. City of Knoxville website
   City of Knoxville Mayors page
   www.ci.knoxville.tn.us/mayor/mayors.asp as of February 20, 2006

   This surprising source has a list of the mayors of Knoxville, beginning in 1816 through present day. Several of the mayors are included in Amos Hitchcock's journal: James Park, Willaby B. Ramsey, M. M. Gaines, Joseph King, George White, and James H. Cowan.

4. Advanced Book Exchange website
   A wonderful resource for hard-to-find and out-of-print books. Over 13,500 booksellers list millions of titles.
   www.abebooks.com

References

1. *American Tract Society, The*
   Promotional pamphlets and website.
   1624 North First Street, Garland, Texas 75046-2008
   www.atstracts.org

2. *Historical Celebration of the Town of Brimfield, Hampden County, Massachusetts* Published by Vote of the Town, 1879.

3. Morse, Jason. *Annals of the Church in Brimfield.* Springfield, Massachusetts 1856.

4. Nord, David Paul. "Religious Reading and Readers in Antebellum America." *Journal of the Early Republic.* Summer 1995, Vol. 15, No. 2. Society for Historians of the Early American Republic: Purdue University.

5. Nord, David Paul. "Systematic Benevolence: Religious Publishing and the Marketplace in Early Nineteenth-Century America" *Communication and Change in American Religious History.* Edited by Leonard I. Sweet. William B. Eerdmans Publishing Company, Grand Rapids, Michigan.

6. Smith, Jonathan Kennon Thompson, transcriber. *Death Notices from the Christian Advocate, Nashville, Tennessee 1874-1876.* Transcription copyright: Jonathan K. T. Smith, 2000. Found at: www.TNGenWeb.org.

7. Smith, Jonathan Kennon Thompson, transcriber. *Genealogical Abstracts from Recorded Deaths, the Nashville Christian Advocate, 1887-1899.* 2002. Found at: www.TNGenWeb.org.

8. *Southern Christian Advocate Marriage Notices, 1867-1878* Published by the Methodist Conferences. Found at: www.FamilyMarriageRecords.com.

9. Thompson, Lawrance. *The Printing and Publishing Activities of the American Tract Society from 1825 to 1850*. Bibliographical Society of America. 1941.

10. *Twenty-first Annual Report of the American Tract Society*. Presented at New York, May 13, 1846.

11. United States Federal Census 1860, Alabama, Talladega County.

12. United States Federal Census 1870, Alabama, Talladega County.

13. *Vital Records of Brimfield Massachusetts to the Year 1850*. The New England Historic Genealogical Society. 1931.

14. United States Federal Census 1880, Alabama, Talladega County, Fayetteville.

15. American Antiquarian Society. Website: http://www.americanantiquarian.org/ATS.htm. Found January 2003.

INDEX

Primarily, only people, places, organizations, and publications are indexed. While there are some exceptions, most "things" are not indexed. For example, things such as postage, contributions, saddles, and most other common nouns are not indexed.

Index Key:

1. *Multiple entries on the same page.*

    Even if a word appears on a page more than once, there will only be one index entry for that word per page. For example, the index indicates that "Wm. H. Smith" is found on page 22. "Wm. H. Smith" is found three times on page 22. So, check the page's entire text for multiple entries on each page referenced.

2. *People Names.*

    A. Titles.

    i. When a person's title and name are given, it is listed in parentheses after the given name. For example, Dr. J. M. Hammer is indexed: Hammer, J. M. (Dr.).

    ii. Titles not in parentheses means that only the title is recorded with the surname name, no first name is given. For example, Dr. Hammer is indexed: Hammer, Dr.

    B. Asterisks.

    i. *Names and/or page numbers, which are followed by one asterisk, are names and page numbers where the surname of the person is not actually given. However, other journal entries suggest or prove that this first name and surname belong together.

    ii. **Names which are followed by two asterisks, signify a name not clearly legible in the original journal, but clarified through other records, such as a U. S. Federal Census.

    iii. ***Amos Hitchcock records Louisville as being in Knox County. However, Louisville is in Blount County. Blount County was formed in 1795 from Knox County.

3. *Place Names.*

    A. When a county, town, or other place, such as a Post Office, is associated with a state, they are indexed under that state. When a town is associated with a county it is indexed under the state and then the county.

    B. When Amos doesn't associate a town or place with a county or state, the town or place is listed under its name only, even if the county or state is common knowledge for today's readers.

    C. County and state boundaries change. Just because Amos listed a town or place in a certain county doesn't necessarily mean that it is in that county today. Place names are indexed as Amos designated.

4. *Publications.*

    Publications mentioned by Amos Hitchcock are not indexed according to their appearance in the text but are arranged alphabetically by title in "Appendix 1," which is indexed.

A. T. S....See: American Tract Society

Academia...See: Tennessee Knox County, Academia

Ackley, J....58, 163

Adams
Johnson (Reverend)...64, 81, 106, 109

Advanced Book Exchange...197

Aikman, [Also listed as Mr., T. H., Tho. A., Brother Aikman,T. H. A., "my associate In Roane County" but refers to the same person]
Thomas H....4, 7, 15, 18, 19, 20, 21, 22, 23, 24, 26, 27, 28, 29, 30, 88, 90, 118, 119, 123, 126, 128, 170, 171

Alabama...180, 182, 183, 200
<u>Talladega County</u>...180, 182, 183, 200
Childersburg...180, 183
Fayetteville...180, 183, 200

Alarm to Unconverted Sinners in a Serious Treatise on Conversion, An...Publication. See Appendix 1.

Alleine, Joseph [When referring to Alleine's publications, Amos usually wrote "Alleine."]...36, 187, 190

American...v

American Antiquarian Society...200

American Bible Society [See Also: Bible Society]...74, 162

American Board of Commissioners for Foreign Missions...190, 195

American Education Society...61, 154

American Messenger...Publication. See: Appendix 1.

American Revolution...179

American Sunday School Journal...Publication. See: Appendix 1.

American Tract Society [Also written: A.T.S.; A.T. Society; the Society; Tract Society]...i, iii, iv, 3, 4, 5, 6, 7, 8, 11, 12, 13, 14, 15, 17, 18, 20, 21, 22, 23, 26, 28, 30, 31, 33, 37, 38, 41, 43, 44, 45, 47, 52, 53, 56, 57, 59, 60, 61, 62, 63, 67, 68, 69, 70, 71, 72, 75 87, 88, 90, 92, 93, 94, 96, 98, 102, 103, 104, 111, 114, 115, 116, 117, 118, 120, 122, 125, 127, 129, 133, 135, 138, 140, 143, 147, 148, 149, 150, 154, 155, 157, 158, 159, 160, 161, 163, 164, 166, 179, 180, 181, 187, 188, 189, 190, 191, 192, 193, 194, 195, 197, 199, 200

American Tract Society of Boston...6

Amos...See: Hitchcock, Amos.

Anderson, [Also See: Craig, Pope & Anderson]
Isaac (Reverend-D. D.)...72, 83, 108, 158
James (Colonel)...82, 108

Anderson County...See: Tennessee, Anderson County

Anderson Woods...80, 109

Andes,
John 81, 109

Annals of the Church in Brimfield...183, 199

Anxious Inquirer After Salvation, The...Publication. See: Appendix 1.

Armstrong,
Addison...79, 109
Robert...79, 109

Ashevill[e]...15, 89, 189

Athens...See: Georgia, Athens

B. Life...Publication. See: Appendix 1.

B.S. Life...Publication. See: Appendix 1.

Backslider: Or an Enquiry into the Nature, Symptoms and Effects, The...Publication. See: Appendix 1.

Baily, [Possibly Boily], John...80, 109

Bank [Also See: Savings Bank; Bank of America; Bank of Cape Fear]...15, 89

Bank of America...15, 89

Bank of Cape Fear...15, 89

Baptist...18, 40, 64, 70, 106, 122, 134, 157, 188

Barber,
Lucinda...180

Bayless,
Reese (Esquire)...79, 109

Baxter, Rev. [When referring to Baxter's publications, Amos usually wrote "Baxter."]
Richard...5, 19, 20, 30, 33, 36, 38, 39, 41, 42, 46, 47, 48, 52, 58, 88, 190, 194

Beaver Dam...18, 92

Beecher,
Lyman...33, 52, 54, 194

Beecher Stowe
Harriet...195

Bell, [Also See: Jansen & Bell.]
Esquire...79, 109

Bible Society [Also See: American Bible Society]...14, 30, 175, 194

Bibliographical Society of America...200
Billen,
    Rev. William...37, 132
Birchfield,
    Robert...80, 109
Birdwell,
    Doctor...56, 64, 106
Bishop,
    Deacon...61, 155
Black,
    James...62, 81, 83, 106, 108, 109
Black/s (people) [Also See: Coloured.]... 35, 41, 57, 66, 131, 135, 146, 154
Blair,
    Hugh...65, 69, 80, 109, 156
    James (Reverend)...80, 109
    Robert...79, 109
Bledsoe,
    Giles S. (Mr.)...82, 108
Bliss,...181
    Aaron...70, 158, 181
    Isaac... 181
    Lucy Hitchcock...181
    Lucy H....57, 162, 163, 181
    Ruth C....58, 59, 162, 163, 181
    Ruth Hitchcock...181
    Samuel Hopkins...181
    Seth (Reverend)...7, 61, 62, 63, 64, 66, 67, 68, 69, 70, 71, 107, 148, 150, 157, 158, 159, 181

Blount County...See: Tennessee, Blount County.
Bogert,
    Esquire...80, 109
Bogle,
    Albert...81, 109
    Andrew...61, 73, 81, 83, 106, 107, 108, 109, 156
    Hugh...56, 68, 81, 83, 108, 109, 157, 166
    Joseph...81, 109
    Matthew (Colonel)...81, 109
Boily...See: Baily.
Boston... See: Massachusetts, Boston.
Boston Recorder... Publication. See: Appendix 1.
Bounds,
    Francis...79, 109
Bowman,
    John...82, 108
    Samuel...60, 82, 107, 108
Boyd,
    Campbell (Reverend)...81, 107, 109
    Thomas...63, 82, 106, 107, 108
Boyd's Creek...See: Tennessee, Sevier County, Boyd's Creek.
Boyd's Creek Church...36, 132
Brabson, John (Esquire)...80, 109
Brabson...See: Brabson & Toole.
Brabson & Toole...19, 58, 59, 118, 158, 160
Brainerd, David...188, 190, 192
Brewer,
    David...79, 109
Brig "Clint"...11, 12, 110, 179
Brigs,
    Mr....79, 109
Brimfield...See: Massachusetts, Brimfield.
Brock [Possibly" Bruck"]
    James...81, 109
Brooks,
    General Joseph A....79, 109
Brown,
    C. R....60, 154
Bruck...See: Brock.
Bryant,
    Gamaliel (Reverend)...81, 109
Bryon,
    W. M. (Esquire)...80, 109
    William (Esquire)...67, 156
Bunker Hill...74, 163
Bunyan, John...190, 193
Burke,
    Joseph...180, 182
    Ellen Hitchcock [See: Hitchcock, Ellen]
Burns...68
    Widow...81, 109
Butler,

    Horatio...56, 102
Cade's Cove...See: Tennessee, Blount County, Cade's Cove.
Caldwell
    John (Esquire)...80, 109
Caler [Possibly "Cales"],
    Eli...81, 109
Cales...See: Caler.
Call to the Unconverted to Turn and Live, A... Publication. See: Appendix 1.
Callahan,
    John C....60, 154
Campbell,
    James (Captain)...82, 108
    John ...80, 109
    John (Esquire)...32, 82, 100, 108
    Mrs. J....35, 100
    Mrs. John...53, 100
Campbell's Station...See: Tennessee, Knox County, Campbell's Station.
Cannon,
    John...81, 109
    William...81, 109
Cape Fear, Bank of...15, 89
Carter
    Amos...79, 109
    Martin B....79, 109
Cause and Cure of Infidelity, Including a Notice of the Author's Unbelief and the

Means of His Rescue,
The*...Publication. See: Appendix 1.*
Census*...See: "United States Federal Census..."*
Childers,
  Mr....79, 109
Childersburg*...See: Alabama, Talladega County, Childersburg.*
Children's Tracts*... Publication. See: Appendix 1.*
Childs,
  David...79, 109
Christian Advocate*... Publication. See: Appendix 1.*
Christian Almanac*... Publication. See: Appendix 1.*
Christian Focus Publications, Ltd 193
Christian Library, A Weekly Republication of the Most Popular Religious Works*... Publication. See: Appendix 1.*
Christian Mirror*... Publication. See: Appendix 1.*
Church Grove*...See: Tennessee, Knox County, Church Grove.*
Church of England*...194*
Clark, Samuel*...194*
Clark W. Bryan Company*...183*
Clinton*...See: Tennessee, Anderson County, Clinton.*
Cockran,
  Mr...12, 112
Coldwell*...See: Caldwell.*
College*...See: Tusculum College.*
Collen*...See: Cullen.*
Colliers,
  Wd. [Widow]...80, 109
Colored*...See: Coloured. Also see: Blacks.*
Coloured *(people) [Also See: Blacks]...24, 126*
Columbia*...See: Tennessee, Blount County, Collumbia.*
Communication and Change in American Religious History *...199*
Compton,
  Colonel...43, 137, 201
  J. S. (Colonel)...72, 159, 201
  John S. (Colonel)...83, 108, 201
Conatser,
  Andrew (Reverend) ...80, 109
Concord*...26, 93*
Connecticut, New Haven*...179, 182*
Cook,
  R. S. (Reverend)... 57, 58, 59, 162
Congregational *...179, 181, 188, 189, 194*
Copeland,
  Andrew C....79, 109
Coram *[Possibly "Cannon"],*
  Reverend John S....73, 82, 108, 156
Cornhill [Street]*...5, 61, 62, 63, 64, 66, 68, 69, 70, 107, 148, 150, 157, 159, 195*
Cote,
  Thomas (Esquire)...80, 109
Cowan*, [Also See: Cowan and Dickinson.]...112, 114, 175*
  Captain...30
  J. H....32, 175
  James Dickinson ...83, 108
  James (Esquire)... 72, 158
  James H. (Esquire) ...33, 59, 82, 89, 108, 162, 197
  Lucinda F---te...83, 108
  Margaret...83, 108
  Mary...83, 108
  Mr....4, 13, 15, 19, 88, 115
  Nancy Estabrook ...83, 108
  Percy** Dickinson ...83, 108
  Susan Perriman [Also see: Perriman] ...83, 108
Cowan and Dickinson *...7, 14, 26, 28, 45, 46, 88, 104, 114, 116, 118, 166*
Craig*, [Also See: Craig, Pope, and Anderson.]*
  Colonel...80, 109
  John S. (Reverend) ...62, 83, 106, 107, 108
Craig, Pope, and Anderson*...59, 162*
Creswell,
  William...32
  William E....65, 72, 81, 106, 109, 156
Crispin,
  Esquire...79, 109
Cullen*, [Possibly "Collen"]*
  Archibald...80, 82, 108, 109
Cumming/s,
  Esquire...81, 109
  James (Reverend)...66, 81, 83, 108, 109,157
Cunningham*, [See Also: Dunn, Cunningham.]*
  Major...48, 140
  Major David...81, 109
D'Aubigne, Jean Henri Merle *[When referring to his publications, usually written simply "D'Aubigne"] ...191, 192*
Daguerreotype*...74, 163*
Dairyman's Daughter, An Authentic

Narrative...Publication. See: Appendix 1.
Dake,
    Henry (Reverend)...80, 109
Danish...187
Davis,
    Jeptha (Major)...80, 109
    Jessee (Esquire)...82, 108
    Morgan (Esquire)...80, 109
Dayspring...Publication. See: Appendix 1.
***Death Notices from the Christian Advocate**, Nashville, Tennessee, 1874-1876...183, 199*
Debates of Conscience with a Distiller, a Wholesale Dealer, and a Retailer...Publication. See: Appendix 1.
Derrick,
    Asa...80, 109
Dickinson, [Also see: Cowan and Dickinson.]
    Mr....59, 102
    Mrs....71, 158
Dickinson Cowan,
    James...83, 108
    Percy**...83, 108
Discourse on Meekness and Quietness of Spirit, A... Publication. See: Appendix 1.
Doddridge, Philip...44, 46, 47, 49, 190, 193
Dorlan...See: Doulan

Doulon [Possibly "Dorlan"],
    Archibald...79, 109
Drennins,
    Mrs...53, 100
Duggen,
    Wilson (Colonel)...80, 109
Dunn,
    Cunningham...81, 109
    Levi (Mr.)...81, 109
Dutch...187
Dying Thoughts of the Reverend Richard Baxter...Publication. See: Appendix 1.
East Tennessee...See: Tennessee, East Tennessee.
East Tennessee University...65, 157
Eastman,
    O. (Reverend)...58, 62, 71, 107, 159, 163
Edmundson,
    Baxter [or Beseter]...79, 109
Edward [Associated with Mrs. Whitney.]...67, 154
Edwards,...190, 192
    James (Reverend)...80, 109
Ellijoy...See: Tennessee, Blount County, Ellijoy.
Ellis,
    James...81, 109
    Wm. (Reverend)...80, 109
Emily [From other references or associations this is probably Emily Porter.]...65, 149
England...194
English...187, 188, 199
Episcopal...189
Episcopalian...64, 106
Ernest,
    Daniel...80, 109
    Frederick (Reverend)...81, 109
Estabrook, [Also See: Cowan, Nancy Estabrook.]
    Joseph (President)...65, 72, 157, 159
    Joseph (M. A.)...82, 108
Eton,
    Wd. [Widow]...60, 154
Evangelical and Family Library The... Publication. See: Appendix 1.
Family Christian Almanac, The... Publication. See: Appendix 1.
Fayetteville...See: Alabama, Talladega County, Fayetteville.
Female Tract Society...13, 17, 46, 115, 122, 139
Fer. Evangelical Society...73, 162
Ferel...See: Ford
Flavel, John...30, 34, 191, 192, 193
Fool's Pence, The... Publication. See: Appendix 1.
Ford, [Possibly "Ferel"] Wm (Dr.)....80, 109
Fountain of Life, Or a Display of Christ in His Essential and Mediatorial Glory... Publication. See: Appendix 1.
French...187
Friends of the Bible...36, 129
Fuller, Andrew...188
Gaines,
    M. M....15, 89, 197
Gallaher,
    Geo....80, 109
Gallaudet, Rev. T. H....8, 17, 194
Gamble,
    Alexander (Esquire)...67, 81, 109, 156
Gant, [Possibly "Gout"] Parker...80, 109
Gap Creek...See: Tennessee, Knox County, Gap Creek.
Garvin [Possibly "Gorin"] Mrs....82, 108
***Genealogical Abstracts from Recorded Deaths, the Nashville Christian Advocate, 1887-1899*...183, 199
Gentry,
    Aaron...79, 109
Georgia...iv, 11, 12, 14, 179, 189
    Athens...12, 14, 112,

114
Griffin...11, 12, 15, 92, 110, 112
Macon...11, 12, 110, 112
Marietta...11, 12, 112
Savannah...iv, 11, 12, 13, 110, 116, 179
German [publications]...15, 27, 90, 95, 168, 187
Gibbs,
Jacob...79, 109
Wm....79, 109
Gist, [Also See: Porter, Gist & Company.]
Angela (Mrs.)...30, 106
Angelina F (Mrs.)...61, 65, 82, 106, 108, 156
Joshua...67, 80, 109, 156
Mimsa...42*, 82, 100, 106, 108
Mrs...51, .53, 100
Spencer C.(Lieutenant) [Also written: Lieu. S. C. Gist, Lieu. S. C. Gist, U.S.N.]...70, 72, 82, 108, 159, 160
St. Paul...42*, 60, 82, 100, 106, 108
Ted...42*, 100
Gorin...See: Garvin.
Graham, Mrs.
Isabella...30, 192, 193
Graves [Possibly "Greves"]
Geo. (Esquire)...79, 109
William (Reverend)...83, 108
Great Bend...23, 125
Green County...See: Tennessee, Green County.
Greene,
James H....80, 109
Greenville...See: Tennessee, Green County, Greenville.
Greves [See: Graves]
Griffin...See: Georgia, Griffin.
Groner [Possibly "Grover"],
Jessee...79, 109
Grover...See: Groner
H. On Meekness... Publication. See: Appendix 1.
Hallock, William A....192
Hampden County...See Massachusetts, Hampden, County
Hammer,...201
Jonathan M. (Dr.) [Also written: Dr. J. M. Hammer]...64, 71, 82, 106, 108, 156, 159, 201
Samuel B....55, 56, 73, 80, 102, 109, 145, 156
Hardin*...157
George...72, 73, 82, 108, 156, 158
Gibson...80, 109
John...80, 109
Hardy...
J. F. E....15, 89
Harlan Page... Publication. See: Appendix 1.
Hart,
Mr....81, 109
Harvey...6, 7
Harris,
Mr....12, 112
Hawck...See: Houck.
Hauk...See Houck.
Hawn...See Hown.
Henderson,
George...80, 109
Henderson & Toomey...58, 102
Henry,...6, 7, 5, 58, 102
James...83, 108
Jane...83, 108
John...57, 72, 73, 146, 156
John Sr....32, 60, 64, 65, 67, 73, 83, 106, 107, 108, 156, 157
Margaret Elizabeth...83, 108
Margaret (Miss)...58, 102
Matthew...190
Rachel...83, 108
Samuel...60, 83, 106, 108
Wm. Jasper...83, 108
Henry's Cross Road...See: Tennessee, Sevier County, Henry's Cross Road.
Highway to Your Immortality: A Comparative Religious Study of Eternal Life... Publication. See: Appendix 1.
Hill,
Green...80, 109
Widow...80, 109
Hillsman,...20
Esquire...20, 29, 118, 128
John (Esquire)...62, 64, 73, 82, 106, 107, 108, 156
Joseph...23, 83, 108, 172
Historical Celebration of the Town of Brimfield, Hampden County, Massachusetts...183, 199
History of the Reformation of the Sixteenth Century... Publication. See: Appendix 1.
Hitchcock/s...i, 179, 180
Abigail...182
Abner...59, 60, 63, 74, 75, 154, 155, 162, 165, 180
Alice C....180, 182
Alvin P....180, 182
Amos [Also written: "Amos" or "Mr. Hitchcock."]...iii, iv, v, 3, 4, 5, 6, 7, 11, 15, 20, 23, 87, 89,

91, 92, 93, 95, 96, 99, 105, 111, 113, 115, 117, 119, 149, 151, 159, 161, 165, 167, 168, 170, 178, 179, 180, 181, 182, 187, 188, 189, 191, 192, 194, 195, 197, 201

Artemas...181

Ellen F. [Also See: Burke, Ellen Hitchcock.]...180, 182

Elizabeth Porter... [Also See: Porter, Elizabeth]...180, 182

Ira...179, 182

J. F....63, 154

Jane...See: Mullendore, Jane Elizabeth Hitchcock...83

John...179, 182

Joseph...179, 182

Lucinda Barber...[See: Barber, Lucinda.]

Lucy N [Also See: Bliss, Lucy]...180, 182,

Luke...179, 182

M....32, 100

Mother...68, 69, 70, 155, 181

Mr....Same person as Amos.

Nathaniel...179, 182

Patience Stebbins... 179, 182

Persis [Same person as Persis Newell. Also see: "Hitchcock, Mother."] ...179, 182

Percy...Same person as Persis Hitchcock.

Ruth...[Also: See Bliss, Ruth Hitchcock.] 179, 181, 182

S....37, 100, 150

Sally...180, 181

Sarah...58, 59, 62, 74, 87, 151, 154, 162, 163, 180, 181

Sarah (Miss)...68, 70, 148, 157

Thomas...180, 182

William....64, 68, 154, 156, 181

Hitchcock Mullendore,
Jane Elizabeth...See: Mullendore, Jane Elizabeth Hitchcock.

Hodge,
Reverend Wm.....80, 109

Homer [Possibly "Homes"],
Linus...68, 70, 75, 155, 165
S....65, 155

Homes...See: Homer.

Hotel Maryville...58, 102

Houck [Possibly "Hauk," "Hawck," "Houk."]
Adam...80, 109
Jordan...71, 80, 109, 156

Houk...[See: Houck.]

Howard,
John (Major)...80, 109

Hown [Possibly "Hawn"],
Andrew L....80, 109

Hubbard,
N. S....59, 60, 69, 74, 155, 163
S...59, 60, 69, 74, 155, 163

Huffaker,
Christian [?] (Reverend)...80, 109
Henry (Esquire)...32, 37, 80, 100, 109, 166
Jacob (Reverend)...80, 109
James (Reverend)...71, 82, 108, 159
James N. S. (Reverend)...71, 158
Wesley (Esquire)...59, 64, 68, 82, 106, 107, 108, 157

Humphrey,
Herman...190

Huskey,
Wm....80, 109

Indian...40, 100

Indiana University...i, 187

Intemperance... Publication. See: Appendix 1.

Irish...68, 155

Italian...187

James, Rev. John Angell...188

Jansen & Bell...iii, 6, 88

Jernigan...See: Jornigan.

Johnson,
Deacon...23, 125
Elijah (Deacon)...69, 83, 108, 156
Esquire...38, 82, 108, 133, 187
Harvey [See Henry]
Henry [Possibly "Harvey"]...80, 109
J. (Esquire)...80, 109
Jonathan...80, 109

Jones,
Widow...80, 109

Jonesborough...See: Tennessee, East Tennessee, Jonesborough

Jornagin [Possibly "Jernigan"],
John (Esquire)...64, 72, 82, 106, 108, 156

Journal of the Early Republic...199

Keeping the Heart... Publication. See: Appendix 1.

Keith,
Andrew...79, 109

Kennear...See: Rennear

Kennedy, Walter...80, 109

Kimbrough,
Isaac (Reverend)...81, 109
Robert (Reverend) ...62, 79, 106, 109

Kindles, [be Rindles]
John...81, 109

King,
John T....14, 15, 16, 116
Joseph (Esquire)...83, 108, 197

King James...194

Kingsbury...See: New

York, Kingsbury
Kingston...17, 118
Knob District...44, 137
Knox County...See:
   Tennessee, Knox County
Knoxville...See:
   Tennessee, Knox County,
   Knoxville
Knoxville Register
   ...Publication. See:
   Appendix 1.
Ladd,
   Nelson...80, 109
Lamb,
   Mr....59, 102
Lane Theological
   Seminary...195
Lawson,
   Colonel...80, 109
Layman [Possibly
   "Loymen."]
   Asa...80, 109
   Widow...80, 109
   C---n...80, 109
Lee,
   Preston...79, 109
Legg,
   Mr...12, 112
Leyman...See: Layman
Lenning,
   Teresa Ann...83, 108
Lenox...74, 163
Liem, H. G....191
Life of the Reverend
   David Brainerd...
   Publication. See:
   Appendix 1.
Lithgo,
   James [Possibly
   "Lethgo"]
   ...80, 109
Little Pigeon Sabbath
   School...67, 157
***Louisville**...See:
   Tennessee, Knox County,
   Louisville. Some original
   entries look distinctly like
   "Loveville."
Love [Also See: Low]
   Samuel H....79, 109
Loveday,
   Geo....80, 109
Lovelace,
   Wm....79, 109
Low [Possibly "Love"]
   Lawson...80, 109
Lowe [Possibly "Love"],
   Samuel (Major)...80,
   109
Loymen...See: Layman
Lyman,
   Mrs....60, 154
Lyon,
   Thomas (Master)...12,
   110
Mabery,
   Colonel Geo...80, 109
Macon...See: Georgia,
   Macon
Malcom,
   Widow...80, 109
Maria* [Other references
   suggest this is Maria
   Porter]...8, 65, 67, 89,
   149, 180
Marietta...See: Georgia,
   Marietta
Martin, Joseph...193
Marx Nyquist,
   Mary...i
Maryville...See:
   Tennessee, Blount
   County, Maryville
Massachusetts [Also see:
   University of
   Massachusetts]...i, iv, 3,
   4, 11, 12, 13, 20, 57,
   58, 59, 61, 62, 66, 68,
   69, 70, 74, 100, 150,
   157, 158, 162, 179,
   181, 182, 183, 195,
   197, 199, 200
   Amherst...197
   Boston...4, 5, 8, 59,
   61, 62, 63, 64, 65,
   66, 67, 68, 69, 70,
   71, 72, 74, 98, 107,
   148, 150, 157, 158,
   159, 161, 163, 181,
   188, 195
   Brimfield...iv, 3, 4, 11,
   12, 13, 20, 26, 58,
   59, 69, 92, 93, 102,
   154, 155, 157, 162,
   163, 179, 179, 180,
   181, 182, 183, 199,
   200
   Hampden County...iv,
   3, 179, 183, 199
   Holland...68, 157
   Springfield [Also see:
   Springfield Gazette]
   ...67, 68, 74, 75,
   56, 157, 163, 179,
   82, 183, 195, 199
   Warren...57, 58, 61,
   63, 70, 74, 150, 158,
   162, 181
Mathes,
   Archibald A.
   (Reverend)...80, 109
Maver,
   Mrs...12, 110
Maynard,
   Horace (Esquire)...82,
   108
McBath [Or McBoth],
   Robert (Esquire)...79,
   109
McCampbell,
   Isaac...79, 109
McCloud,
   Levi...22, 116, 118
   Levi (Esquire)...79,
   109
McCroskey,
   D....68, 69, 70, 155,
   157
   David...60, 64, 65, 69,
   71, 82, 106, 108,
   157, 158
   Eliza...82, 108
   Oscar...82, 108
McGilvray,
   D. F....62, 154
McInnis,
   Reverend Mr....83,
   108
McIntosh,
   Melinda...i
McKinley,
   Samuel...79, 109
McLain [Or: McLoin],
   James...79, 109
McMillen,
   Gaines...79, 109
   John...79, 109
McMullen,
   Mr....18
   R. B. (Reverend)... 71,

82, 108, 158

Reverend Mr....17, 46, 122, 139

Mecklenberg See: Tennessee, Mecklenberg

Meek,
Joseph (Esquire)...iv, 64, 68, 69, 73, 82, 107, 108, 155, 156, 157

Memoirs of Harlan Page of the Power of Prayer and Personal Effort for the Souls of Individuals ... Publication. See: Appendix 1.

Memoirs of Mrs. Graham ...Publication. See: Appendix 1.

Messenger, The... Publication. See: Appendix 1.

Method of Grace in the Holy Spirit's Applying to the Souls of Men the Eternal Redemption Contrived by the Father and Accomplished by the Son...Publication. See: Appendix 1.

Methodist...29, 55, 128, 145, 180, 189, 199

Michigan
Grand Rapids...199

Middle Creek...56, 102

Miller's Cove...58, 147

Mimsa...See: Gist, Mimsa

Mitrisin,

Kristin...i, 194

Montgomery,
Widow...81, 109
Wm. H.(Doctor)...79, 109

Moore,
Martin...61, 64, 107, 188
R. H....28, 93

Morris,
Wm. (Esquire)....80, 109

Morse,
Jason...183, 199

Moses
J. C....69, 105, 157
James (Esquire)...60, 107
James C. (Esquire) 66, 70, 82, 108, 156, 158

Moulton,
David...72, 151

Mullendore,
Abraham Lafayette ...82, 108
Esquire...48, 140
Elijah Lunidas...83, 108
J....154
Jane Elizabeth Hitchcock ...83, 108
John (Esquire)...60, 66, 67, 72, 82, 86, 104, 105, 106, 107, 108,157, 158
Mary Amanda...82, 108
Nancy Matilda...83, 108

Robert Bruce...83, 108
Susan Catherine...83, 108
William Wallace...82, 108

Muny,
John (Esquire)...79, 109

Murray,
Mr. and Mrs....25, 93

Myers,
Henry...81, 109
John...58, 67, 81, 102, 109, 156
Rev...46, 139

Mynatt,
Calvin...70, 156
Gordon (Reverend) ...62, 82, 106, 108
John (Esquire)... 60, 82, 107, 108
Joseph...79, 109
Martyn L. (Esquire) ...79, 109

Nances,
P....8, 89

Nashville...See: Tennessee, Nashville.

Nassau Street [See: New York, Nassau Street]

Nelson, [In journal, when referring to publications by David Nelson, Amos Hitchcock usually wrote "Nelson"]
David (Reverend or Dr.) ...5, 22, 25, 33, 36, 46, 124, 188

Nelson Tucker,
Shanna...i

New England...iv

New England Historic Genealogical Society, The...183, 200

New Orleans...18, 122, 189

New York...iii, iv, 4, 5, 8, 11, 12, 13, 15, 18, 19, 20, 21, 23, 25, 26, 37, 57, 58, 59, 60, 62, 67, 71, 72, 73, 92, 107, 111, 115, 116, 118, 157, 158, 159, 164, 166, 179, 189, 194, 195, 200
Kingsbury...45, 164
Nassau Street...iii, 5, 6, 23, 71, 88, 118, 158, 189

New York Religious Tract Society...4

Newell,
Persis...[Also See: Newell, Persis; Same person as Persis Hitchcock]...179, 182

Nichols,
John...81, 109

Nicholson,
Reverend John...80, 109

Nord,
David...i, 8, 187, 199

Nown [See Hown]

Norman,
Wilson J....79, 109

Nyquist,
Mary Marx...i

Ogle,
Wm. (Reverend)...80,

109
Oil of spike...30, 93
Page, Harlan...20, 52, 191, 192
Park,
    James...28, 99, 197
Pate,
    Samuel (Reverend)...41, 136
    Sam...80, 109
Patrick...56, 102
Partrige,
    Mr. and Mrs....67, 154
Pennimon [See: Perriman Cowan]
Perriman Cowan,
    Susan [Also see: Cowan, Susan Perriman]...83, 108
Persuasives to Early Piety, Interspersed with Suitable Prayers...Publication. See: Appendix 1.
Philadelphia...74, 163
Physiology...74, 163
Pickle,
    Jacob...80, 109
Pigeon River...49, 141
Pike, John Gregory [In journal, when referring to publications by J.G. Pike, Amos Hitchcock usually wrote "Pike."]...36, 193
Pilgrim's Progress...Publication. See: Appendix 1.
Poindexter,
    John A.....80, 109

Pope [Also see: Craig, Pope, and Anderson], Fielding (Reverend)...83, 108
Porter,...180
    Belinda (Miss)...82, 108, 180
    Elizabeth...67, 71, 157, 158, 180, 182
    Elizabeth (Miss)...82, 108
    Ellen (Miss)...82, 108
    Emily...See: Emily Gilbert...82, 108
    George...82, 108
    Hannah (Mrs.)...68, 82, 108, 156, 180
    J. C....60, 71, 72, 74, 106, 158, 163
    Jackson...82, 108
    James...67, 157
    James C....63, 65, 67, 71, 107, 108, 156
    James C. (Mr.)...60, 82, 107, 108
    Maria [Also See: Maria]...65, 67, 71, 72, 157, 158, 159, 180
    Maria (Miss)...82, 108
    Virginia (Miss)...82, 108
Porter, Gist, & Company...64, 106
Portugese...187
Power of Faith Exemplified in the Life and Writings of the Late Mrs. Isabella Graham, The...Publication. See: Appendix 1.
Preeders [religious sect]...34, 130
Presbyterian [Also See: Second Presbyterian Church]...194
Printing and Publishing Activities of the American Tract Society, The...200
Purdue University...199
Ramsey [Possibly "Remsey"],
    Francis A....82, 108
    J. M. (Dr.)...66, 156
    John M. A....66, 82, 108, 156
    Maragret E....82, 108
    Mary Ann...82, 108
    Willaby B....82, 108, 197
Rawhoof,
    Mr...79, 109
Reeder,
    Wm....79, 109
Religion and Eternal Life or Irreligion and Perpetual Ruin, the Only Alternative to Mankind...Publication. See: Appendix 1.
Religious Tract Society Of London...6, 194
Remsey [See: Ramsey]
Rennear [Possibly "Kennear"], Lewis (Esquire)...81, 109
Richmond, Rev. Legh...189
Rise and Progress of Religion in the Soul, The...Publication. See: Appendix 1.
Revival/s...20, 27, 122, 127
Reynolds,
    Wd. [Widow]...80, 109
Roane County...See: Tennessee, Roane County
Roberts,
    Andrew...79, 109
    Eli (Reverend)...64, 83, 106, 108
    John (Reverend)...82, 108
Rogers,
    Esquire...80, 109
    James (Doctor)...82, 108
    Marion W....81, 109
    Thomas (Colonel)...69, 157
    Thomas (Esquire)...63, 82, 106, 108
    Wm. (Doctor)...82, 108
    Wm. (Reverend)...23, 27, 172
Russell,
    Patterson...80, 109
Russum [Possibly "Russon"],
    John (Reverend)...81, 109
Saint Indeed or the Great Work of a Christian Opened and

Pressed, A...
Publication. See:
Appendix 1.
St. Paul...See: Gist, St. Paul
Saint's Everlasting Rest, The...Publication. See: Appendix 1.
Salmon [Possibly "Solmon"],
    Wm. W....79, 109
Sanford,
    Reverend Mr...68, 157
Savannah...See: Georgia, Savannah
Savings Bank...74, 163, 165
Sawyers,
    Josiah...82, 108
    Wm. (Esquire)...82, 108
Scott,
    Ham....79, 109
Scripture Biography for the Young with Critical Illustrations and Practical Remarks...Publication. See: Appendix 1.
Scripture Promises or the Christian's Inheritance...Publication. See: Appendix 1.
Scruggs,
    Archibald...81, 109
Sears,
    H. (Reverend)...17, 63, 65, 106, 107, 122

Homer (Reverend)...64, 82, 107, 108
    Mr....15, 47, 92, 139
    Reverend...46, 139
Seaton,
    Esquire...80, 109
Second Presbyterian New School Church [Written: "2nd Presbyterian"]...17, 122
Sermons...Publication. See: Appendix 1.
Sevier County...See: Tennessee, Sevier County
Sevierville...See: Tennessee, Sevier County, Sevierville
Shaddon,
    Joseph...80, 109
Sharp,
    James...80, 109
Shiloh...43, 100
Shinneberry,
    Geo....79, 109
Shipe,
    Alex...79, 109
Shults,
    Philip...80, 109
Sinner's Prayer, The...Publication. See: Appendix 1.
Six Sermons on the Nature, Occasions, Signs, Evils, and Remedy of Intemperance...Publication. See: Appendix 1.
Skaggs,
    Eli...79, 109

Slave...21, 124
Smith,
    Brother [William H.]...19, 123
    John (Deacon)...60, 65, 66, 68, 69, 72, 73, 82, 106, 108, 156, 157
    Jonathan Kennon Thompson...183, 199
    Philip...79, 109
    Thomas...63, 70, 72, 82, 107, 108, 156, 158, 159
    William H....4, 5, 7, 15, 18, 22, 27, 28, 29, 30, 31, 61, 88, 90, 106, 119, 121, 169, 201
    William Harvey [Possibly "Henry"]...4
Snapp,
    Joseph...80, 109
Sneider,
    Peter...81, 109
Snoddy,
    Reverend Mr.....82, 108
Society, The...See: American Tract Society
Society for Historians of the Early American Republic...199
Sodom...23, 125
Soli Dei Gloria...193
Solmon..See: Salmon.
Southern Christian Advocate Marriage Notices, 1867-1878...199

Sovereign Grace Publishers...193
Spanish...187
Spirit of Popery: An Exposure of Its Origin, Character, and Results in Letters from a Father to His Children...Publication. See: Appendix 1.
Springfield...[See: Massachusetts, Springfield]
Springfield Gazette...Publication. See: Appendix 1.
St. Paul...See: Gist, St. Paul
Stebbins,
    Patience...179, 182
Stephens,
    Rufus M.(Reverend)...82, 108
Stowe,
    Harriet Beecher...194, 195
    William...69, 157
Swan,
    Mr....65, 106
Swedish...187
Sweet, Leonard...199
Talladega County...See: Alabama, Talladega County
Ted...See: Gist, Ted
Temple,
    Harvey...See: Henry
    Henry [Or: Harvey]...80, 109

Jackson...80, 109

Miss...13, 115

Tennessee [Also see: East Tennessee]...iv, 3, 4, 5, 7, 11, 12, 13, 19, 22, 59, 60, 61, 62, 63, 64, 65, 66, 67, 68, 69, 70, 71, 72, 73, 74, 79, 108, 109, 154, 155, 160, 162, 163, 179, 180, 183, 191, 199

<u>Anderson County</u>...iv, 4, 5, 7, 19, 82, 108, 123

Clinton...64, 72, 82, 106, 108

<u>Blount County</u>...iv, 32, 56, 61, 62, 64, 65, 67, 68, 72, 73, 80, 81, 83, 106, 107, 108, 109, 146, 156, 157, 201

Cade's Cove...80, 109

Collumbia...59, 162

Columbia [See Collumbia]

Ellijoy...32, 61, 62, 65, 68, 72, 73, 83, 106, 108, 156, 157

Maryville...11, 12, 13, 19, 32, 58, 59, 60, 61, 62, 64, 65, 67, 69, 72, 73, 83, 94, 102, 106, 107, 108, 112, 118, 156, 157, 158

Tuckaleechee Cove...67, 156

Tuckaleechy...58

Tuckaleechy Cove [Also See: Tuckaleechee Cove]...81, 100, 102, 109

<u>East Tennessee</u>...iv, 3, 5, 11, 22, 59, 60, 61, 62, 63, 64, 65, 66, 67, 68, 69, 70, 71, 72, 73, 105, 106, 107, 108, 124, 125, 156, 157, 158, 159, 160, 179, 180, 191

Jonesborough...57, 71, 158, 159, 163

Tuckahoe...82, 108

Weir's Cove...48, 64, 106, 140, 164

<u>Mecklenberg</u>...66, 82, 108, 156

<u>Green County</u>...62, 68, 155

Greenville...62, 68, 106, 107, 155, 157

<u>Knox County</u>...iv, 60, 62, 63, 64, 65, 67, 68, 69, 70, 79, 106, 107, 155, 156, 157, 159, 201

Academia...iv, 60, 63, 64, 68, 69, 70, 72, 73, 106, 107, 156, 157, 158

Campbell's Station...69, 72, 156, 157

Church Grove...60, 62, 70, 82, 106, 107, 108, 156

Gap Creek [Also See: Third Creek]...60, 80, 82, 107, 108, 109,

Louisville...60, 62, 63, 65, 67, 68, 82, 106, 107, 108, 156, 157, 189, 201

Knoxville...11, 13, 14, 15, 17, 19, 20, 23, 38, 45, 46, 47, 59, 60, 62, 63, 64, 65, 66, 68, 69, 70, 71, 72, 73, 80, 82, 83, 89, 106, 107, 108, 109, 112, 114, 115, 116, 117, 122, 124, 133, 139, 140, 154, 156, 157, 158, 159, 162, 166, 175, 197

<u>Nashville</u>...183, 189, 199

<u>Roane County</u>...5, 7, 18, 19, 20, 21, 22, 24, 25, 80, 109, 118, 124, 126

<u>Sevier County</u>...iv, 35, 55, 61, 63, 64, 65, 66, 67, 68, 69, 70, 72, 81, 107, 109, 131, 155, 157, 159

Boyd's Creek...36, 37, 59, 61, 64, 69, 71, 82, 106, 107, 108, 156,

Henry's Cross Road...67, 80, 109, 156

Sevierville...46, 51, 60, 61, 64, 65, 66, 67, 68, 69, 70, 71, 72, 73, 82, 106, 107, 108, 139, 146, 156, 157, 158, 159

Walden's Creek...66, 81, 83, 108, 109, 157

Texas,

Garland...5, 197, 199

Third Creek [Written: "3rd Creek." Possibly "Gap Creek."]...15, 23, 125

Thomas,

Mr....37, 134, 166

William (Mr.)...61, 69, 106, 157

William...72, 82, 108, 159

Thompson,

Lawrance...200

Tinker,

Obadiah...79, 109

Wm....79, 109

Tolmer...74, 163

Toole...Also See: Brabson & Toole,

J. M....13, 92

J. M. (Colonel)...59, 103

James M. (Colonel)...61, 64, 67, 69, 83, 106, 107, 108, 157

Toomey [Also See: Henderson & Toomey], Pinckney H. (Esquire)...66, 82, 108, 157
Tract Society...see: American Tract Society
Tract Society of Knoxville...14, 15, 115
Treatise on Keeping the Heart...Publication. See: Appendix 1.
Trotter,
  Wm....80, 109
Trundle,
  Daniel L....80, 109
  John...80, 109
Tuckahoe [See: East Tennessee, Tuckahoe]
Tuckaleechee Cove...See: Tennessee, Blount County, Tuckaleechee Cove.
Tuckaleechy...See: Tennessee, Blount County, Tuckaleechey. Also see: Tennessee, Blount County, Tuckaleechee Cove.
Tucker,
  Shanna Nelson...i
Tusculum College...68, 157
Twenty-first Annual Report of the American Tract Society...200
Uncle Tom's Cabin...195
United States Federal Census
  1860...183, 200
  1870...183, 200
  1880...183, 200
University...See: Purdue University; East Tennessee University; Indiana University.
University of Massachusetts...i, 197
Village in the Mountains, The...Publication. See: Appendix 1.
Vital Records of Brimfield Massachusetts to the Year 1850...180, 183, 200
W.E.B. Du Bois Library...i, 197
Waded,
  G. [or S.}...72, 158
Walden's Creek...See: Tennessee, Sevier County, Walden's Creek.
Walker,
  Archibald...29, 62, 68, 82, 106, 108, 128, 157
  Elijah...80, 109
  W. W....82, 108
Wallace,
  C...45, 166
War...27, 127
War of 1812...179
Warren...See: Massachusetts, Warren.
Waters,
  John S....79, 109
Wayland,
  Wm....80, 109
Weaver,
  John (Deacon)...79, 109
Webster,
  Mrs....66, 154
Weir's Cove...See: Tennessee, East, Tennessee, Weir's Cove.
Wells,
  Rev. Shepherd...57, 58, 59, 162, 163
Welsh...187
West,
  Samuel B. (Reverend)...80, 109
Westerfield,
  Dr...26, 93
  John (Doctor)...82, 108
Whitney,
  Edward [Name associated with Mrs. Whitney] ...67, 154
  Mrs...67, 154
White (people)...24, 126
White,
  Geo. (Esquire)...83, 108, 197
  Gideon S. (Reverend)...60, 82, 106, 108
  H....15, 89
William B. Erdmans Publishing Company...199
Williams,
  Mr....56, 102
  Richard...81, 109
  Solomen...80, 109
Willis, Nathaniel...195
Wills,
  Caroline...67, 82, 108, 156
  Caroline (Miss)...60, 106
  David...68, 72, 156, 157
  David Jr....82, 108
  David (Mr.)...62, 69, 106, 107, 157
  Elisa [Or: Eliza]...62, 82, 106, 108
  John...82, 108
  Will...82, 108
Winn,
  Ashley (Reverend)...69, 81, 109, 156
Wright, Dr....80, 109
Www.abebooks.com...197
Www.atstracts.org...197
Www.ci.knoxville.tn.us...197
Www.FamilyMarriage Records.com...199
Www.library.umass.edu...197
Www.TNGenWeb.org...183, 199
Yett [Possibly "Zett"], John C. (Esquire)...80, 109
Young,
  Robert (Reverend)...80, 109
  Wd. [Widow]...80, 109
Youth's Christian Library...Publication. See: Appendix 1.
Youth's Companion...Publication. See: Appendix 1.
Youth's Dayspring...

Publication. See: Appendix 1.

To Purchase

Tennessee Travels 1844-1847,
Journal of Amos Hitchcock

Online: www.lulu.com or
LilyLeeDesigns.com

By Mail: Lily Pond Books
P. O. Box 986
Liberty Hill, TX 78642

By Phone: 512-355-9852

www.ingramcontent.com/pod-product-compliance
Lightning Source LLC
Chambersburg PA
CBHW080539170426
43195CB00016B/2615